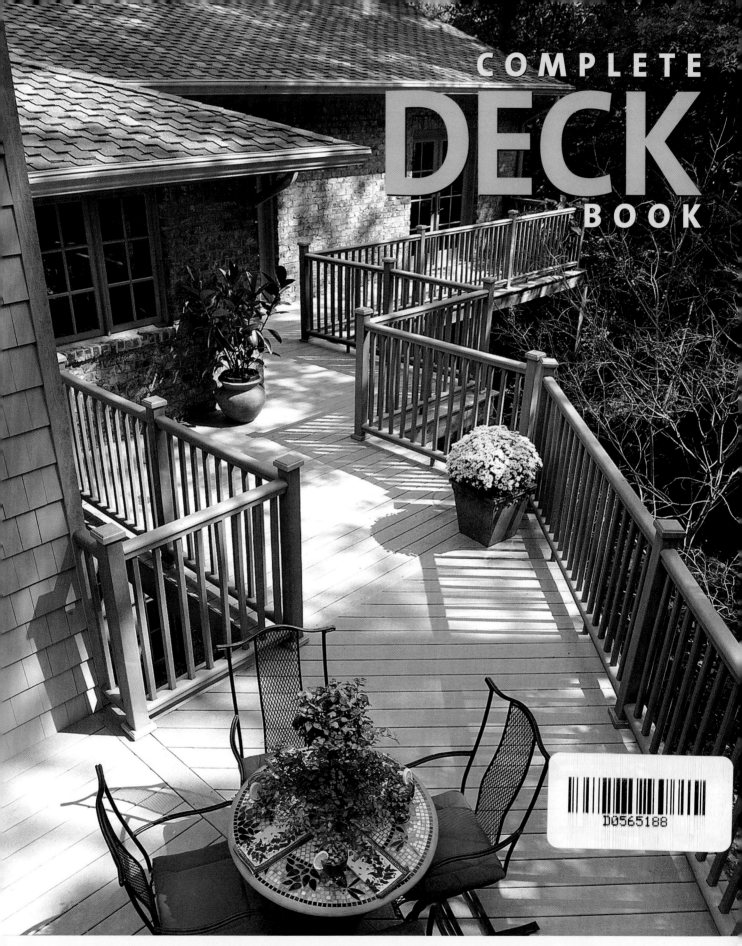

COMPLETE
DECK
BOOK

By Steve Cory and the Editors of Sunset Books, Menlo Park, California

SUNSET BOOKS

VP, GENERAL MANAGER
Richard A. Smeby
VP, EDITORIAL DIRECTOR
Bob Doyle
DIRECTOR OF OPERATIONS
Rosann Sutherland
MARKETING MANAGER
Linda Barker
ART DIRECTOR
Vasken Guiragossian
SPECIAL SALES
Brad Moses

STAFF FOR THIS BOOK

SENIOR EDITOR
Ben Marks
DESIGNER
Susan Paris
PREPRESS COORDINATOR
Eligio Hernandez
COPY EDITOR
Cynthia Rubin
PRODUCTION SPECIALIST
Linda M. Bouchard
PROOFREADER/INDEXER
Jennifer Block Martin

Cover photograph: Laurie Black
Deck design: Northwest Exteriors by John Breiling

1 Decks for Today | 4

Designer Decks • Small Decks • Defined Use Areas • Decks for Dining • Decks that Connect • Shade Structures • Ponds, Pools, Spas • Destination Decks • Enclosed Decks • Multiple Levels • Up on the Roof • Planning for Plants • Finishing Touches

2 Planning Your Deck | 32

Anatomy of a Deck • Parts of a Deck • Envisioning Your Deck • Know the Codes • Drawing Plans • A Tale of Two Decks

3 Materials, Tools, Techniques | 52

Choosing Lumber • Deck Fasteners • Other Materials • Tools of the Trade • Special Deck Tools • Squaring for Layout • Power Tools

4 Footings and Ledgers | 80

The Right Foundations • Layout Basics • Footing Holes • About Concrete • Pouring Concrete • Attaching a Ledger

5 Framing | 110

Framing Options • Beams • Framing with Supports • Aboveground Posts • Joists • Framing Variations • Framing a Curve • Building a Low Deck • Using Precast Piers

6 Decking | 146

Decking Patterns • Prepare for Decking • Decking Techniques • Synthetic Surfaces • Hidden Fasteners • A Custom V-Shape

7 Stairs | 170

Planning Stairs • Concrete Landing Pad • Brick Landing Pad • Stair Dimensions • Notched Stringers • Other Stair Options

8 Railings | 190

Codes and Safety • Railing Styles • Railing Products • Non-Wood Railings • Wood Railing Designs • Railing Posts • Installing Rails • Installing Balusters • Working with Synthetics • Stairs and Hybrids

9 Deck Extras | 214

Benches • A Custom Bench • Planters • Overheads • Skirting • Lighting Options • Low-Voltage Lighting • Outdoor Counters

10 Finishes and Repairs | 236

Finishing a Deck • Inspecting and Repairing

11 Deck Plans | 246

Simple and Modern • Hardwood Entry Deck • Seating Deck • Deck for a Sloping Site • Split-Level Spa Deck • Deck with Ramps • Transitional Deck

Resources | 268

Credits | 269

Index | 270

decks for today

A GOOD DECK CAN CAPTURE A VIEW, CREATE A COMFORTABLE OUTDOOR ROOM, AND ADD A FEELING OF SPACIOUSNESS TO YOUR HOME BY BLURRING THE BOUNDARIES BETWEEN INTERIOR AND EXTERIOR SPACES. DECKS ARE ALSO ECONOMICAL: FOR A FRACTION OF THE COST OF MOST INDOOR REMODELING PROJECTS, YOU CAN BUILD A DECK THAT EXPANDS YOUR LIVING AREA.

DESIGNER DECKS

OF ALL THE GOALS AN AMATEUR OR PROFES-
SIONAL DECK BUILDER could aspire to, creating
a structure that is harmonious with its adjoining house is probably pretty high on the list.
Yes, expanding one's living space in a cost-
effective way is a worthy aim. And using a deck to tame an otherwise difficult site is a natural—if your home sits on a steep slope,
it's probably easier and less expensive to build a deck than to
engineer terraces; if your home came with an ugly patio, covering
it with a deck is a simple solution. Any deck can do those sorts
of things, but only a deck that echoes the design of the home will
blur the boundary between a home's interior and exterior spaces.

LEFT: Constructed of the same materials as the abutting porch, this modest
deck differentiates itself from its cousin only through its decking, which runs
at a right angle to the porch's. Like the porch, the low deck needs no railing.

ABOVE: A whimsical partial wall, with trim and siding that matches the home and even a sliding window, divides this expansive deck into a pair of outdoor rooms.

RIGHT: A Japanese-style overhead gracefully shelters a conversation area; on the other side of a low wall is a walkway that invites you to enjoy the view.

OPPOSITE: When the decking blends with the color of the house, its relationship to the home's design is clear. Here, cedar decking is finished with a pale stain that complements the house's white-stained cedar shingles. The deck's design has one area for dining, another for gathering around a firepit.

SMALL DECKS

JUST BECAUSE YOUR NEIGHBORS HAVE A DECK big enough to land a helicopter on doesn't mean you need one too. When you build your deck, build it to please yourself, not to impress others. If you have a small amount of space to work with, you may not have much choice, but that needn't keep you from creating a deck that suits your lifestyle. An area about 120 feet square will accommodate a small table and four chairs. You may want to give your deck an L shape to form a smaller area where you can place a lounge chair or perhaps a small barbecue. Plant low ground covers or taller bushes along the outskirts of the deck, or mount planters to the railings to soften its edge.

LEFT: Surrounded by lush greenery and the sound of running water, this modest deck is perfect for small gatherings or relaxing with the Sunday paper.

BELOW: This freestanding cedar deck is blessed with a woodsy setting and dappled shade. Casual furniture creates an inviting outdoor room, ideal for conversation and just spacious enough for a dancing child or two. Note the planters on the railing.

ABOVE: This classic stained redwood deck gracefully extends the home's living space to the outdoors. Tall bamboo and other plants offer privacy and shade, while butterfly chairs beckon to those still inside. The single wide step is also a great place to sit and talk.

INSET: Four comfy chairs and a coffee table mimic the furnishings of an indoor living room, but all are made of materials that will hold up to rain and sun. The area is in plain view of the house, yet partially shielded by a small tree in a large planter.

DEFINED USE AREAS

DECKS CAN SERVE ALMOST ANY PURPOSE, be it entertaining, cooking, dining, gardening, or just relaxing. The best decks are designed to have designated use areas (page 43) with each of these activities in mind. Start by thinking through the traffic flow between the deck areas and the rest of the yard—make sure your family, friends, and pets are able to move about without creating bottlenecks or disturbing those seeking to cook, dine, or relax. Next, push the perimeter of your deck beyond the standard rectangle—think of the space you need for, say, a table and six chairs as a wing off the deck's main structure. Finally, choose furniture and grills that will comfortably fit in the spaces allotted for them—if you purchase a pair of chaises when you really only have room for two Adirondack chairs, you'll frustrate yourself.

LEFT: With recliners for basking in a sunny nook and a shady gazebo retreat at its far end, this spacious deck allows for privacy as well as communication between its sections. The contrast between the dark decking and the white railing and trim highlights the deck's unique lines.

BELOW: Another way to define a use area is by adding a level. Here, an eating area near the kitchen is partially protected from early evening sun by a trellis, which also serves as a divider for a seating area below.

ABOVE: Cascading levels and angled shapes provide numerous clearly defined areas for sitting, dining, and lounging. Shady umbrellas and well-placed pieces of furniture also help establish separate spaces. Though the deck is large, its natural wood finish and proximity to big plants and trees give it the feeling of a cozy retreat.

RIGHT: Composite decking in three colors is used to create an eye-catching pattern, which helps define the spaces. Several seating areas radiate from the design.

DECKS FOR DINING

A DECK IS A WONDERFUL PLACE to enjoy warm-weather meals with friends and family. Most people keep their grill and food preparation area near the kitchen door, while the dining area tends to be farther away. To create a semisecluded eating area on a rectangular deck, consider adding a bump-out section. Or place the dining area a step up or down from the main deck. Choose a spot that has a pleasant view, perhaps facing a flower bed or nestled in trees and shrubs. Outdoor kitchen counters and grills can also be placed on a deck or built into a railing. Enhance the atmosphere by choosing lighting and accessories that complement those on your home's exterior.

LEFT: **A separate wing of a deck provides privacy and seclusion for a dining area. Shielded by walls on two sides and opening to the yard on a third, this little nook is clean and unaffected by foot traffic.**

OPPOSITE: With a blazing fireplace as its focal point, this deck is an outdoor version of the classic great room, with a cooking area, living-room-style seating, and a tree-shaded space for dining. The ruglike shape in front of the fireplace is easy to achieve when you install different hues of composite decking.

RIGHT: A palette of bright colors—napkins, place mats, chair cushions, flowers in pots—contributes to the cheerful character of this compact outdoor dining area.

BELOW: At home in its arid climate, a rooftop cedar deck features a sheltered cooking area and a curved dining counter with a solid-surface top for easy cleaning.

DECKS THAT CONNECT

TO MAKE THE MOST OF THEIR OUTDOOR SPACES, homeowners have gotten pretty creative about deck placement. Many homes now feature more than one deck, or a deck plus a patio. Typically one is attached to the house while another is freestanding. Decks situated away from a house let you enjoy the shade of a favorite tree or the peace and privacy of a quiet corner of a yard. To connect these different areas, paths are sometimes constructed out of a series of linear decks. Such connector decks may be built like standard decks, with footings, framing, railings, and the rest, or you can purchase modular decking, also called duckboards (page 161). The direction of the decking can be played with to signal the direction of the path, or alternate the decking from one section of the path to the next.

LEFT: In this straightforward design, a house is actually divided in two by a deck that is placed between them. This arrangement provides unobstructed views of the ocean and a nearby stand of cypress trees.

BELOW: Two pond-side decks are linked by steps made of sandblasted glass. The decking's dark stain blends well with the colors of the water and the lily pads.

BELOW: A boardwalk made of treated wood meanders through a fern-filled field, evoking the feel of a nature walk. Exposed posts remind walkers where the deck's edges are.

ABOVE: Running along the length of the upper story of a house, this composite deck, whose decking is secured by hidden fasteners, employs a charming zigzag design to maximize views of the woods below. It also provides a separate exterior route for residents to get from one end of the house to the other.

SHADE STRUCTURES

OFTEN THE BEST SPOT FOR A DECK is also the sunniest, but during warm months the heat can make such places sweltering. If you need full shade, consider installing an awning or a screened-in room. Overhead structures, often called pergolas, also offer serious shade (page 222). Most designs use several layers of wood, each layer composed of smaller pieces spaced closer together than the last. An overhead is easier to build at the same time as you build the deck, but adding one to an existing structure is usually not too difficult. Aim for a height that will block the sun when you most need shade, and plant vines to grow over the top for added color and protection.

LEFT: Looking out onto an ocean view, an ironwood deck is shaded by a stunning overhead. The curved beam is painted, dark-stained joists rest atop the beam, and stained 1 × 2s crown the structure. The posts are covered with decorative trim.

ABOVE: In addition to blocking the sun's rays, this overhead's evenly spaced top pieces are attractive architectural elements that define the use areas below them.

RIGHT: A professionally built welded metal overhead, thick with vines, lets filtered light through to the eating area below. The railing balusters are also made of metal.

OPPOSITE: Each of these beams is supported by cylindrical metal posts sunk deep in concrete, so they provide strong lateral support. Most of the shade is created by vigorously bushy climbing vines (think of the pergola as the plant's armature). Two of the beams serve as a frame for a swinging bench.

PONDS, POOLS, SPAS

A DECK IS A PLACE TO RELAX AND UNWIND, so what better place for a hot tub or spa? Some spas must rest on concrete foundations, with a deck built around them. Others can be installed on the deck itself, in which case the deck's framing will need serious beefing up. If you have a pool, consider surrounding it by a deck rather than concrete. Wood and composite decking are great surfaces for relaxing after a dip, and they're inviting to nonswimmers who may simply want to hang out. Decks also work well next to fish ponds and water gardens; since these will attract birds and butterflies, the deck becomes a platform for backyard nature watching.

LEFT: A gently curving edge is all it takes to give this deck a strong connection to an adjacent pond. The short section of railing between the table and pond follows the curve.

OPPOSITE: Redwood decking, left unstained so it can "go gray," neatly abuts a swimming pool. Wood soaks up a fair amount of water, so it's a comfortable surface to rest on after a swim. But it requires care and sanding to keep it splinter-free.

RIGHT: A hot tub raised 16 inches or so above a deck is easy to enter and exit. Here, a roof made of wood rafters and translucent panels provides shelter and support for plants in containers.

BELOW: Water cascades from a small spa to a larger one on its way to a decorative pond with underwater lights.

DESTINATION DECKS

SOME DECKS ARE DOGGED WORKHORSES, flat expanses of sure footing over unsightly or difficult terrain. Others are the main event—the destination, if you will. These decks please us by virtue of their proximity to, or views of, the local landscape. Sometimes they lure us to an edge of a yard for grand, unexpected vistas; other times they just provide some peace and quiet. Placed near a vegetable garden, a favorite tree, or at the top of a series of terraces, a destination deck can be an invitation to family and friends to appreciate the work you've put into your yard. Even if your property has no such beguiling features, you can easily add a focal point.

LEFT: Tactfully built into the landscape, this deck lures visitors to the water's edge and provides a comfortable place to sit and enjoy the view. Cutouts in the decking allow bamboo to grow tall.

ABOVE: A stairway leads to a deck near a river's edge, where one can take in the view of whatever happens to be floating by. Because of its location, this is one deck where it would not be wise to cut corners on footings and railings.

RIGHT: Walking along this scalloped deck path is its own reward, a chance to stop and smell the flowers on the way to a breathtaking view.

OPPOSITE: Set in the midst of a sloping garden and facing the ocean, this deck is a destination brimming with natural beauty, a perfect place for a cup of tea or a good book. The vegetation hides the deck walkway from most points of view, making the deck itself appear even more secluded.

ENCLOSED DECKS

NOT EVERYONE IS BLESSED with a golf-course-size lawn or a backyard stretching to the horizon. Most of us are hemmed in on at least a few sides, which means our decks are too. Such decks are like the floors of small outdoor rooms. The good news here is that a little bit goes a long way—if your materials list is short, you can afford to buy the good stuff, and a handful of accessories and artistic touches is all you need. One strategy is to treat the outdoor room like a part of the interior living space, so that furniture and color schemes echo those inside. For example, choose outdoor pots that are similar to the ones indoors. And consider using end tables for food and drinks—if you must have a dining table, choose a round or oval design to save space.

LEFT: This small side-yard deck is private and stylish. A deck this size can be built at a reasonable cost even if you use expensive materials and pay for fine craftsmanship and joinery, as in the overhead above.

BELOW: A table with chairs that fold for easy storage adds versatility to this small deck. The umbrella and lights draw the eye upward, making the space seem larger.

ABOVE: This painted deck has all the charm of a traditional front porch. The built-in bench adds seating without taking up space, and the wide stairs offer additional inviting seating, as well as places for potted plants. The unobtrusive overhead is handsome and carefully joined.

RIGHT: This shady little deck with a bamboo-topped overhead is small but feels open thanks to its simple design and the spare furnishings, proving that the principles of feng shui can be applied to outdoor rooms.

MULTIPLE LEVELS

DECKS WITH MULTIPLE LEVELS have long been favored by homeowners looking to increase the horizontal surface areas of sloping lots. As a rule, building a deck over a steep slope is easier and less expensive than building terraces. But multilevel decks are also popular with the owners of multistory homes. Such a deck can offer sweeping views from its upper level as well as a cozy outdoor dining spot on the level below. Keep in mind that the steeper the terrain, the higher the deck will be off the ground, and in some cases special footings and post structures, beyond those shown in this book, will be required. Fortunately, most multiple-level decks consist of only a step or two, which is usually all it takes to create a unique space.

LEFT: A small upper deck is connected by a stairway to an expansive lower deck. Painted metal balusters contrast handsomely with the stained wood. Building a stairway like this one is not easy, so don't be shy about turning to the pros.

BELOW: This simple multilevel deck has a one-step descent to the lower level. Building such a deck is not complicated. Make sure the step ascends 6 to 7 inches, so it will feel like a normal stair step.

ABOVE: A deck with multiple level changes as well as angles and turns makes for a pleasant jumble, creating lots of interesting nooks and crannies. The gazebo anchoring the far end helps bring order to the chaos by providing a destination.

RIGHT: This composite deck has a curved step at its bottom, plus a set of four stairs leading to a jut-out that's just the right size for a pair of easy chairs. Running the decking in the direction of the upper level draws the eye into the overall structure.

UP ON THE ROOF

ON HOT SUMMER EVENiNGS it's usually cooler up on the roof. Building a roof deck has its challenges, but the reward is well worth the effort. Make sure that the roof is flat and strong, that the deck is attached without damaging the roof (which could lead to leaky ceilings), and that water is able to flow freely underneath the decking; check with your local building department for the codes that apply in your area. One popular solution is to install modular decking units (also called duckboards), which can be easily removed if you need to repair the roof. You will also want to install a strong railing. As for plants, choose ones that like hot, direct sun.

LEFT: In cities, where morning and afternoon sun is often blocked by buildings, the best spot for a garden can be the roof. This urban oasis provides its owner with a steady supply of vegetables and flowers all summer long.

OPPOSITE: The ocean views surrounding this beach house are terrific, but from this rooftop deck they are positively stunning. Notice how the decking seems to lead to the access door, while a pair of folding chairs is tucked into a notch so they are out of the way of traffic.

RIGHT: Roses and boulders bring a bit of the countryside to Manhattan. Plants in containers add color and variety to the rooftop landscape, without adding too much weight to the decking.

BELOW: Surely the envy of the workers toiling in the office building across the way, this rooftop deck showcases fir shrubs to give the space a woodsy feel. The decking is modular, so it can be removed if needed.

PLANNING FOR PLANTS

PLANTS ADD A NATURAL SOFTENING ELEMENT to a deck. Lush green and bright colors bring an outdoor room to life, and make people feel more relaxed. Plants can also define deck areas and break up large expanses to provide privacy, add shade, hide an unsightly view, highlight an entryway, or lend color to a seating area. Whether on the deck or next to it, plants help the deck blend into the yard. Large plants can mimic permanent structures: For instance, four tall potted plants can establish the corners of an outdoor dining area, or they can be lined up to create a privacy wall behind a pair of chaises. You can custom-build planters to fit your deck's contours (page 220). Or choose from an array of pots that sit or hang—hanging plants pull the eye's focus up and make a space seem larger.

LEFT: On this curving section of a larger multilevel deck, flowerpots sit on the decking itself, hang from the railing to provide color for the level below, and are mounted to the house's exterior wall. Wherever you place your pots, be sure to protect the decking from standing water.

BELOW: Grasses and sun-washed deck boards with a matching bench have a muted appeal, creating a natural setting that encourages contemplation and conversation. When planting like this, make sure water drains away from the deck's footings rather than into them.

ABOVE: Gleaming galvanized troughs, available at farm supply stores, serve as the base of a wall of potted bamboo, softening the edges of this deck's modern metallic railing. The area under the deck is carefully landscaped with sun- and shade-loving plants, chosen according to their placement.

RIGHT: The simple lines of a rustic wooden railing are neatly accented by a prim row of evenly spaced terra-cotta pots.

FINISHING TOUCHES

OFTEN IT'S THE LITTLE DECORATIVE DETAILS that are the most memorable parts of a deck. Outdoors, the scale of accessories can be pumped up to increase their visual impact; objects like candles and candle holders should also be large and heavy enough to remain stable under windy conditions. Or place a self-supporting hammock at the far end of a deck to create a lounging area. Beyond accessories, peruse the possibilities in the lighting section of your deck store or home center, where you'll find everything from unobtrusive lights built into railings and risers to bold beacons that double as post caps, which themselves are available in a variety of styles. As for the decking, let nature dictate the lines by building around obstacles such as boulders or trees.

LEFT: To produce a table and seating reminiscent of a Japanese restaurant, a section of this deck has been lowered; diners sit on the decking and dangle their feet below.

BELOW: It's not difficult to build a deck around a favorite tree, and the shade the tree provides makes it worth the effort. Make sure the framing is located away from the tree, so you can cut back the decking to accommodate its expanding trunk.

ABOVE: A wraparound built-in bench adds extra seating, making it possible for the deck to accommodate a number of guests while retaining a spacious, open feel. Other details include the small light built into the riser and skirting made from decking boards.

INSET: Here, a grill has been built into a railing to free up valuable space on a small deck. Note the angled support extending from the post to the outside of the deep top rail. Surfaces near the grill should either be made of composite material or sealed for easy cleaning.

planning your deck

OFTEN THE DIFFERENCE BETWEEN A PROFESSIONAL-
LOOKING DECK AND ONE THAT APPEARS AMATEURISH
CAN BE TRACED TO THE PLANNING STAGE. IN THIS
CHAPTER WE BREAK DOWN A DECK INTO ITS COMPONENT
PARTS TO HELP YOU PRODUCE THE DRAWINGS YOU'LL
NEED TO SATISFY YOUR INSPECTOR, STAY ORGANIZED,
AND KEEP EVERYTHING PLUMB AND LEVEL.

ANATOMY OF A DECK

TO HELP YOUR IDEAS TAKE SHAPE, YOU'LL NEED TO UNDERSTAND A DECK'S STRUCTURE. Even if you are not planning to build your deck yourself, it's good to know the name and purpose of each component so you can converse with a builder or architect. If you do intend to build your own deck, the right terms will be invaluable when you're talking to the people down at your local lumberyard or home center. The component names given here are common throughout much of the country, though different terms may be used in your neck of the woods.

Skip Ahead

To learn more about the components of a deck, please turn to the following pages:

FOUNDATIONS

| Footings | page 82 |
| Ledgers | page 84 |

FRAMING

Posts	page 112
Beams	page 116
Joists	page 130

DECKING

| Wood | page 152 |
| Composite | page 158 |

STAIRS

Pads	page 174
Treads & Risers	page 180
Stringers	page 182

RAILINGS

Rails	page 194
Posts	page 202
Balusters	page 208

AMENITIES

Benches	page 216
Planters	page 220
Overheads	page 222
Skirting	page 228
Lights	page 230

LEDGERS. Most decks attach to the house via a ledger. Aluminum or vinyl flashing tucks up under the house's siding and folds over the ledger to keep water away from the house. A deck can be built without a ledger; in some areas, building codes actually require that decks remain unattached.

JOISTS. Usually made of 2 × 6s, 2 × 8s, or 2 × 10s and spaced at regular intervals, joists rest on top of the beam. Joist hangers, hurricane ties, post anchors, and beam anchors tie the framing (the posts, beams, and joists) firmly together. Building codes specify exactly which hardware pieces should be used, and where.

BEAMS. Posts support beams, which are typically made of doubled 2× lumber.

FASCIA. Fascia boards, usually made of the same material as the decking, often cover visible framing pieces. If the deck is raised, the area under the joists may be covered with skirting.

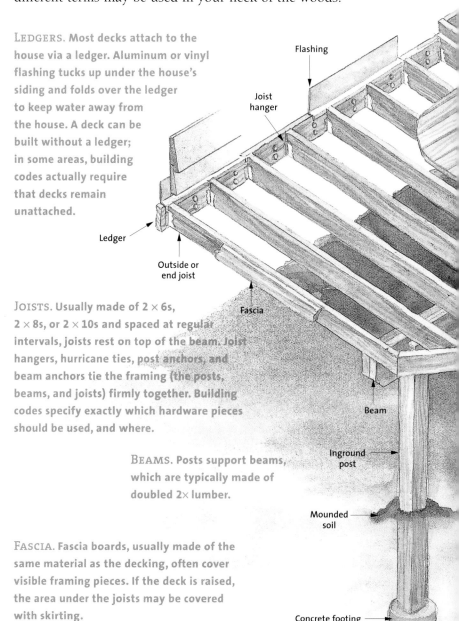

Flashing

Joist hanger

Ledger

Outside or end joist

Fascia

Beam

Inground post

Mounded soil

Concrete footing

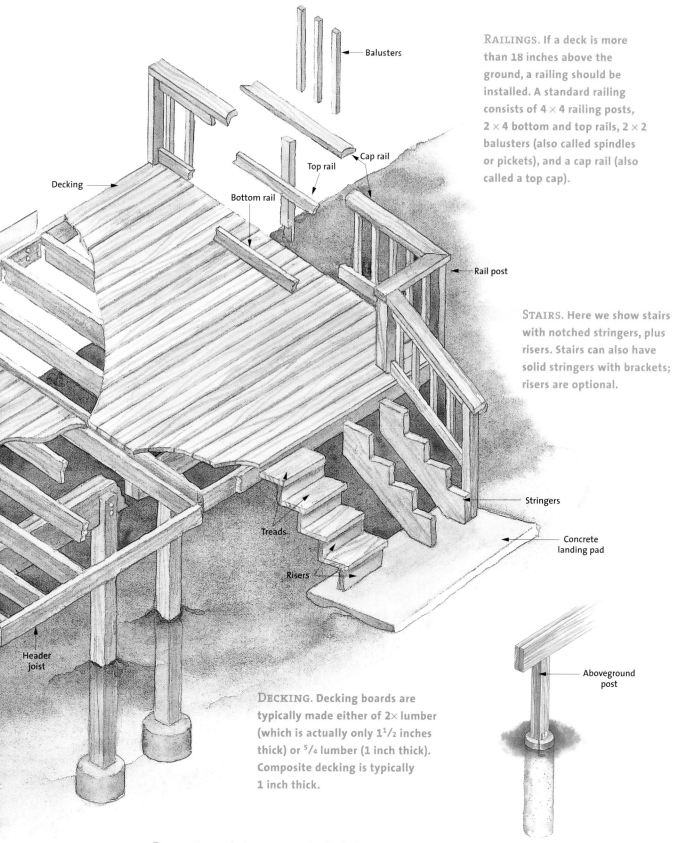

Balusters

Decking

Top rail

Cap rail

Bottom rail

Rail post

Treads

Risers

Stringers

Concrete
landing pad

Header
joist

Aboveground
post

RAILINGS. If a deck is more than 18 inches above the ground, a railing should be installed. A standard railing consists of 4 × 4 railing posts, 2 × 4 bottom and top rails, 2 × 2 balusters (also called spindles or pickets), and a cap rail (also called a top cap).

STAIRS. Here we show stairs with notched stringers, plus risers. Stairs can also have solid stringers with brackets; risers are optional.

DECKING. Decking boards are typically made either of 2× lumber (which is actually only 1½ inches thick) or 5⁄4 lumber (1 inch thick). Composite decking is typically 1 inch thick.

POSTS. Beneath those parts of a deck that are not supported by a house, posts made of 4 × 4s or 6 × 6s do the job. Posts typically rest on concrete footings (also called piers). The footings may rise above grade with aboveground posts (see inset, right), or they may rest underground with inground posts (above and left).

PARTS OF A DECK

LET'S BEGIN WITH A DECK'S STRUCTURAL COMPONENTS, which usually include concrete footings, a ledger, posts, beams, joists, and the hardware that holds it all together. Consult your local building department to learn the specific code requirements for each. The span chart on page 45 is a good guide to how large and closely spaced joists and beams should be, but again, be sure to follow your local codes.

No matter which material you are using for decking and railing (i.e., composite or real wood), your deck's structural components should be built with pressure-treated lumber; any part that touches or comes near the ground should be made from lumber rated for ground contact (pages 54–55).

Posts and Footings

Posts must rest on firm concrete footings (also known as piers). In many parts of the country, temperatures often dip below freezing in late fall and early spring. If this describes your locality, you may be required to dig footing holes that extend below the frost line. The two basic post-footing arrangements are described below. Your building department may require one or the other.

The second-story deck above this patio has an underlying rooflike covering to keep the patio dry when it rains. The inground posts have been finished simply with paint.

Inground posts rest on a pad of concrete poured at the bottom of a post hole, which means much of the post is below ground. Posts are usually made of 6 × 6s or 4 × 6s, although 4 × 4s can be used. With this method, you dig the holes first and then construct much of the framing with temporary supports (pages 118–125). You can then pour the concrete and set the posts to line up with the framing. One advantage of this method is that you do not need to precisely dig the holes or place the footings.

Some people fear that an inground post may rot. But post lumber that is rated for ground contact is virtually impervious to the elements. To be on the safe side, mound the soil around the post in a conical fashion to help ensure that rainwater will flow away from it. Ratings aside, if the soil in your area stays wet for long periods, it may be best to build with aboveground posts.

PRO TIP

If your deck is low to the ground or if it has skirting, its structural posts are all but invisible, so build in whichever manner is easiest for you.

Aboveground posts rest on footings that rise several inches above grade. Usually, 4 × 4s are used. Typically, a tube form is used to produce a cylindrical footing. A bolt is inserted into the wet concrete (or attached later with a masonry drill and epoxy cement), and a post anchor is attached to the bolt. When the concrete has set, the posts are attached and cut to height, and the beams are set on top of the posts.

Some inspectors prefer aboveground posts because they keep the posts from contact with the soil, thereby guaranteeing against rot. If you use this method, the footings and bolts must be placed with a fair amount of precision—footings in a row must be lined up exactly. Mistakes in placement are common because it can be difficult to visualize the correct locations before the framing is built. But aboveground posts are still within reach of a careful do-it-yourselfer.

The Ledger

A ledger is a horizontal piece of lumber that attaches to a house's framing and provides stability for a deck. Using a ledger instead of a beam near a house means that you have fewer post holes to dig and footings to pour. For these reasons, most decks have ledgers.

In areas where soil is unstable, however, ledger-attached decks may sink downward and damage the houses they are attached to. Consequently, ledgers are not permitted in some locales.

Ledgers can be attached in several ways. It is probably most common to cut away a ledger-size section of the house's siding, slip in building paper, add flashing, and attach the ledger to the house's framing between the building paper and the flashing. Some deck builders don't like the idea of removing siding from a house, so they install what's called a held-off ledger, or they may simply mash the ledger against the house—if your

home has smooth siding, this may be the best method. If your home is clad in stucco or brick, you will need to use special techniques described on pages 108–109.

Beams and Joists

Deck structures are usually built out of three layers of lumber—joists rest on top of beams, which rest on top of posts. The joists attach to the ledger (if there is one) via joist hangers; at the other ends, they attach with nails or screws driven through a header joist. Some codes may call for installing joist hangers at the header joist as well as at the ledger.

If a deck is very low to the ground, there may not be room for all three layers. In that case, joists may run into the beams and attach with joist hangers rather than resting on top. In this arrangement, the beam is essentially a beefed-up header joist.

It was once common to make beams using heavy 4× lumber. Now most beams are made by laminating—nailing or screwing together—two or more pieces of 2× lumber. It does not take long to build a beam like this, and the result is stronger than an unlaminated beam of the same thickness.

A side-by-side beam (page 113) is made by bolting or screwing 2× boards to either side of a post. This technique is not as common as it once was, and is disallowed by many building codes.

Deck joists are usually installed 16 inches apart on center, but if you are running composite decking at a 45-degree angle, you may need to install them 12 inches apart.

Decking

Decking installed in a typical way—say, parallel to the house—has a classic appeal. But for a fairly modest investment of time and energy (especially compared to the time it takes to build the structure), you can add visual interest by installing decking in a pattern. For some patterns, the framing may need to be modified at certain points. See pages 148–149 for the most common configurations.

The decking material you choose has its own design possibilities. Cedar, redwood and tropical hardwoods such as mahogany can be stained to obtain a variety of colors. If you install them in patterns such as V shapes or herringbones, the result can be stunning. You can also alternate different widths of decking boards to create a pinstriped effect (see inset above).

Composite and vinyl decking runs from subdued to vivid. A light-colored composite installed in a pattern will yield a subtle effect. As a group, composites are remarkably flexible—they can be installed in curves to produce everything from gentle wavelike effects to outlandish designs—and require little or no maintenance after installation.

Hammers vs. Guns

Decide in advance how you will attach the framing pieces, as well as the decking and rails. Your options are hand nailing; a nail gun; a drill equipped with a screwdriver bit; or a screw gun. Hand nailing works fine, but it can be slow and arduous. A nail gun (which you can rent from a home center) is by far the quickest and easiest option, especially for attaching wood decking. Screws drive fairly quickly into most woods and all but disappear into composite decking.

Railings

From the street or the yard, a deck's railing may be its most visible feature. Almost all deck railings have the same basic components—posts, rails, balusters, and perhaps top caps and post caps. As a rule, the most successful railings are ones that complement the look of the home they are attached to. For a selection of railing designs, see pages 194–201.

Railings are typically built from the same material as the decking, although railings that contrast with the decking can be stunning. If you have a great view, materials like cable and acrylic are less obstructive than closely spaced balusters made of wood or composite materials.

Fascia and Skirting

The exposed faces of the end and header joists, as well as any exposed parts of a stairway, are traditionally covered with fascia made of decking material. To create contrast, apply several rows of narrower boards.

The area below the deck can be left open or hidden behind skirting. You will need to install framing for skirting, which can get a bit complicated because it needs to be attached to the beams or posts. Skirting can be made of common lattice panels from your local home improvement center, vertical or horizontal decking boards, or customized to echo your home's design.

Stairs

A stairway may be simply a way to get on and off your deck, or it can be both functional and stylish. Widening and deepening your stairway can create an inviting place to sit and converse between deck levels, as shown above. A landing pad made of concrete or patio pavers should support the bottom of any stairway that's frequently used and rests on bare ground. For more about landing pads, see pages 176–179.

Many stairs are built with notched stringers (also called carriages). For a quicker way to install stairs—and one that allows you to install wide stairs with fewer stringers—check out the adjustable stair brackets shown on page 187.

Amenities and Extras

Extra touches can give your deck that homemade, custom feel. Many amenities can be added later (a planter that rests on a rail, for example), but most are usually easier to build along with the rest of the deck. Check out the possibilities—overheads, benches, planters, and lighting—shown in Chapter 9.

ENVISIONING YOUR DECK

THE MOST COMMON PLACE FOR A DECK IS ALONG A HOUSE'S BACK WALL, with easy access to the kitchen or dining room. Which is not to say that that's the only place to put your deck. The plans in the back of this book, for example, suggest that no two decks need be alike. To help you find the design and placement that's right for you, begin by mapping out your future deck's contours.

A small deck just off the kitchen door allows for pleasant outdoor dining and makes it easy to enjoy the backyard.

Working from a Base Plan

Many people find it helpful to noodle things out on paper, even before they sit down to create their actual plan drawings (whether by hand or computer). The first step is to measure the primary dimensions of your backyard and your home's exterior walls. A survey or other form of property map, if you have one, is a useful reference. If you don't have such a document, you may want to have your land surveyed, to be sure you know the exact location of your property lines.

Transfer your measurements to graph paper or enter them into the design software of your choice and gradually add detail. Focus on the portion of your house that is most relevant to your deck's dimensions. Add elements such as exterior electrical outlets, hose bibs, casement windows, French doors that open outward, major landscape features such as trees that you plan to keep, and structures such as sheds.

Draw a north arrow, then note shaded and sunlit areas. If you are designing on a computer, it will probably be easy to see how these areas change, both during a single day and with the seasons. Also note any microclimates—a perennially sunny hot spot, an always-shady cold area. Indicate the direction of prevailing winds to identify parts of your deck that may require protection. Once you've captured all of this data, make five or six versions of your base plan; now is the time to experiment!

A Trial Run

If your site is fairly flat, you can gain a vivid view of a proposed layout by actually positioning lawn furniture, a barbecue, and other deck furnishings on the ground. Use a hose to outline the deck's perimeter, and have family members sit in chairs and walk around.

To see the effect that a railing will have on the view from inside your house, set up a clothesline at the railing's proposed height and take a gander from behind the window. If your view is obstructed, consider lowering your deck by a step or two.

Defining Use Areas

Think of your deck in terms of activity areas that are joined by invisible pathways. How much space should be allocated for a particular area? Here are some general rules of thumb:

• A typical round or square table requires an area that is 10 to 12 feet square, and a rectangular table for eight calls for an area 10 to 12 feet by 16 to 18 feet.

• A chaise or hammock accompanied by a small end table for drinks will fit comfortably into an area about 4 by 8 feet.

• Barbecue areas should include space for at least one small preparation table. A 6-by-8-foot space will accommodate a cook and a couple of advisers.

• A 3-foot-wide pathway is fine for light traffic.

KNOW THE CODES

IN MOST AREAS YOU WILL NEED TO GET A PERMIT FROM YOUR LOCAL BUILDING DEPARTMENT BEFORE YOU START BUILDING. You may also need to schedule inspections in advance. Codes vary from region to region, even from town to town. The purpose of codes is to establish minimum requirements for variables like footings, lumber, spans, railings, and stairs. Over the years codes have become more strict, so much so that many new decks are often stronger than the old houses they are attached to.

Your first step is to visit your town's building department and ask for information on deck codes—in some communities you may be able to download all the information you need from the Web. Following the guidelines provided, make your drawings and create a materials list, then schedule an appointment with an inspector. At that meeting you will review your plans and make alterations on the spot as needed; in some cases you may be asked to redraw your plans.

In some towns or neighborhoods, local zoning codes dictate where—and even if—you can build a deck. For instance, setback requirements may state that the deck must be at least 6 feet from the property line. If you live in a historic preservation zone, rules may govern the style of railing and skirting, and you may need to present your plans to a committee.

Typically there are three inspections during construction: after the footing holes are dug; once the framing is complete; and after the deck is finished. Be sure not to cover up anything the inspector needs to see, or you may have to tear out some of your work.

Your deck is exposed to the elements and comes in for constant use. Following building codes ensures it will endure, be safe, and stay attractive.

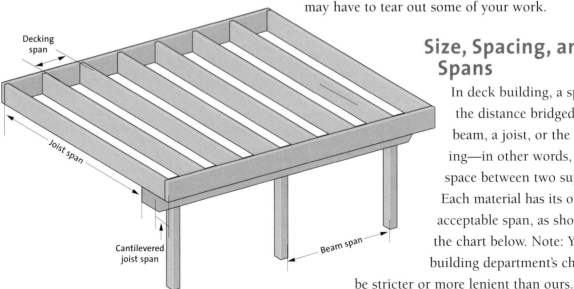

Decking span

Joist span

Cantilevered joist span

Beam span

Size, Spacing, and Spans

In deck building, a span is the distance bridged by a beam, a joist, or the decking—in other words, the space between two supports. Each material has its own acceptable span, as shown in the chart below. Note: Your building department's chart may be stricter or more lenient than ours.

Spacing is the distance between the centers of parallel posts, beams, and joists. As you might guess, spacing is dictated by a given material's allowable span. For example, the distance a chosen decking can safely span determines the joist spacing, the allowable span for the joists determines the distance from ledger to beam (or beam to beam), and the beam spacing determines the post spacing. The spacing between joists can also depend on your chosen decking pattern.

You can use the following span chart to help determine which materials and dimensions are best for your deck's framing. It is usually easiest to build a deck using a single beam plus a ledger, but doing so may force you to use larger joists than if you had installed more beams. Similarly, you may be able to reduce the number of posts (and post holes) if you use a larger beam.

Typical Beam Spans
Southern pine and Douglas fir, No. 2 or Select Structural grade

NOMINAL BEAM SIZE	ON-CENTER SPACING BETWEEN BEAMS						
	6'	7'	8'	9'	10'	11'	12'
4 × 6	6'						
Doubled 2 × 8	7'	7'	6'	6'			
4 × 8	8'	7'	7'	6'	6'	6'	
Doubled 2 × 10	9'	8'	8'	7'	7'	6'	6'
Doubled 2 × 12	10'	10'	9'	8'	8'	7'	7'

Typical Joist Spans
Southern pine and Douglas fir, No. 2 or Select Structural grade

NOMINAL JOIST SIZE	ON-CENTER SPACING BETWEEN JOISTS		
	12'	16'	24'
2 × 6	10'3"	9'4"	8'2"
2 × 8	13'6"	12'3"	10'9"
2 × 10	17'3"	15'8"	13'8"

Typical Decking Spans

DECKING	NOMINAL	MAXIMUM
Redwood,	⁵⁄₄ × 4	16"
Western red cedar,	⁵⁄₄ × 6	16"
Douglas fir	2 × 4	24"
	2 × 6	24"
Southern pine	⁵⁄₄ × 4	24"
	⁵⁄₄ × 6	24"
	2 × 4	24"
	2 × 6	24"
Composite	2 × 6	Varies by product; typically 16"

DRAWING PLANS

ONCE YOU HAVE DETERMINED YOUR DECK'S BASIC CONTOURS AND DIMENSIONS, contacted the building department, and chosen your materials (if you haven't done so already, feel free to skip ahead to pages 54–61 for an overview of choices), it's time to make final drawings. These pages show the types of deck drawings most commonly required by building departments.

Don't rush through the process of drawing plans. If you take the time to identify the location of every board now, you will almost certainly avert mistakes and avoid pitfalls during construction.

If pencils and rulers fill you with dread, consider designing your deck on your home computer. The price of basic design programs has dropped dramatically in recent years, though if you are only using the software to design one deck, it is probably not worth the time it could take you to learn how to use it. Finally, you may also choose to have a professional make drawings for you, which you would then submit to the building department.

Most decks are like this one— simple enough to design yourself. Don't hesitate to throw in a level change or an angle.

Elevations and Details

An elevation drawing is a side view. It typically captures important information about footings, posts, and railings. A single elevation drawing may suffice, but it's a good idea to draw elevations showing at least two sides of the deck and at least one that shows the stairway. Detail drawings present close-ups of particular features of a deck, such as the stairs, a railing, or a built-in bench.

The Plan View

A plan view, or overhead, is drawn to scale, with accurate dimensions and structural details. Many building departments require only one plan view, indicating both decking and framing. Others require two overhead drawings, one that shows the decking and the railing, and another that is devoted exclusively to the framing. Whether you produce one plan view drawing or two, be sure to include all the beams, ledgers, and joists. Use dotted circles to indicate posts and footings.

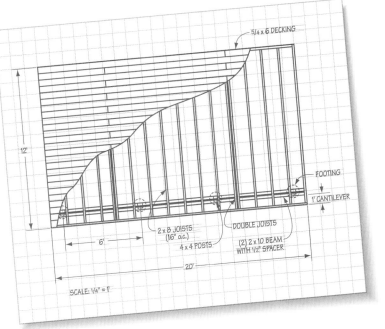

The Materials List

Use your drawings to generate a complete list of all the materials you will need. The lumber list should include ledgers, posts, beams, joists, decking, and materials for railings and stairways. Also list hardware, such as joist hangers and hurricane ties, as well as concrete and concrete tube forms.

Joist and Beam Cantilevers

If a beam cantilevers past the posts and the joists cantilever past the beam, construction will be easier because the footing locations will not need to be precise. Cantilevering also helps hide the deck's structure, but be sure to check local codes to find out how far you can cantilever. Some codes say you can safely overhang the joists by up to a third of the ledger-to-beam (or beam-to-beam) distance. Thus, if the joists travel 9 feet from the ledger to the beam, the joists can overhang the beam by up to 3 feet. As a practical matter, however, some codes simply limit the cantilever to a specific length—usually no more than 2 feet.

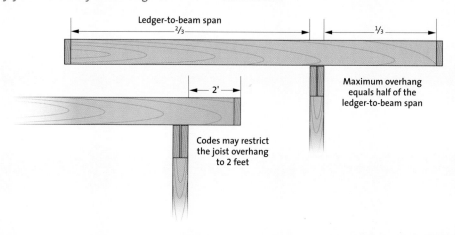

A TALE OF TWO DECKS

THE NEXT FOUR PAGES OFFER QUICK SNAPSHOTS OF TWO DECKS DURING THEIR CONSTRUCTION. One has cedar decking and railings, with inground posts and angled corners. The other is finished with composite materials and is not attached to the house. You can employ a mixture of materials and techniques used to build each of these decks—at many points throughout the rest of this book we will return to these decks to give you detailed, step-by-step instructions for implementing each of these deck's various features.

Deck 1: Wood

The deck shown on these pages features:

- Sunken footings and inground posts
- Ledger attached to the house
- Angled corners
- Two decking levels
- Cedar decking that is power-nailed
- A cascading stairway
- Custom cedar railing

Footings, ledger, and partial framing. The site is laid out using the triangulation method and marking the ground with spray paint (page 87). A rented power auger bores large holes for inground posts (the holes can be 2 or 3 inches out of alignment, and it will not matter). For the ledger, the siding is cut away, roofing felt is stapled to the exposed sheathing, a piece of flashing is slipped up under the siding, and a ledger is installed (pages 100–109). The ledger steps down where the deck's level changes.

For each level, the outside joists and header joists are assembled and held up with temporary supports (pages 118–125). Miter-cut pieces are used to create angles at the corners. The resulting boxes are checked for square. Beams are assembled, positioned directly above the post holes, and attached to the underside of the joists using temporary cleats at either end. Concrete is poured into the bottoms of the holes and allowed to set for at least 12 hours.

All the visible parts of this deck are cedar, which will be stained to a color just slightly darker than unfinished wood. A cascading stairway and distinctive light posts give it a rich, unique appearance.

Finishing the framing. Massive 6 × 6 posts are notched and cut to length, so they support the beams when resting on the concrete at the bottom of the footings. The posts are checked for level and attached to the beams. The rest of the joists are installed, using joist hangers at the ledger and nails at the header. The temporary supports for the joists and the beams can now be removed.

Decking and fascia. Cedar $5/4$ decking, running at angles, is installed quickly with gun-driven nails. The boards are butted together side by side; gaps will appear naturally later as the wood dries. Chalk lines are used to mark the perimeter cuts, after which the edges of the decking are slightly rounded with a router. Fascia boards are installed to cover exposed joists.

Railing. The railing posts for this deck are custom built to accommodate wiring and a light fixture at the top. The railing posts are bolted to the sides of the joists, through the fascia boards. Custom-made post sleeves slip over the posts. Two horizontal rails and a top cap are cut to fit between the post sleeves, and 2 × 2 balusters are attached at regular intervals to the rails.

Deck 2: Composite

The deck shown on these pages features:
- Aboveground footings and posts
- Posts and footings near the house, since there is no ledger
- Rectangular shape, on a single level
- 4-foot-high stairway
- Skirting to cover the underside of the deck
- Composite decking installed with a screw gun
- Composite railings

Footings and posts. The triangulation method is used to mark the positions of the footing holes. One row of footings is positioned close to the house since there is no ledger board. String lines ensure that the footings in each row line up exactly. Small-diameter holes are dug using a hand-operated auger. A tube form is cut for each hole and set about 2 inches above grade. Concrete is poured into the forms at the end of each row, and bolts are inserted into the wet concrete. String lines are used to make sure intermediate forms and their bolts line up precisely.

Once the concrete hardens, metal post anchors are attached to the bolts. Posts are set in and nailed to the anchors. A laser level is used to mark all the posts for cutting to height.

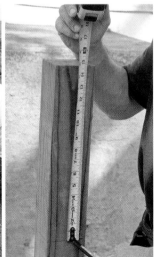

Framing. Beams are built, though not yet cut to length, and attached to the tops of the posts. The two outside joists, also not cut to length, are attached to a header joist by the house and are set on the beam and checked for square; the beams can now be marked for cutting. Once the beams are cut, all the joists are attached with joist hangers to the header near the house. The joists are aligned and attached to the beams. With a chalk line used for marking, all the joists are now cut to length. A header joist is attached to the ends of the joists.

Rail posts and decking. Composite rail posts are attached to the inside of the joists for extra strength. Composite decking is run at an angle to the house and screwed down easily using a stand-up screw gun. A spacer tool is used to maintain consistent gaps between the boards. Where the decking meets a post, the decking is notched to fit. Chalk-line cuts ensure straight lines around the perimeter.

Railing and skirting. Framing for the skirting is built out of 2 × 4s. The skirting is made of vertical decking pieces that reach all the way to the ground. A fascia board covers the top of the skirting boards, and a narrow nosing piece covers the ends of the decking. Simple access panels are made using the same materials.

   A composite railing system has pieces that fit together like a kit. Special tools are used for maintaining baluster spacing, so assembling a railing section is a snap. Once assembled, each section is cut to fit between posts, then attached using special clips that attach to the posts.

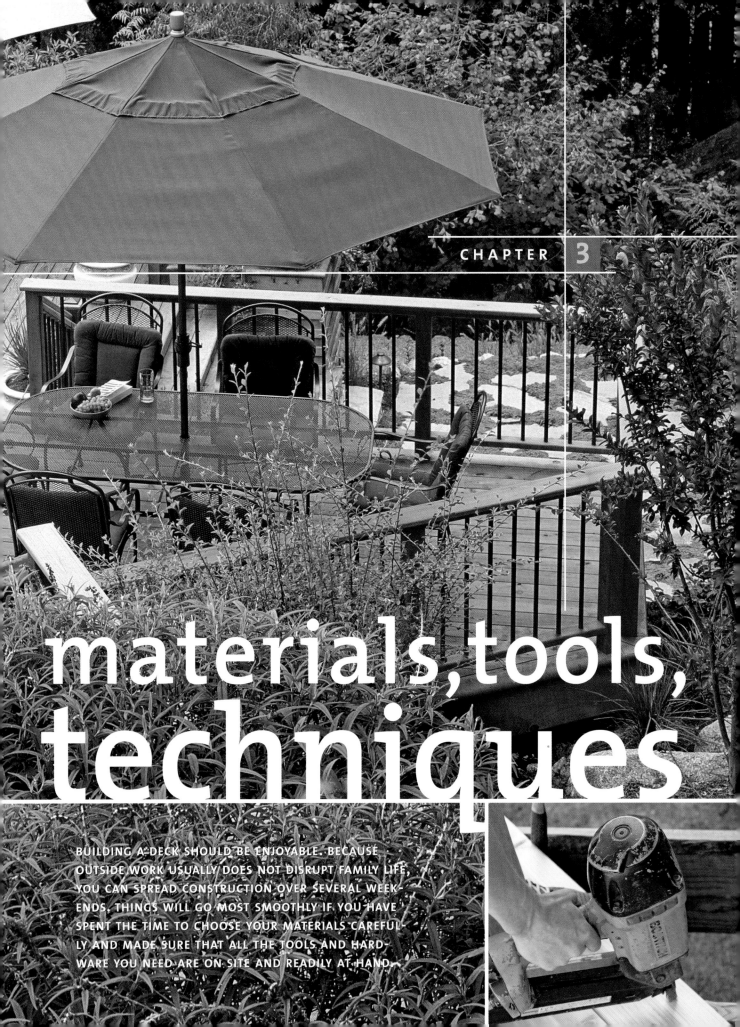

materials, tools, techniques

BUILDING A DECK SHOULD BE ENJOYABLE. BECAUSE
OUTSIDE WORK USUALLY DOES NOT DISRUPT FAMILY LIFE,
YOU CAN SPREAD CONSTRUCTION OVER SEVERAL WEEK-
ENDS. THINGS WILL GO MOST SMOOTHLY IF YOU HAVE
SPENT THE TIME TO CHOOSE YOUR MATERIALS CAREFUL-
LY AND MADE SURE THAT ALL THE TOOLS AND HARD-
WARE YOU NEED ARE ON SITE AND READILY AT HAND.

CHOOSING LUMBER

DECKS ARE EXPOSED TO A WIDE RANGE OF ELEMENTS—not only rain, and in some climates snow, but also radical temperature changes, ultraviolet rays, mildew, and wood-boring insects. When purchasing lumber for your deck, be sure to ask about its track record of durability in your area. Pressure-treated lumber is designed to stand up to the elements, making it the logical choice for your deck's structure. But when it comes to decking, railing, and fascia, you have an array of options, all of them with strong points in their favor.

Lumber that is stacked tightly and horizontally is more likely to be straight than lumber stacked loosely or vertically. Save the straightest and best-looking boards for places that are most visible. In particular, the cap rail should be made of the best boards you can find.

Treated Lumber for the Structure

Wood that has been factory-treated with preservatives will last longer than untreated wood. Pressure-treated lumber is only marginally more expensive than untreated lumber, so most codes require it for all structural components. Don't skimp; untreated wood—even many types of cedar and redwood—will rot in only a few years.

Treatment types and strengths. For many years, most wood was treated with the preservative chromated copper arsenate (CCA). CCA-treated lumber that's rated for "ground contact" or with a treatment content (also known as a retention level) of .40 or greater is nearly indestructible. However, because of concerns about its arsenic content, CCA has been banned for most residential use.

Newer, more environmentally friendly treatments include ammoniacal copper quaternary (ACQ), copper azole (CA), and copper borate azole (CBA, or CA-B). Copper is the active ingredient in all of these treatments. Tests have confirmed that these treatments are very effective at eliminating rot, as long as the boards are installed correctly.

Newer treated lumber costs more than CCA, because it has a higher copper content to replace the arsenate. To reduce costs, manufacturers produce boards with different levels of treatment. Decking typically receives the lowest chemical-retention level. Structural boards made for aboveground use—that is, most 2× lumber—contain more treatment, and structural members used for ground contact—4× and 6× material—have the highest levels.

SAFETY TIP

Borate-based treatments, which use disodium octaborate tetrahydrate (DOT), are perhaps the safest variety of pressure-treated lumber. Unlike copper-based timbers, DOT lumber can be burned (which means you can use scraps and end pieces for kindling), but DOT products are currently not rated for ground contact.

Pressure-treating and wood species. Treated Douglas fir is very strong and stable, but it may not be available in your area and tends to be expensive. Because fir does not readily accept treatment, it typically has a grid of slits incised during the treating process. Southern pine is also strong, though a bit more likely to crack. It readily accepts treatment, so there are no incisions.

Treated Douglas fir

Using the right fasteners. The copper content of new pressure-treated lumber is corrosive to steel, which means that many types of galvanized hardware—screws, nails, joist hangers, flashings—will deteriorate quickly if used to fasten pressure-treated wood. Look for hardware that is clearly labeled as safe for your type of treated wood.

Many new decking screws and nails are protected with both galvanizing and a polyester coat, to make them safe to use with ACQ- or CA-treated lumber. You can also choose hardware with G-185 galvanizing (as opposed to the G-60 or G-90 galvanizing that was once common). Stainless-steel fasteners will not corrode, but they are expensive.

Treated Douglas fir, stained

Finishing pressure-treated wood. Most treated lumber is a greenish color, which will fade in time to gray. You can buy stains designed to beautify green or graying pressure-treated lumber. However, if the lumber has slits from the treatment process, they will never disappear. Be sure to allow the wood's treatment to completely dry before applying finishes. In arid areas, the wood may dry in a few weeks; it may take up to half a year in humid climes.

Treated Southern pine

Read the Label

A typical treated board has a plastic tag stapled to its end. Look for these nuggets of information:
- Description such as "GROUND CONTACT" or "ABOVE GROUND"
- The type of treatment, often ACQ or CA-B
- The treatment retention level
- The initials AWPA (American Wood Preservers' Association) or ALSC (American Lumber Standard Committee)
- The name of the treatment company

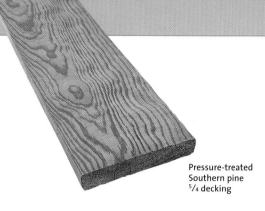

Pressure-treated
Southern pine
⁵/₄ decking

Pressure-treated decking can be
bleached and stained to colors
that mimic redwood or cedar.

Decking and Railings

As we have just seen, lumber types for the
structural portions of your deck are generally
dictated by code. For the visible portions
of your deck, on the other hand, you have
a wide variety of options. Your local home improvement center
probably carries a decent selection, and you'll find even more
choices at deck-supply stores and larger lumberyards. Some products can be ordered online. In addition to choosing the wood
species, you may also need to choose boards according to grading
(page 58).

Pressure-treated. This is probably the least expensive choice.
Treated wood goes on green and turns a dirty sort of gray if left
untreated. However, properly stained treated lumber can be
quite attractive (pages 238–239). In fact, it may cost less to
have a company refinish treated decking yearly for 15 years
than it would to buy more expensive decking to begin with.

Redwood. This material has great beauty and stability. It can be
stained to maintain rich wood tones or left unfinished to turn a
silvery gray. As with cedar, only the dark heartwood is naturally
resistant to rot. All of that said, the biggest problem with redwood
is its price, which continues to increase as sus-
tainable supplies dwindle.

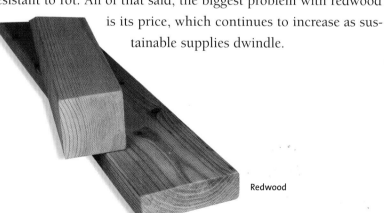

Redwood

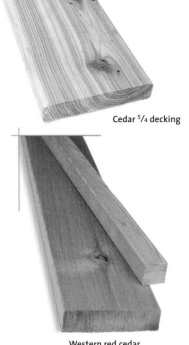

Cedar ⁵/₄ decking

Western red cedar

Cedar. This species is naturally good-looking and tends not to warp or crack too much. However, only the heartwood—which is darker in color—is reliably rot resistant; the lighter-colored sapwood may rot within a few years if not sealed. Western red cedar is the most abundant type, but in some areas you can find northern white, Alaska yellow, and others. Most cedars are fairly soft, but that is usually not a concern unless you expect especially heavy traffic—sealers add to the strength of the wood. Cedar is available in all sorts of dimensions, but ⁵/₄ decking (which is 1 inch thick and 5½ inches wide) is the most commonly used material for decks. It has rounded edges and is often installed butted tightly together; once it dries it will shrink, producing ⅛-inch gaps between boards.

Tropical hardwoods. Often called ironwood, tropical hardwoods include species such as Ipé, Cambara, Pau Lopé, and meranti. These woods are amazingly strong, so often a 1× board can span the same distance as a 2× softwood board. They are expensive, but fairly popular because of their lasting good looks. Boards are often perfectly straight, with close grain and very few knots. Some types are so full of natural oil that they will not accept stain for a year or so. Working with hardwoods is sometimes difficult. You may need to drill pilot holes before driving each fastener.

Mahogany and teak, more familiar hardwoods, are similarly hard, with dense, straight grains. The quality of these materials varies greatly, however. Some people swear by them, while others find the wood splits and warps. Check with your dealer or a professional deck builder in your area to make sure these boards will perform well for you.

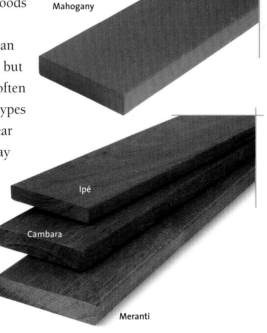

Mahogany

Ipé

Cambara

Meranti

Siberian Larch

This lumber is new to the American market, though it has been in use in Europe and Asia for decades. Siberian larch is naturally rot resistant even though it is light in color. It is harder than pine but not as hard as ironwood, and most of the boards are straight and splinter-free. If larch is not available in your area, check online.

Spend as much as you can afford to buy high-quality decking, and choose the individual boards carefully. You'll be rewarded by a deck that looks great for years.

Lumber Grading

Most boards display a grading stamp or sticker that gives important details about the board's quality. Grading systems vary dramatically from one species of wood to another, but here are some of the most common designations.

Lumber is often rated Select (or Select Structural), No. 1, No. 2, or No. 3. Another system uses the terms Construction, Standard (or Standard and Better), and Utility. Avoid using No. 3 or Utility. Standard and No. 2 boards are strong enough for most structural work, but your local codes may require a better grade.

Cedar and redwood are graded for appearance and heartwood content. When buying redwood, choose boards with a label that contains the word "heart." If the label on a piece of cedar doesn't contain information about the board's heartwood content, choose darker-colored boards.

A board with a high moisture content is more likely to warp and shrink; the drier the board, the more stable it will be. If a board is labeled S-DRY or its moisture content is 20 percent or less, shrinkage and warping should not be a problem. Pressure-treated lumber labeled KDAT (kiln dried after treatment) is the driest and most stable; you may want to buy KDAT boards for the cap rail of a railing or for other very exposed parts of your deck.

Fascia Boards

You can leave the outside and header joists exposed and unfinished but most people prefer a cleaner look. When building a wood deck, it is common to cover joists with 1× fascia material that is made out of the same wood as the decking—say, cedar, redwood, or appearance-quality pressure-treated lumber. If you use cedar or redwood, you may choose to showcase its rough side to give your deck a pleasant woody appearance. If you plan to install skirting, you may not need fascia at all.

Vertical and Flat Grain

Depending on how it was cut at the sawmill, a board may have either vertical grain—narrow, parallel grain lines—or flat grain: wide grain lines that form wavy V shapes. Many boards contain both vertical and flat grain. Vertical-grain lumber is less likely to cup or twist and is stronger than flat-grain lumber. Whenever possible, choose boards with primarily vertical grain.

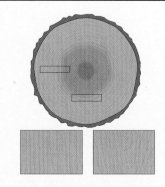

Checking for Defects

If possible, you should pick up and examine each board before purchasing. First check the board's surface for obvious defects, then raise one end and look down its length to make sure it's fairly straight. Few boards are perfect, but you should make sure none of yours are damaged in a way that will harm the deck's structure. Here are the major defects to watch out for:

● **CROOK.** A severe warp (more than an inch on an 8-foot-long piece) along the edge line. If the warp is not severe, it is called a crown, and can be straightened out on decking boards. Joints are installed with the crown side up.

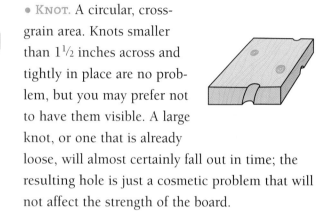

● **BOW.** A warp on the face of a board from end to end. Unless the bow is extremely pronounced, it usually can be straightened during installation.

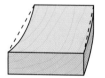

● **CUP.** A hollow across the face of a board. This is difficult to straighten out, so reject a board with a severe cup.

● **CHECKING.** Cracks that run along the length of a board but do not go all the way through. If the check is wider than $1/16$ inch or deeper than half the board's thickness, the checked portion must be cut off.

● **KNOT.** A circular, cross-grain area. Knots smaller than $1^1/2$ inches across and tightly in place are no problem, but you may prefer not to have them visible. A large knot, or one that is already loose, will almost certainly fall out in time; the resulting hole is just a cosmetic problem that will not affect the strength of the board.

● **SPLIT.** A crack that goes all the way through the board. This usually occurs at one of the board's ends. Plan to cut off the split portion.

● **WANE.** Missing wood or untrimmed bark along the edge or corner of a board. Unless a major portion of the board is missing, this is only a cosmetic problem.

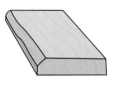

● **TWIST.** Multiple bends in a board. Twists are usually difficult to straighten.

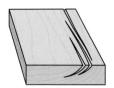

Many types of composite decking have a look that recalls natural wood but with cleaner lines and no possibility of splintering.

Synthetic Decking and Railings

In recent years many people have been drawn to decking products made in whole or part of synthetic materials. These products—which range from composites of plastic and wood to "boards" made entirely of vinyl—are generally expensive, but the payoff is that they are virtually maintenance free. Or, at least, some of them are. While it is certainly true that synthetics are easier to care for than wood, not all synthetics perform the same, and no synthetic is perfect.

The information below is intended to help you choose the right synthetic product for your situation. As with wood, it's a good idea to talk with deck owners and staff of building-supply stores that supply at least several types of synthetics to learn how different products perform in your area.

Some products have a fairly smooth surface; others have a deeply embossed wood-grain pattern. Still other products have variegated colors meant to further approximate the look of wood.

Synthetics can only be used for decking, railing, and fascia; they are not strong enough to be rated as structural members. As of the writing of this book, more than 80 manufacturers were producing synthetic decking and railing.

Composite products are the most common type of synthetic. Made of recycled plastic and ground-up waste wood, composites are an ecologically sound choice. At least three types of plastic are used in composite materials: standard polyethylene, which is fairly soft; polypropylene; and high-density polyethylene (HDPE). Composites engineered with last two kinds of plastic are harder and more stain- and scratch-resistant than composites containing standard polyethylene. The wood particles in many composites are not, as you might expect, entirely shielded from moisture, which means many composites are still subject to mildew and fungus. To eliminate this problem, some products are made with a process that encapsulates the wood fibers.

All-vinyl decking has no wood particles and is usually made with virgin rather than recycled plastic. These products are generally more expensive than composites, but they resist staining and fading better. The trade-off is that they tend not to have a convincing woodlike appearance—some don't even pretend to.

Composite hardwood

Though it has the look of old-world craftsmanship, a synthetic railing like this assembles easily and quickly.

When choosing a synthetic, consider these factors:

● FADING. Some synthetics fade faster than others. Still, many can be painted to restore their original color.

● FASTENERS. Buy your fasteners when you buy your synthetic lumber. Railing systems are usually sold with their own special clips; some brands of decking require special invisible fastening systems.

● MILDEW. Just because a product is synthetic doesn't mean it's immune from mildew, especially in humid climates or chronically shady locations.

● MUSHROOMS. Driving a nail or screw through a synthetic board usually produces a small raised bump, or mushroom, around the screw head. In many cases, these mushrooms can be eliminated by tapping them lightly with a hammer. Or, use a self-tapping composite deck screw which cuts its own counterbore hole.

● SCRATCHING. Synthetics scratch fairly easily, although some are engineered for scratch resistance. You can erase scratches with a heat gun, but try this technique on a sample first to get the hang of it.

● STAINING. Oil from a bicycle, grease from the barbecue, rust from patio furniture, and even suntan lotion may produce stains that are difficult to remove. Some synthetics resist staining, but to varying degrees.

● SWELLING. All synthetics swell at least slightly; some swell a lot. Be sure to leave gaps between boards as specified by the manufacturer.

Vinyl

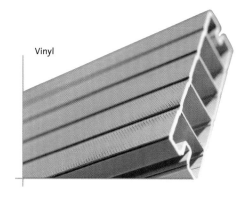

Composite softwood

Decking nails
for nail gun

DECK
FASTENERS

EVEN THE BEST-QUALITY FASTENERS ACCOUNT FOR ONLY A MODEST PORTION OF THE COST OF A NEW deck—they are well worth the investment. Choose fasteners that not only hold firmly but also resist corrosion. To ensure a strong deck, purchase fasteners that exceed the requirements of your local code.

Ring-shank nail

Galvanized spiral-groove nail

Stainless-steel spiral-groove nail

Joist hanger nail

Finish nail

Galvanized decking screw

Stainless-steel screw

Stainless-steel trim screw

Nails

Nails are commonly used for fastening deck structures because they can be installed so quickly. Whether you choose to hand-drive or use a power nailer, be sure to choose nails that will not corrode when driven into pressure-treated lumber (page 55). The somewhat chunky surface of galvanized nails not only inhibits rust, but also adds to the nail's grabbing power. Spiral-groove galvanized nails hold even better and are a good choice for decking.

Many people assume they should use screws on their decking. But nail heads present a less-obtrusive appearance. Hand-driven nails look great, but it takes patience and practice to drive nails without marring the decking surface. Gun-driven nails sink below the surface, and many types of wood will nearly cover up the hole in time.

Screws

Equipped with a strong drill and a screwdriver bit, you can drive screws quickly. If you rent a screw gun and buy screws that come in long clips, you can put down your decking even faster.

Stainless-steel screws are classy looking and impervious to corrosion, but they are also expensive. Decking screws are typically double-coated, to resist corrosion. (Even if you are installing nontreated decking, the screw must drive into treated wood, so don't scrimp on decking screws.) Standard Phillips-head screws strip easily. Instead, buy screws that use a square drive bit or a special deck-screw bit.

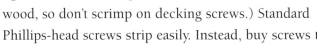

Square drive bit

Decking screw bit

Decking screws for screw gun

PRO TIP

For sizable decks, you will probably want to rent a power nailer, which drives nails with machine-gun speed. Take the time to adjust the nailer's depth setting so it drives nail heads just below the surface of the wood.

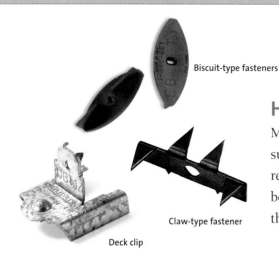
Biscuit-type fasteners

Claw-type fastener

Deck clip

Hidden Fasteners

Many people dislike the sight of nail or screw heads dotting the surface of a deck, especially if the decking itself is top-notch. In response to that concern, several types of hidden fasteners have been developed. They cost more and take longer to install, but the results can be worth it.

Bolts and Lag Screws

Bolts are heavy-duty fasteners intended to carry larger loads than standard nails and screws. Carriage bolts and lag screws are used to connect ledgers, railing posts, and other critical framing members; your building code will likely specify the exact size and number of such fasteners. Carriage bolts, which require a nut and washer, are usually stronger than lag screws, but cannot be used if the back side of the fastener is not accessible. Carriage bolts and lag screws both require pilot holes. Anchor bolts (or J-bolts) are used to secure post anchors to concrete footings. Use a washer whenever driving a lag screw or a bolt.

For ledgers or other boards that must be fastened to masonry, options include expanding anchors, masonry screws, and lag screws with masonry shields. Special ledger screws have greater shear strength (to resist downward pressure) and can sometimes be used instead of lag screws.

Anchor bolt

Carriage bolt

Lag screw

Screw with masonry shield

Framing Hardware

A variety of items, including joist hangers and metal straps, are made specifically for connecting various components of a deck. Be sure to buy connectors that are coated for use with your type of treated lumber.

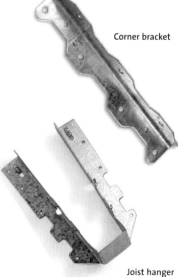
Corner bracket

Angled joist hanger

Seismic strap

Post cap

Post base

Joist hanger

OTHER MATERIALS

YOUR CHOICE OF DECKING, RAILING, AND FASTENERS WILL HAVE A MAJOR IMPACT ON THE LOOK OF YOUR DECK, but equally important are the choices you make about materials that add to your deck's durability. In particular, materials that prevent moisture from causing damage to your house's protective sheathing are critical. Concrete is required to anchor and support your deck. And to protect wooden decks from premature aging, choose a top-quality finish and apply it regularly.

Moisture Barriers

The area where the house and deck framing connect must be protected so moisture will not collect and cause damage to either structure. Your building department may require specific products. You will likely have to staple or nail roofing felt (also called tar paper) directly to your home's sheathing. Choose a metal or vinyl flashing that is Z shaped, so it slips up under the siding above and wraps around the ledger board.

Building departments may call for applying a flexible, self-adhering membrane, sometimes called self-stick flashing. This product can be used instead of flashing to protect the ledger board. Some installers apply a similar product to the tops of all the joists.

You'll probably need caulk as well. Choose a high-quality exterior-rated caulk such as silicone, latex/silicone, or butyl.

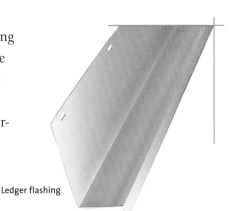

Self-adhering membrane

Ledger flashing

Gravel and Weed Block

If you live in a humid part of the country, it may be a good idea to excavate away the sod from under the deck and replace it with weed block and gravel. Fibrous weed block allows water to seep through but blocks the sun so plants cannot grow. Gravel placed on top of the weed block keeps it in place and prevents puddles.

Concrete

You will, of course, need concrete to form foundation footings and piers; you may also need it to create a landing pad at the bottom of a set of stairs. See pages 94–95 for various ways of mixing concrete. If you are building a large deck with many deep holes to fill, it may be best to have ready-mixed concrete delivered. Usually, however, for smaller decks, it is easy enough to mix bags of dry-mix concrete on site in a wheelbarrow, trough, or small rented power mixer.

To create cylindrical concrete footings, use tube forms, which are well worth their price and may be required by code. Tubes are available in various diameters and can be cut to length with a handsaw or a circular saw.

Post Caps

One of the easiest things to protect is the exposed grain at the tops of posts. A post cap will do the trick nicely, while adding a lovely finishing touch to your railing. Home centers, deck specialty stores, and online sources offer a dizzying array of post caps, so there's really no excuse to leave your posts unprotected.

Wood Finishes

The essential ingredients for deck longevity include thoughtful design, careful construction, and, if you've selected wood for your decking and rails, routine coatings with a good-quality finish. All wood decks last longer if they are regularly coated. Finishes are available in a variety of colors and formulations (pages 238–239). Choose the type of finish you will use when you design the deck—it is, after all, an important aspect of your deck's design. In general, you should apply a finish to your deck as soon as possible.

TOOLS OF THE TRADE

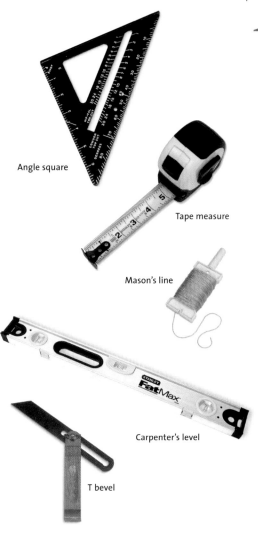

Angle square

Tape measure

Mason's line

Carpenter's level

T bevel

ONE OF THE GREAT THINGS ABOUT BUILDING A DECK IS THAT DESPITE IT BEING A SERIOUS PROJECT THAT YOU can really get immersed in, you don't need a lot of tools. Most of the tools required are of the standard construction variety, so you may already have many of them in your garage. If you do have to purchase a few new tools, take heart in the knowledge that you will likely use them again for other home-improvement projects. Basic hand tools are discussed here; power tools are covered on pages 72–79. As for accessories, don't deny yourself a good, strong tool belt.

Measuring and Laying Out

A 25- or 30-foot tape measure will probably handle most of your measuring needs. If your deck is very large, purchase a 50- or 100-foot model to complement your 25-footer. A framing square allows you to quickly check corners to make sure they are square, and it is ideal for marking stringers for stairs. A smaller angle square is handy for marking cut lines on lumber, guiding the base of a circular saw, and marking precise angle cuts. You may also need a T bevel to duplicate unusual angles. Colored mason's line is superior to standard string for laying out your deck. Use a chalk line to quickly mark long, straight lines.

To check structures for level and plumb, a carpenter's level will usually do the job. A post level lets you check a post for plumb in both directions at once, leaving your hands free to position the post as you secure it. For more on leveling, see page 70.

Framing square

Post level

Chalk line

Fastening and Cutting

Even if you rent a power nailer to lay down your decking, a curved-claw hammer will be a constant companion, so buy one that is comfortable to work with. If you are hand nailing, be prepared to use a nailset to drive nails below the surface of your decking without marring it. For quick cuts, a handsaw is occasionally useful. Wood chisels are invaluable for cleaning out notches in decking around posts and for completing cuts at inside corners. A flat pry bar can be used to coax crooked deck boards into place. And since we all make mistakes, a cat's paw can help you to remove misplaced nails in your framing.

A caulking gun is essential for sealing joints with caulk. For securing nuts, bolts, and lag screws, an adjustable wrench is okay but a socket wrench with correctly sized sockets is better. A variety of clamps will help you pull boards into alignment or hold them in place while you fasten. You may also need a pair of tin snips to cut metal flashing. Finally, a hand sanding block is often the fastest way to round off wooden edges.

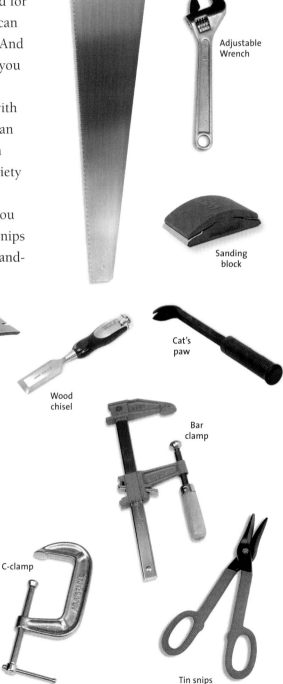

Handsaw

Adjustable Wrench

Sanding block

Caulking gun

Cat's paw

Wood chisel

Bar clamp

Nailset

Pry bar

Curved claw hammer

Socket wrench

Squeeze clamp

C-clamp

Tin snips

SPECIAL DECK TOOLS

IN ADDITION TO A CARPENTRY TOOL KIT, you'll need tools for digging, mixing concrete, and smoothing the ground. Other tools help you lay out the site and keep everything level and plumb. Some of these tools can be rented. Others are inexpensive enough to be purchased, even if you never intend to build another deck in your lifetime. A few have uses beyond the building of a deck.

Mortar hoe

Mortar tub

Digging bar

Square-bladed spade

Garden rake

Pointed spade

Excavation and Concrete Tools

If you have a lot of footing to dig, you should probably rent a power auger to dig your holes, but you'll still need a hand post-hole digger to clean out the dirt and perhaps widen the hole. A digging bar (also called a wrecking bar) is a great help when you encounter a thick root or a large rock. A square-bladed spade is better than a pointed spade for cutting away sod, and a simple garden rake is all you need to smooth soil or gravel in the area under the deck.

Unless you are renting a power mixer or are ordering ready-mix from a truck, mix concrete in a mortar tub or a wheelbarrow (rinse it thoroughly after use). A mortar hoe is the best tool for mixing dry ingredients with water.

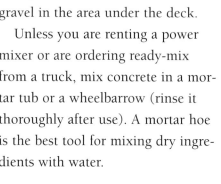

Post-hole digger

Carpenter's level

Safety Equipment

Though it may be a bit annoying and make you feel like a dork, you really should wear safety goggles when cutting boards and when driving fasteners—protect your eyes! Wear gloves when handling wood that may splinter. And if you will be spending a lot of time on your knees nailing or screwing down the decking, a pair of knee pads will make the task significantly more comfortable.

Eye protection

Hand protection

Stand-up
screw gun

Power Fasteners

Nowadays it's not unusual for a do-it-yourselfer (or his neighbor) to have a power nailer, also known as a nail gun. If you can't borrow one or don't want to buy one, you can rent a power nailer from most home improvement centers. You'll need a compressor, plus at least one gun. A typical framing gun drives nails from 2 to $3\frac{1}{2}$ inches long, so it can be used for both framing and decking. Smaller nailers are designed to make quick work of driving joist-hanger nails. Another option is to go cordless, which many people prefer since there is no compressor and hose to deal with. A typical cordless nailer has a rechargeable battery and a small gas canister, which can drive about 1,000 3-inch nails.

Cordless
nail gun

If you choose to secure your decking with screws instead of nails, you can use a standard corded or cordless drill with a screwdriver attachment instead of a drill bit. But with a screw gun, the work will go faster and you won't have to worry about your drill overheating. Screw gun screws are packaged in a clip, so you can drive 50 or so before having to reload. Stand-up models are easy to use and will help save your knees.

SQUARING FOR LAYOUT

THE CARDINAL RULE OF CAR-
PENTRY CAN BE SUMMARIZED
AS FOLLOWS: BUILD IT PLUMB,
LEVEL, AND SQUARE. "Plumb"
means true to a vertical plane.
A plumb object takes maximum advantage of gravity, transfer-
ring loads directly to the earth. "Level" means true to a horizontal plane. When a plumb object meets a level object, they
form a 90-degree angle, which is the basis of "square."

Establishing Plumb

Deck posts need to be plumb in both directions (i.e., to your
left and right; in front of and behind you). Hold a carpenter's
level against the post and move the post until the bubbles are
centered in the two end vials. Then check the other direction. Or
use a post level, which checks in both directions at once and frees
your hands. You can also check for plumb using a plumb bob (above),
which hangs perfectly straight down from a piece of string.

A post level simultaneously
checks for plumb and level in
both directions, so you can con-
centrate on fastening.

Finding Level

Check beams, joists, and decking with a carpenter's level placed
in the horizontal position. When the bubble is centered in the vial,
the object is level. To check for level over a long distance (say,
from the ledger to a far post), the simplest method is to place a
level atop the center of a long, straight board (secure it with tape).
This turns a 4-foot level into an 8-, 10-, or 12-footer. Because
boards are often crowned, meaning they rise up in the middle,
you'll usually get the most accurate measurement if you place
the level in the center of the board.

A laser level makes quick work of
checking for level over a long distance—inexpensive models are widely
available. A water level also works well,
though it is a bit slow to use.

Checking for Square

Most decks are rectangular or made of several adjoining rectangles. If the corners of the frame are not square, the decking will be harder to install and the results will look unprofessional. Continually check for square when laying out for post-hole locations, when installing footings and posts, and when building framing (bottom, right). You can check a small structure for square by simply placing a framing square against the edge of two boards that are supposed to be at a right angle to each other. For larger structures, however, use measurements.

To quickly determine if a rectangle is square, measure both diagonals. If they are identical, the corners are square. Be aware, however, that this method works only if parallel sides are exactly the same length.

To check a single corner for square, use the "3-4-5" technique. Measure along one side 3 feet, along a perpendicular side 4 feet, then measure the diagonal formed between these two spots. If it equals 5 feet, the corner is square. For greater accuracy, use a set of larger numbers that have the same ratio, such as 6-8-10, 9-12-15, or even 30-40-50.

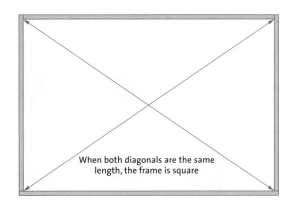

When both diagonals are the same length, the frame is square

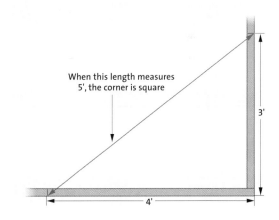

When this length measures 5', the corner is square

3'

4'

Laying Out for Joists

Joists must be spaced evenly—usually 12, 16, or 24 inches apart, on center. To ensure on-center joist placement, hook a tape measure to the outside of the first joist, and make marks on your ledger or beam every 12, 16, or 24 inches. Then make another series marks on the ledger or beam 1½ inches away from the first ones, to mark the other side of the board's thickness (below). Use a square to draw straight lines down from the marks. Each joist's end should be positioned between the lines.

POWER TOOLS

THE TWO MOST ESSENTIAL POWER TOOLS IN A DECK BUILDER'S ARSENAL are definitely a reliable circular saw and drill. If you don't own either, or are still making do with the tools your father gave you too many years ago when he was cleaning out his garage, now is a good time to make a modest investment. Stay away from low-cost models, which are frequently underpowered and may be poorly constructed. Midpriced tools are often the best choice for a homeowner—to build a deck, and for occasional work around the house, you do not need top-of-the-line professional-grade tools.

PRO TIP

To ensure straight cuts, keep your saw's base plate perfectly flat on the board you are cutting. If you are cutting near the edge of a board, hold the saw so the widest part of the base plate rests on the board. Otherwise, you will likely wobble as you cut, and your cuts will not be square.

An Ode to the Circular Saw

In deck building and most carpentry tasks, no power tool sees more action than a circular saw. The most common style takes a $7\frac{1}{4}$-inch blade, which will cut to a depth of about $2\frac{1}{2}$ inches.

Choose a saw that feels comfortable and is easy to operate. Make sure that you can clearly sight along the notch in the base as you cut. It should also be easy to adjust the base plate, both for cut depth and to produce bevel cuts. Read the fine print in the saw's manual: A quality saw will be rated at more than 12 amps and will use ball or roller bearings rather than sleeve bearings.

Purchase at least one carbide-tipped blade with at least 24 teeth. Such a blade will last longer and produce smoother cuts than less expensive blades. When the blade starts to labor rather than glide during cutting, replace it or have it sharpened.

A circular saw is a serious tool that demands respect. Always follow the manufacturer's safety recommendations. Practice on scrap pieces of wood until you are skilled at making straight cuts.

Checking the blade. If the blade is not square to the base, your cuts will be slightly beveled rather than square. This can create unsightly gaps when cutting decking boards that will be butted together. Unplug the saw, turn it upside down, retract the blade guard, and use a square to check the blade. For a more accurate test, cut two boards, and butt them together; if the ends do not meet precisely, the blade needs to be adjusted.

Adjusting the depth. Before making a cut, unplug the saw and adjust the saw depth to about $1/4$ inch below the bottom of the board you are about to cut. This adjustment is easiest to make with the saw on the top of the board.

Making a cross cut. You can use an angle square to mark a board for cutting, but you can also this tool as a guide for making accurate 90- and 45-degree cuts. Hold the saw's base against the square, pull the trigger, and push forward. Avoid micromanaging the cut; aim for a smooth motion.

Making a rip cut. To rip a board (that is, to cut it lengthwise), mark the cut line with a chalk line. If you are unsure of your abilities to cut a straight line, you can clamp a straight board alongside the saw's base plate to act as a guide. For a quicker guide, skilled carpenters use a thumb and knuckle: Start the cut, pinch the front inside edge of the saw's base plate so that the side of your finger slides along the board's edge, then continue the cut.

Jigsaw

You will need a jigsaw (also called a saber saw) to cut curves in decking and other boards. Invest in a substantial jigsaw that pulls at least 5 amps and has a stable base plate; cheaper models make it difficult to execute smooth, accurate cuts.

Cordless drill

Drills and Screw Guns

Screws are often used for fastening decking and railing. They can also be used to fasten framing, but nails are more common for structural work.

You will need a drill to make pilot holes for screws and bolts. Add a screwdriver bit to your drill, and you can use it to drive screws. If you will be screwing down decking for a large deck, a standard drill may overheat. Use a heavy-duty corded drill rated at 7 amps or more. Better yet, rent or buy a screw gun.

You will appreciate having two or more drills available as your deck-building project moves along. A corded drill is handy for regular use, while a cordless drill is often more convenient in tight or remote spots. Choose a cordless drill rated at 14 volts or better; an 18-volt cordless drill is as powerful as many corded drills. If you need to drill holes in concrete, you will be thankful that you have a hammer drill, which can also serve as your regular corded drill.

TIME SAVER

If you are using a cordless drill, buy an extra battery and set up a battery charger in a convenient location. That way, one battery can always be charging while the other is being used.

Hammer drill

Pilot Holes for Bolts

When installing carriage bolts, drill a pilot hole all the way through the lumber using a bit that is the same size as the bolt's shaft. Lag screws, which are often used to attach posts, require two drilling steps, as shown at right. For $\frac{1}{2}$-inch lag screws, first drill a $\frac{1}{2}$-inch-diameter pilot hole completely through the first board. Then change to a smaller drill bit—about $\frac{5}{16}$ inch—and drill a second hole into the second board. Put a washer on the lag screw and tighten it using an adjustable wrench or a socket wrench.

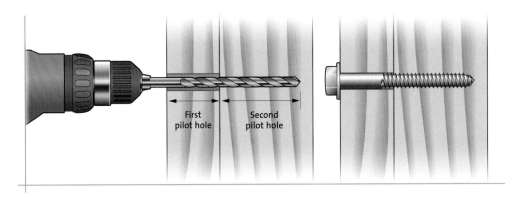

First pilot hole   Second pilot hole

Angle-Driving Screws and Nails

When you need to attach the end of a board to another board at right angles to it, often you need to drive nails or screws at angles, a process often called toenailing. If you drive several nails or screws through each side of the board, the bond will be quite strong. However, the joint will be made stronger if you add a joist hanger or an angle bracket after toenailing.

If you are using a nail gun, simply hold the gun's nose about $1\frac{1}{2}$ inches from the end of the board, angled at about 45 degrees, and pull the trigger.

To drive a toenail by hand, start by holding the nail at a right angle to the board, and tap once or twice until it barely sinks in (top, left). Place the board a little to the side of the layout line; driving the toenail will usually cause the board to move over $\frac{1}{8}$ inch or so. Grab the nail, change its angle to 45 degrees, and drive it home with the hammer (top, center). When you sink the nail's head, the hammer will make a fairly large dent in the wood. You can avoid this by using a nailset, but if you are framing, don't spend a lot of time and energy making cosmetic fixes that no one will ever see.

To drive an angled screw, first drill an angled pilot hole in your board. Start two or more screws until they barely poke out through the end of the board. Then place the board about $\frac{1}{8}$ inch to the side of the layout line and finish driving the screws (top, right).

Pilot Hole Shortcut

When driving nails or screws near the ends of boards, you stand a good chance of splitting a board, and thus weakening the connection to other boards. To prevent that, whenever driving a fastener within 2 inches of a board end, first drill a pilot hole using a drill bit slightly smaller in diameter than the screw or nail. Then drive the fastener.

Many professional deck builders skip this step to avoid having to go back and forth from drill bit to screwdriver bit; instead, they simply use the screwdriver bit to drill a short "cheat" hole, then drive the screw. This shortcut works particularly well with softwoods like cedar, but if you have pressure-treated or harder wood you will probably need to drill "honest" pilot holes in order to prevent splitting.

Drill pilot holes (or "cheat" holes) at slight angles before driving the fasteners.

Power Miter Saw

Many well-built decks have been constructed with only a circular saw. But a power miter saw, or chop saw, ensures straight cuts and clean joints. It can also dramatically speed up the deck-building process, making short and neat work of miters and bevels. For repetitive tasks, such as cutting dozens of balusters to identical length, a power miter saw set up with a stop block is unbeatable.

Anchor the chop saw on a stable, table-height surface. Some saws have a clamp that holds the lumber tight during cutting. To test whether the saw is cutting accurately, cut two boards at identical 45-degree angles. Flip one of the boards 180 degrees, then butt them together—they should align to create a straight board.

MONEY SAVER

A 10-inch power miter saw is the most common size for homeowners, but if you need to miter the ends of 2 × 6s at 45-degree angles, it may be smarter to rent a 12-inch saw than to buy a 10-inch one that won't perform this task.

Cutting the balusters, angled seat supports, and 45-degree angles in the decking of this small deck was easy with a power miter saw.

Table Saw

A portable table saw is the best tool for making long rip cuts, or for cutting notches in railing posts. It's not a tool you should buy for just one deck, though, so only make the investment if you are contemplating future building projects around your home.

You can set up a table saw on an actual table, but it's nearly as easy to use it on the ground. Adjust the blade so it cuts about $3/8$ higher than the thickness of the board you are cutting. Use a tape measure to adjust the saw's guide, or fence, then rip a test piece to make sure you are cutting at the correct width. Press the board firmly against the rip guide as you feed the board smoothly; avoid any turns, which can cause the blade to bind. If the saw binds and stops, turn the saw off immediately, back up, and start again. For long boards, have a helper on the other end pull gently as you push.

Reciprocating Saw

A reciprocating saw can cut in places a circular saw cannot reach, making it handy for demolition work. It also cuts more quickly than a handsaw. If you are cutting off the tops of 6 × 6 posts, for instance, first cut around the perimeter of the post with a circular saw, then finish the cut with a reciprocating saw. The tool is also excellent for cutting a notch for a beam into the top of a post, as shown above and left.

When cutting with a reciprocating saw, sympathetic vibration is your greatest enemy; if the piece is shaking while you are cutting, it will take a long time to cut, and the cut will likely be ragged. Have a helper hold the piece still while you cut.

You can also use a reciprocating saw to surgically cut through hidden screws and nails. This makes demolition easier, and makes it possible to do things like slip flashing under siding.

Driving Nails

There's nothing wrong with hand nailing, but the work is slow and tiring. Where the nail heads will show—on the decking and railing, for example—it takes a fair amount of skill to drive the nails just flush, with no indentations. A miss will create a "smile" or "frown" in the wood.

A nail gun is much easier to use. In most cases, it will set the nail head slightly below the surface of the wood, and will do so consistently to create an even appearance. You can drive a nail by pressing the gun's nose into the wood and then pulling the trigger, or pulling the trigger and then tapping the gun's nose onto the wood. The second technique is faster, but less accurate.

Power Sanders

If the ends of your decking are a bit rough, a random-orbit or vibrating sander will smooth them out with little trouble, although the results will be less uniform than what you'd achieve with a router. Practice on scrap pieces. Some woods sand quickly, and with these you'll need to take precautions against digging in; harder boards are virtually impossible to over-sand. As you sand, keep the tool moving and hold the sandpaper flat against the edge; stopping in one place or tilting the tool could cause it to dig in. Belt sanders are not recommended for use on decks because they dig into the wood a lot.

 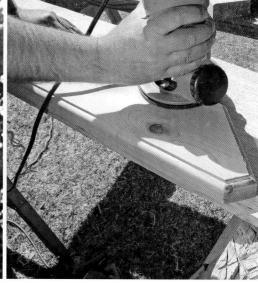

Router

For most deck work requiring a router, an inexpensive one will suffice. To create neat, smooth edges on decking, posts, handrails, and stair treads, use a router equipped with a self-guiding round-over bit that produces a $^3/_8$- or $^1/_2$-inch radius edge. A carbide-tipped bit with a ball-bearing pilot will give the best results. To create 45-degree beveled edges, use a chamfer bit.

You can also use a router to create ornate edges for post caps and other finish pieces. Ogee bits (top, right) are most commonly used for this purpose; several ogee styles are available. Install the bit, and practice on scrap pieces until you get the depth you desire. Hold the router's base plate flat on the board with the bit an inch or so away from the edge. Turn on the router, slide it over until the bit starts cutting, and move the router along the edges using smooth motions. As long as you keep the base plate flat on the board, it is virtually impossible to make a mistake.

Extension Cords

You should have enough outdoor extension cords and plugs so that you do not have to repeatedly unplug one tool and plug in another. Purchase heavy-gauge cords made for tools; household extension cords can over-heat dangerously. All cords and power strips should be GFCI (ground fault circuit interrupter)-protected. If no GFCI outlet is available, use a cord with an in-line GFCI.

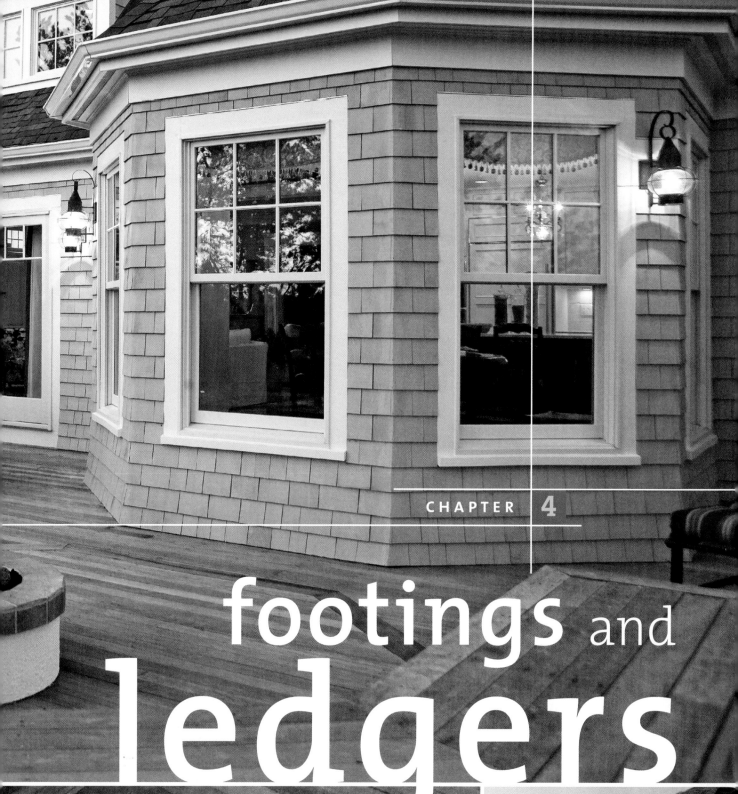

footings and ledgers

A DECK'S FOUNDATION SUPPORTS THE WEIGHT
OF YOUR STRUCTURE AND ANCHORS IT TO PREVENT
SHIFTING. CONCRETE FOOTINGS CAN BE SET BELOW
GROUND OR ABOVE. IN THIS CHAPTER WE SHOW
YOU HOW TO DO BOTH, AS WELL AS HOW TO SAFELY
ATTACH A LEDGER TO YOUR HOME'S FRAMING.

THE RIGHT FOUNDATIONS

DECK-BUILDING MISTAKES ABOVE-GROUND CAN BE CORRECTED LATER, but the foundation will be hard to access once the structure is in place. Therefore, plan your foundation carefully. Heavy accessories—such as an outdoor kitchen counter or a very large planter—may require you to beef up the foundation; consult with your local building department to be sure.

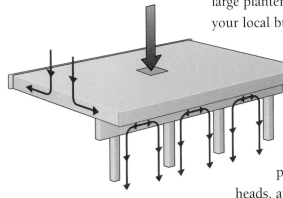

The curved arrows indicate how load is carried through joists, beams, and posts from the deck to the earth. Additional load is carried through the ledger to the house and its foundation.

Supporting the Load

There are two kinds of weight, or load, that a deck must support. "Dead load" is the weight of the structure itself plus all of its permanent components, such as railings, overheads, and built-in benches. "Live load" consists of variable factors, such as people, portable furniture, and snow. The typical code requirement is that decks be able to support a dead load of 10 pounds per square foot and a live load of 40 pounds per square foot, for a total maximum load of 50 pounds per square foot. In areas with loose and unstable soil, extra-large footings may also be required.

Footing Types

For a deck, as with a house, the foundation anchors the structure to prevent settling and shifting. It also distributes the weight of the deck and its contents onto the earth. But while most house foundations are composed of a masonry wall around the entire perimeter, most deck foundations consist of a series of individual concrete piers or footings.

Local building codes govern the size and spacing of foundations and specify how deep into the ground they must go. Typical codes call for 16-inch-square or 18-inch-diameter footings that are 8 inches thick at the bottom; a pier may rise up above the ground as well.

In cold climates, codes often also require that the bottom of the footing extend below the frost line. If it does not go this deep, ice can form beneath it and push up the deck an inch or more, a process called frost heave. In some circumstances this movement can seriously weaken the deck or damage the house. However, if the deck is not attached to the house, codes may allow the deck to "float" independently; in that case, footings can be above the frost line. Codes provide

LINGO ALERT

In the parlance of many building departments, a "pier" is the vertical portion of a foundation; a "footing" is a horizontal piece, often located at the bottom of a pier. Terminology varies, so in this book we generally refer to the entire concrete structure as either the "footing" or the "foundation."

detailed specifications for several types of foundations. For years, the most common footing has been a cylindrical pier that rises above the ground. Lately, many building departments have been showing a preference for the inground post, supported by an 8-inch-thick concrete footing at the bottom. If frost heave is not a concern, you can use precast piers set on tamped soil, a concrete footing, or a tamped gravel bed. There's even a type of footing that requires the post to be embedded while the concrete is wet; the upper portion of the post hole is later filled in with gravel or compacted soil.

INGROUND POST

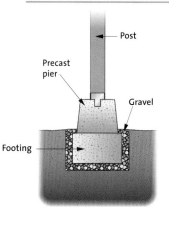

Post

Soil

Footing

POST ON SOLID CONCRETE

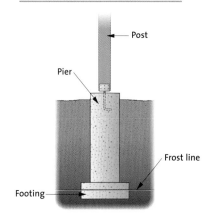

Post

Pier

Frost line

Footing

POST IN CONCRETE FOOTING

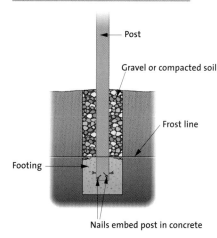

Post

Gravel or compacted soil

Frost line

Footing

Nails embed post in concrete

POST ON PRECAST PIER

Post

Precast pier

Gravel

Footing

Supporting a Freestanding Deck

An alternative to a ledger-mounted deck is a free-standing deck, which is not connected to the house at all. Instead of being bolted to a ledger, the part of the deck alongside the house rests on an extra row of posts and an additional beam. This approach eliminates the need to attach a ledger, which can be a complicated task (see pages 100–109). However, freestanding decks generally require extra work to add all those extra posts and footings, which may need to be dug extra deep to reach undisturbed soil (the area near the house was probably deeply excavated when the house was built). If the deck is more than 3 feet above the ground, extra bracing may also be required.

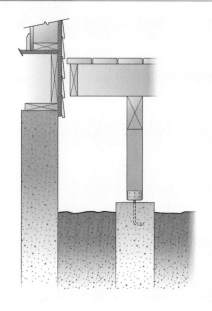

LAYOUT BASICS

WHEN YOU LAY OUT YOUR DECK'S FOOTINGS, you will use either the tape measure method (pages 86–87) or the more precise batterboard method (pages 88–89). On these two pages, we discuss general principles that you can use on a variety of layouts, and we use batterboards to illustrate those principles.

How Precise Do You Have to Be?

Most decks are built of footings supporting posts supporting beams, on which rest the joists. Joists typically cantilever, or overhang, beams by 2 or 3 feet. This means that the post footings can be off by several inches in relation to the house and it will not affect the deck's look or structural integrity. Similarly, if you are digging large-diameter holes for inground posts, the holes can be off by several inches and there will still be room to adjust the posts. However, footings supporting the same beam must be in a perfectly straight line.

If the deck's design does not have joists cantilevering over a beam, you will probably need to position the footings precisely in relation to the house, as well as to the beam. Use batterboards and string lines, and double-check the layout before pouring any concrete.

Laying Out with a Raised Ledger

If you are building an elevated deck, attach a plumb bob to each outside edge of the ledger and drop it close to ground level. Drive stakes or install batterboards and mark them, using the plumb lines hanging from the ledger for reference.

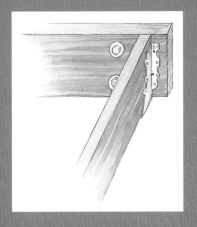

REFERENCING A HIGH LEDGER

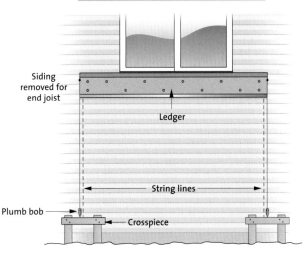

Siding removed for end joist

Ledger

String lines

Plumb bob

Crosspiece

LAYING OUT A RECTANGULAR DECK

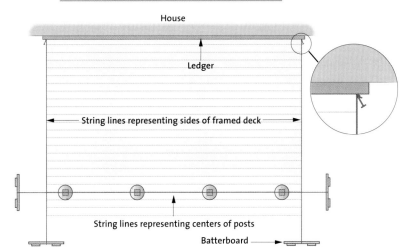

House

Ledger

String lines representing sides of framed deck

String lines representing centers of posts

Batterboard

Rectangular Decks

For a rectangular deck, usually a row of footings supports a beam that runs parallel to the house and stops 2 to 3 feet short of the deck's two ends. A larger deck may have two beams, with two rows of footings and posts. Beams can overhang their outside posts by 2 to 3 feet on either side.

Irregular Shapes

Lay out an irregularly shaped deck using the same approach as for a rectangular deck. If, for example, you are building a deck that wraps around a corner, run a single corner string line out from one of the ledgers (right), to create two rectangles. Then you can check each rectangle for square.

If the deck has mitered corners (below), first establish a rectangular layout as if the miters were not there. Then measure an equal distance on each side of the far string line back to the house to lay out a parallel string line. For more complicated decks, follow the same basic principle: Divide the deck into a series of rectangles and check each for square.

LAYING OUT A WRAPAROUND DECK

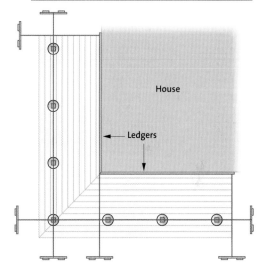

House

Ledgers

LAYING OUT A DECK WITH MITERED CORNERS

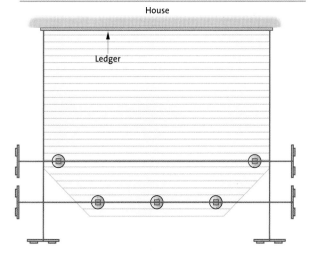

House

Ledger

This deck will be freestanding, so a framing square and a plumb bob (actually, a chalk line used as a plumb bob) is used to mark the ground with spray paint for a row of post holes 16 inches away from the house.

Laying Out with Tape Measures

This layout method uses triangulation to quickly establish the locations of post holes. it is a good option as long as the holes do not have to be placed precisely in relation to the house. You will have ample opportunity to adjust the positions of the posts and/or the footings later (pages 90–93); the larger the hole you dig, the more latitude you will have.

Measure in from the corners. To determine the center of the holes in relation to the corner of a house, measure in by half the width of the hole you need to dig (page 90), plus the length of the beam overhang (usually about 2 feet), plus the length of the decking overhang (usually about 2 inches). How far away from the house you actually dig the hole will depend on the depth of your deck and whether it's freestanding or supported by a ledger. Mark the hole's center with spray paint or a stake.

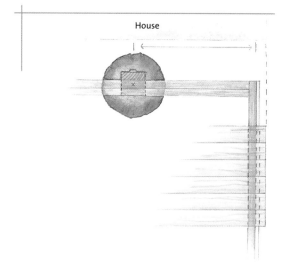

House

In this illustration of the photo above, the post hole is placed 2 feet, 2 inches from the corner of house so that that the edge of the decking is in line with the edge of the house.

Laying out with 3-4-5. The 3-4-5 layout method shown here works best with two tape measures. Starting from the mark you made from the corner of the house (described above), measure along the house in multiples of 3 feet, then away from the first mark in multiples of 4 feet. Leave this tape on the ground. Now find the hypotenuse of your right triangle by measuring from the multiples-of-3 spot to the multiples-of-4 tape, moving the tape to the left or right until the hypotenuse equals a multiple of 5. This spot is now at a right angle to the spot marked at the house, and is ready to be marked with spray paint or a stake. Mark for the other outside post holes in the same way. For more about the 3-4-5 method, see page 71.

Lining up a row. Stretch a string line from outside hole to outside hole. Measure for evenly spaced intermediate holes, and mark their centers—the number of intermediate post holes will depend on the dimensions of the beam (see chart on page 45). Double-check your measurements; all holes should be the same distance away from the house.

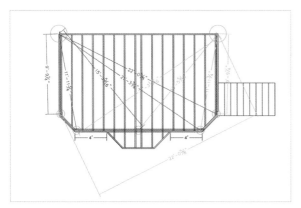

Triangulation. If you purchase professional deck plans, they may include triangulation measurements for post locations. To use this method, simply place stakes along the house at the points specified in the plan, then run two tape measures (you may need long ones) from the stakes, and mark the intersections, which is where the holes should go. Once all the marks are in place, double-check: be sure that posts supporting a single beam will line up, and that the holes are the correct distance from the house.

Digging Holes in Patios

If it turns out that a post hole needs to be dug through an existing sand-laid patio, you can simply pry pavers out. Dig the hole carefully so you don't misalign adjoining pavers. Once the post is installed, cut pavers to fit around it.

If the patio is a concrete slab, use a masonry saw to cut out the area, and pry out the concrete with a wrecking bar. If the slab is thick (they can vary from 2 to 6 inches), consult with your inspector; you may be allowed to set the post directly on top of the patio, or you may need to call in a pro for demolition.

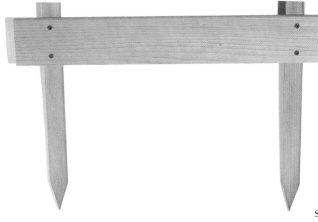

Laying Out with Batterboards

Use batterboards when you need to precisely mark post hole locations. Batterboards also make it easy to double-check locations of footings, post anchors, and posts later on. Make batterboards out of scrap 2× or 1× lumber. The stakes should be pointed; their length will depend on how high they need to be and how soft your soil is. The crosspiece should be about 2 feet long. You'll need two batterboards for each outside corner of the deck.

1 **SET BATTERBOARDS AND LINES.** Establish the centers of the outside post holes in relation to the corner of the house (see page 86), and drive a stake into the ground or a nail into the house at that point. Use triangulation (page 87) to roughly determine the location of each outside post hole center. About 2 feet beyond this point in either direction, drive in batterboards. Tightly stretch mason's line from the house to the batterboard on each end of a row of post holes. The strings should be close to but not touching the ground. Temporarily wrap the lines around the batterboard so you can easily shift their positions. For the line that is parallel to the house, measure to position both ends the same distance from the house.

2 **CHECK FOR SQUARE.** To check a deck's corner for square, mark a spot on the house by a multiple of 3 from the corner. Use a piece of tape to mark the string that runs at a right angle from the house by a multiple of 4. If the distance between the two marks is a multiple of 5, then the corner is square. If not, move the lines as needed. Check the other corner using the same method. Double-check for square by measuring the diagonals, which should be the same length. When you are certain of the lines' positions, nail or screw them in place on the batterboards. Then mark the batterboards so you can remove and correctly replace the lines during construction.

3 **MARK A CORNER.** To mark the ground, dangle a chalk line (or a plumb bob) so that its string nearly touches the intersection of the two guidelines and the weight nearly rests on the ground. Drive a stake or mark the spot with paint. You may choose to mark the batterboards with the positions of the outside edges of the concrete tube forms, so you can quickly move the lines when checking the forms. Remove the lines while digging the holes, and reattach them to check the post anchors (if any) and the posts.

BUILDING TIP

Because you may need to remove and replace layout lines several times during the course of layout and construction, be sure batterboards are securely anchored into the ground.

Easy Option: A Framing Box

If the deck is fairly small and uncomplicated and the site is reasonably level, you can simplify the layout process by building a framing box before you measure for footing holes. Cut two outside joists and the header joist to length; you may also cut and install the ledger as well (pages 100–109). Drive nails or screws to attach the pieces together at the corners and lay the structure on the lawn, positioned against the house as it will be once the framing is installed. Use the 3-4-5 method to check that the box is square, and adjust as needed. Now you can measure from the inside of the box to find the locations of your footing holes.

FOOTING HOLES

IF YOUR SOIL IS SOFT AND YOU DO NOT HAVE MANY POST HOLES TO DIG, this part of the job can be fairly easy. However, hand-digging holes large and deep enough to satisfy codes is usually demanding work. If you have six or seven holes to dig, you may want to hire a high-school kid, or someone else with a strong back, to hand-dig the holes—even if it takes all day, the cost is probably less than hiring a pro. Often, the best solution is to rent a power auger, or hire a company to dig the holes.

ABOVE: A deck like this, though small and low, calls for several beams, each of which must be supported by at least two posts.

Size and Shape

For in-ground posts, digging wide holes (16 to 20 inches in diameter) allows you to adjust their position later. For aboveground posts, narrower holes are typical. Cardboard tube forms are sometimes needed to ensure that the footing is the right diameter to meet codes. If you are using 4 × 4 posts to support your deck, 8-inch-wide tubes are usually sufficient. For 6 × 6 posts, use 10- or 12-inch-wide tubes. If you plan to bury the posts in concrete, dig each hole wide enough so that there will be at least 2 inches of concrete around the post at all points. Codes may require that the bottom of the hole be "flared," or widened, to form a more massive footing. For more about foundations, see pages 82–83.

TIME SAVER

Digging is hard work, so it's only natural to want to move the hole over a bit when you encounter an obstacle. Holes tend to wander just as much with a power auger as when they are dug by hand. Double-check a hole's position by re-measuring when it's about halfway dug.

Digging by Hand

A garden spade may be the only tool you need to dig holes up to 2 feet deep. For deeper holes, you will need a post-hole digger. A digger like the one shown at left is effective for most types of soil. Use a spade to carefully dig around the stake or paint mark that marks the center of the hole (pages 86–89). Dig away all sod, then grasp the digger with the handles held together, stab it into the ground, spread the handles apart, and lift out the dirt. If you encounter large rocks or need to loosen the hard soil, use a wrecking bar. Take your time, and pause for periodic rests and to stretch; unless you are used to this type of work, there is a danger of straining your back.

Common Obstacles

It's highly likely that all sorts of pipes and cables are running under your yard. A post hole will almost certainly be deep enough to reach any of them, so take the time to locate all the lines you can.

Utility lines. Many building departments do not allow you to dig footing holes until you have contacted the gas, electric, and water companies, many of which will mark the locations of gas, water or electrical lines with small flags. Cutting through any of these lines can be expensive, and even dangerous, so be sure to contact your utilities even if it is not required by code.

Sprinkler lines. Utility lines can be located by the gas, water, and electrical companies, but sprinkler lines are usually not well mapped. So it's not unusual to hit a sprinkler line when digging post holes. Make sure the sprinkler system is shut off before you start digging. If you hit a pipe (usually, a flexible tube like that shown at right, but sometimes more rigid PVC), repairs are fairly easy (below, right). Use a utility knife to cut back the tubes so the ends are clean and not frayed or cracked. Use compression fittings or flexible rubber fittings with hose clamps to connect a new piece of repair tubing.

If you cut through the low-voltage wires that trigger your automatic sprinkler system, there is little danger of getting shocked. Use wire strippers to remove about $3/4$ inch of insulation from the wire ends. To make the connections, twist on underground-rated wire nuts—just be sure to keep the wire colors straight!

Using a Power Auger

A rented power auger can remove dirt much faster than a manual digger. But that does not mean it will make the job easy. Choose an auger bit that matches the width of the hole you want to dig. If you do not anticipate difficult digging, a one-person auger works well. If you expect to hit hard soil, clay, roots, or rocks, a two-person auger is a better choice.

Even the best two-person power auger, however, should be used by two strong people who are ready for a tough physical workout. Digging can be a wrenching experience, especially if you encounter a large stone or root. If you are working alone, consider renting a flexible-shaft auger. Its engine is separated from the auger, rather than sitting on top of it, which makes the tool lighter and easier to handle.

1 **START OUT STRAIGHT.** Get in a comfortable position, with your feet about shoulder's width apart for stability. Hold the bit's point just above the mark for a second or two, to allow gravity to straighten the bit. Pull the trigger to engage the bit, and allow the machine's weight to dig down.

2 **PULL OUT WHEN NEEDED.** Once you have dug down about a third of the way, pull the bit up and out to clean out the hole. Then start again. If the digging gets hard or you encounter an obstacle, pull the bit out.

3 **CLEAR OBSTACLES.** If you encounter a small root, cut it with a shovel or clamshell digger. For large roots, you might need a reciprocating saw. For rocks, a digging bar is a good companion to a post-hole digger.

4 **CLEAN OUT.** Once you have achieved the desired depth, use a post-hole digger to clean out the hole.

5 **TAMP THE BOTTOM.** Pound with a 4 × 4 or a hand tamper (shown here) to firm the bottom of the hole.

Hiring a Pro

You may prefer to hire someone with an auger mounted on a truck, tractor, or small earth-moving machine. Check the yellow pages. Often a fence building company or a deck builder will offer this service; prices can vary widely. Some charge by the hole, others by the hour. If your soil is reasonably loose, a heavy-duty machine can usually dig eight holes or so in an hour.

Make sure there will be a clear pathway for the truck or earth-moving machine. Ask for a promise that the wheels won't do permanent damage to your yard; this often depends on whether it has rained recently. The rig must be maneuverable enough to get to all the hole locations without damaging permanent plantings in your yard.

All the holes should be clearly marked before the digger arrives. Machine diggers typically leave several inches of loose soil in the bottom of the holes, so you will need to clean out and tamp the holes after the pro has left.

If the auger tip is inserted precisely on the mark and positioned fairly plumb, the hole should be reasonably accurate. However, if the tip is off or the auger is angled, you may need to readjust the hole's position.

Before the driver leaves, check that the holes are deep enough.

Plenty of dirt will be mounded up around the holes, and you will need to clean out loose soil and tamp the holes.

Controlling Weeds and Puddles

In a dry climate, you may be able to simply build a deck on the lawn, allowing the grass to die over a year or so. However, if you get plenty of rain, water may puddle under the deck and take a long time to dry out. In lush areas, weeds may grow up through a low-lying deck. The usual solution is to remove sod, install landscaping fabric, and cover the fabric with gravel. Consult with a gardening expert at your local nursery or home center for the best type of landscaping fabric and gravel to use in your area.

ABOUT CONCRETE

EARLY ON, DECIDE WHETHER YOU WILL MIX YOUR OWN CONCRETE by hand, use a small power mixer, or have the concrete delivered by truck. The choice largely depends on the number and size of the footings, as well as your budget and time.

Estimating Concrete

A 60-pound bag of dry-mix concrete produces ½ cubic foot of concrete, which will fill about 20 inches of an 8-inch tube form, 13 inches of a 10-inch form, or 9 inches of a 12-inch form. An 80-pound bag contains .6 cubic feet and will therefore fill a few more inches.

For greater precision, determine the amount of concrete in a cylinder with this formula: radius² × inches of depth × 3.14 = cubic inches. Then divide by 1,728 to convert cubic inches to cubic feet. In the example shown at left, the pier contains 1,808.64 cubic inches and the base footing another 1,607.68 cubic inches, for a total of 3,416.32. Divide this by 1,728 to reach the total of 1.98 cubic feet, or roughly four 60-pound bags of concrete, for each footing.

Mixing by Hand

Making concrete can be as easy as adding water to dry concrete mix, or you can create your own mix by combining 4½ shovelfuls of gravel, 2 shovelfuls of Portland cement, and 3½ shovelfuls of sand. Dealing with piles of gravel, cement, and sand is a hassle, so make sure your projected savings justify the work.

Buy the type of concrete mix recommended (or required) by your local building department. Mixes labeled "high strength" or "high early" cost a bit more but ensure a strong footing (so-called "posthole concrete" is not rated for footings). Check the bag's information label to see how soon you can place a post on top of the concrete; you may need to wait a day or two, or just overnight. Concrete can irritate your eyes, lungs, and skin, so wear gloves, long clothing, a dust mask, and eye protection when you work with it.

Mix your concrete in a wheelbarrow or masonry tub. A mortar hoe is the best mixing tool, but a regular hoe or a shovel works nearly as well. Squirt an inch or so of water into your chosen mixing container and pour in a full bag's worth of dry mix. Slowly add more water, mixing and scraping along the bottom and sides of the container.

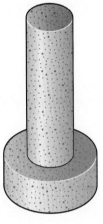

PIER VOLUME
(4" × 4") × 36" × 3.14 =
1,808.64 CUBIC INCHES

FOOTING VOLUME
(8" × 8") × 8" × 3.14 =
1,607.68 CUBIC INCHES

TOTAL VOLUME
3,416.32 CUBIC INCHES

CONCRETE PER POST
3,416.32 CUBIC INCHES ÷
1,728 = 1.98 CUBIC FEET

The Right Consistency

Avoid adding too much water; a runny mixture makes for weak concrete. Aim for a mix that is just barely pourable and that holds its shape when you pick some up with a tool, as shown above.

Using a Small Mixer

A rented electric or gasoline-powered mixer does the job quickly and thoroughly. Spray several inches of water into the hopper; you can clean the sides of the hopper as you do so. Add two bags of dry mix, turn on the machine, and gradually add water until the mix is just pourable.

Ordering Concrete in a Truck

If you need more than 16 cubic feet or so of concrete, it may be cost- and labor-effective to have the concrete delivered in a ready-mix truck. Order ready-mix concrete by the cubic yard (27 cubic feet). Some companies have special trucks for delivering amounts less than a yard. The driver will pour concrete into wheelbarrows, which you then transport to the holes. Be sure to lay down 2 × 10s or strips of ply-wood for wheelbarrow paths. You may need to pay the driver extra if he has to wait more than half an hour.

Wheelbarrow Safety

A wheelbarrow full of concrete is heavy. Start with barrows about half full, then increase the amount as you gain confidence. If you start to lose control while wheeling, push down on both handles to stabilize the wheelbarrow, then start again. If you try to right the barrow, you will likely spill the concrete.

Pouring Concrete

CONCRETE SETS FAIRLY QUICKLY, SO HAVE ALL YOUR DUCKS IN A ROW before you start mixing and pouring. Prepare all the footing holes and perhaps the forms ahead of time. How you form and finish the concrete depends on the type of footing. On these pages we show an above-grade footing for an aboveground post. See page 98 for an in-ground footing.

Above-Grade Footing

Waxed concrete tube forms are convenient and practical, and they are required by many codes. They create smooth-sided piers that resist the uplift caused by frost. They also make it easy to estimate how much concrete you will need. And they hold in moisture while the concrete cures, resulting in stronger footings.

Schedule footing inspections as needed. You may be required to have footing holes inspected before pouring the concrete. Sometimes you may need to flare out the bottom of the hole and add several inches of gravel.

For each row that will support a beam, install the outer footings first, then stretch string lines from either end to guide the placement of intermediate footings.

1 **CUT THE TUBE FORM.** Use a circular saw, handsaw, or reciprocating saw to cut the tube forms. In some installations the forms run the depth of the hole; here, they are used only for the top 2 feet of the footing. If the forms will run down to the bottom of the hole, measure and cut each form individually since hole depths vary.

COMMON MISTAKE

It's easy to install post-anchor bolts either too low or too high, which makes it difficult if not impossible to install the anchors after the concrete has set. Measure an anchor to determine how high the bolts need to be installed, and take care to keep each one at the right height.

2 **POUR THE CONCRETE.** Tamp the hole bottom, and add gravel if required. Mix the concrete as described on pages 94–95, and pour it into the hole.

3 **SET THE TUBE IN THE HOLE.** Once the concrete level is high enough, set in the tube form. Push it down until it is about 2 inches above grade. Use a small level to check that the form is at least close to level at the top. If not, you may need to cut the form.

4 **FILL THE TUBE.** Shovel concrete into the tube form until it nearly reaches the top. Poke a piece of reinforcing bar (rebar) or a 1 × 2 down into the concrete and agitate, working up and down, to remove any air bubbles. Continue adding concrete until the form is just slightly overfilled. You may be required to add rebar at this point.

5 **STRIKE.** Use a short board to level and smooth the surface, a process called striking. Move the board slightly up and down as you pull it across the surface. Fill any low spots with additional concrete.

6 **OUTER FOOTINGS.** Depending on the type of post anchor you will install (page 98), you may need to insert a bolt into the center of concrete at this point. Use a J-bolt or a carriage bolt.

7 **INTERMEDIATE FOOTINGS.** After you have installed the outer footings, use string to align the tube forms for the intermediate forms. After you have poured the concrete, stretch a string line again, this time to line up the intermediate bolts. The post-base hardware that attaches to these bolts will likely be adjustable from side to side, but only by a couple of inches.

Anchoring a Tube Form

If the tube form extends nearly to the bottom of the hole, you may need to support it at the top. Attach 1 × 2 crosspieces to 1 × 2 stakes as shown. Check for level, then drive two screws to hold the form in place. You can also use this method if the footings need to be at precise heights.

Post Anchors for Above-Grade Footings

The most common post anchor (also called a post base) is adjustable and attaches to a bolt that pokes up through the concrete. Place the anchor's main part over the bolt, slip on a washer, and hand-tighten the nut. Check that the anchor is positioned so the post will have a face aligned parallel to the house.

Attach and hand-tighten the outside anchors in a row, then stretch a string line across the intermediate footings to determine the locations of those anchors. Once everything is lined up and hand-tightened, go back and tighten the nuts using a ratchet or a wrench.

Inground Footings

An inground footing can be poured after some of the framing is installed (pages 123–125), so you are certain that it is in the right place. Before pouring, use a level to check that the post will be fairly near the center of the hole. The inspector will likely want to look at the holes before you pour the concrete and may check how many bags of concrete mix you have on hand, to ensure that the footings will be thick enough.

Shortly before pouring, tamp the bottom of the hole (page 92). As you work, take care to keep from spilling loose soil into the hole; if you do, tamp again. Mix the concrete and pour it into the hole. You may be required to check the thickness of the footing.

Unless conditions are very humid, the concrete should set quickly enough to allow you to set posts the next day. To test, tap lightly with a board or a hand tamper, as shown below left. If the concrete feels at all mushy, wait at least a few more hours, then test again. Install posts only when the concrete feels firm.

Setting Inground Posts

Some building departments allow, or require, posts that are set in the ground, with no concrete. To install a post this way, dig the post hole below the frost line, or as required by code. Set the post into the hole, and check it for correct alignment and plumb. Use a sledgehammer to drive the post until it stops sinking when you hit it. Check again for alignment and plumb, and shovel in two feet or so of construction sand, gravel, or soil. Use a 2 × 2 or a piece of rebar to tamp the fill so it is firm. Repeat until you have filled the hole.

In some locales, the preferred method is to surround bottoms of posts with dry concrete mix. After sledgehammering the post, pour in a bag or two of dry concrete mix, check the post for plumb, and fill the rest of the hole with well-tamped construction sand, gravel, or soil. Groundwater will slowly seep into the dry mix, typically creating a firm concrete footing within a month or two.

In some designs, the post is completely surrounded with wet concrete. Installed correctly, this approach produces a rigid frame, which may be necessary for a freestanding or an elevated deck, and may be required where earthquakes are common. The earth itself can serve as the form for concrete, or you can set the post in a tube form. The posts must be carefully plumbed, aligned, and temporarily braced before you pour.

To ensure that an inground post will be stable during construction or while the concrete is curing, drive stakes and install temporary braces in two directions.

Other Anchoring Methods

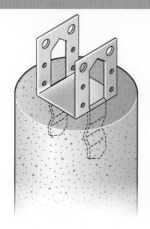

Some builders prefer to add the post anchor bolts after the concrete has set, using threaded studs and injectable epoxy cement. Drill a hole in the dry concrete with a masonry bit, inject the epoxy, and insert the stud. Wait a day or so for the epoxy to cure.

Some codes specify one-piece post anchors (left), which have fins that insert directly into wet concrete. This creates a very strong bond with the concrete, but take extra care to ensure the anchors are correctly aligned, because they cannot be adjusted later.

ATTACHING A LEDGER

THE LEDGER BOARD IS ANCHORED TO THE HOUSE TO SUPPORT ONE END OF THE DECK JOISTS. If you install the ledger as the first deck-building step, it can become the reference point for laying out the rest of the deck. Installing a ledger can be simple or complicated, depending on your plan, the type of siding on your house, and local codes. Check with your building department to make sure your ledger is to code.

A chalk line marks the vinyl siding for a ledger cutout.

Ledger Length and Height

In most cases, you should use the same size board for the ledger as you will for the joists. You can use a wider board, however, if it will permit a stronger connection to the house's framing. As a rule, the length of the ledger should be 3 inches greater than the width of the deck framing (page 84). The decking overhang will keep the ledger's extra length from view.

When determining the ledger's height, take into account how far below the interior floor it needs to be, as well as the thickness of the decking. To keep snow and water out of the house, the finished surface of the deck should be lower than the interior floor of any room leading onto it. To avoid creating a tripping hazard, locate the deck $3/4$ to 1 inch below the interior floor. This distance will produce a safe, clearly visible step from the deck up to the house. Local building codes may offer more specific guidelines.

Alternatively, install the deck a full step—6 to $7\frac{1}{2}$ inches—below the threshold.

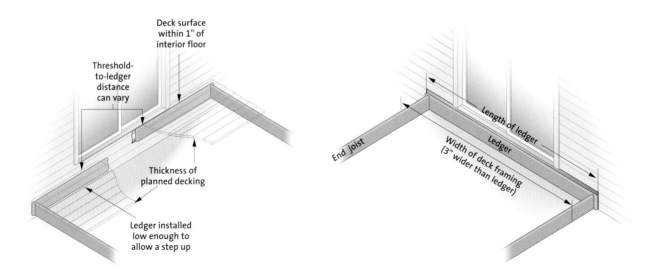

Deck surface within 1" of interior floor

Threshold-to-ledger distance can vary

Thickness of planned decking

Ledger installed low enough to allow a step up

End joist

Length of ledger

Ledger

Width of deck framing (3" wider than ledger)

Anchoring Methods

The correct way to attach a ledger to siding is a matter of debate among deck builders and inspectors. Some say that the ledger should simply be attached firmly up against the siding; others prefer to use spacers to hold the ledger away from the house so that water can drain through; and still others believe that siding (especially beveled siding) should be cut away and the ledger installed in the cutout. All these approaches have pluses and minuses. The best course is to find out your inspector's preferred method and follow it.

However you anchor your ledger, keep in mind that it will be stressed in both downward and outward directions. Therefore, ledgers should be connected securely to the house framing or foundation—never just to the sheathing, which cannot support a deck.

Snugging to the siding. Some deck builders simply mash the ledger up against the siding (right). This is certainly the easiest method, but detractors point out that moisture will be trapped, especially in the case of beveled siding. This method seems to work fine, however, for building in a dry climate or when both the ledger and the siding are made of very rot-resistant materials.

Setting into the siding. Some building departments require that you cut out a section of siding to accommodate the ledger. It is important that the opening is then covered completely by roofing felt, flashing, and caulk; one gap could lead to serious moisture damage to your house.

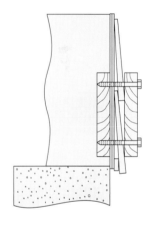

SNUGGING

SETTING
INTO SIDING

PRESSURE-
TREATED
SPACERS

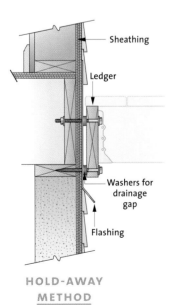

Sheathing

Ledger

Washers for
drainage
gap

Flashing

HOLD-AWAY
METHOD

The hold-away method. This technique leaves a space behind the ledger to allow for drainage. On flat siding, place three or four stainless-steel washers on each bolt, as shown at left. For added protection against moisture infiltration, squirt some caulk into the holes before inserting bolts or lag screws. When you're installing on beveled siding, it's a good idea to add flashing. Alternatively, wood spacers can be cut out of pressure-treated plywood and placed behind the ledger, as shown at right.

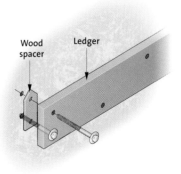

Wood
spacer

Ledger

Typical Ledger Obstacles

The walls of most houses have a number of objects that can get in the way of the ledger—dryer vents, hose bibs (spigots), gutter downspouts, utility meters, and so on. Some of these can be moved or removed, while others must be built around.

- REMOVE NAILS before cutting out siding for the ledger. Partially pull out the nail head by prying the siding, then tapping it back in (left). Now you can pull the nail. You may also need to remove the piece of siding just under the doorway (left, center).

- GUTTER DOWNSPOUTS can be easily moved a short distance to the side, using components available at a home improvement center. If the downspout would need to be moved more than 6 feet, the solution may be to frame around it and run it under the deck. Add a downspout extension so water exits past the deck, away from footings.

- A HOSE BIB may be rerouted by changing the pipes. Or build around it, and provide an access panel in your decking so you can connect hoses and turn the bib on and off. If you no longer need the bib, cap it off inside the house.

- A DRYER VENT can sometimes be moved, but often there is no other place to put it. You may be able to cut a hole in the ledger and run the vent through it. Make sure the vent has at least 6 inches of space all around, so it can freely blow. Provide for occasional access to the vent by building an access panel in your decking or the deck's skirting, so you can check for lint accumulation and replace the vent cap if needed.

- UTILITY METERS may need to be in clear view, though many utilities now use a wireless sensing device to read meters. Check with your electric, water, or gas company to find the best solution.

Working with Vinyl

If the siding of your house is vinyl, you can cut it with a utility knife, tin snips, or a saw of any sort. If the ledger extends to an outside corner, you will need to notch the corner trim piece so the ledger can be set into it.

Installing a Set-in Ledger

Many building departments require that a ledger be set into a section of siding that has been cut out. Perform this work with care, so that rainwater cannot seep behind the ledger and damage the house's sheathing and even reach the framing. In some circumstances, it may be easier to pry out and remove full siding pieces around the area where the ledger will go. After installing the ledger, you can then cut and install siding pieces to fit.

1 **MARK FOR THE CUTOUT.** The ledger—and therefore the cutout for it—should extend $1\frac{1}{2}$ inches past the outside joists (page 84). At the top of the cutout, allow $\frac{1}{8}$ inch for the thickness of the flashing. For most first-floor decks, you don't have to cut the bottom horizontal; simply remove the entire bottom piece of siding. Use a chalk line to mark for the horizontals, and an angle square and pencil to mark for the verticals. For correct positioning and sizing of the ledger, see page 100.

2 **CUT THE HORIZONTALS.** Set a circular saw's blade to cut just through the siding, and not dig into the sheathing beneath. Start with a plunge cut: Set the front of the base plate on the siding, turn on the saw, and slowly lower the spinning blade into the wood. Avoid cutting backwards; always cut moving forward. Cut along the chalk line or guide below the saw, and stop when you reach the vertical pencil lines.

3 **CUT THE VERTICALS.** Set the blade deeper, so it can cut through the full thickness of the siding. Cut the verticals (again using a plunge cut), stopping when you reach the horizontal cut lines.

4 **FINISH THE CORNERS.** Use a hammer and chisel to cut out the corners.

continued ▶▶

5 **MAKE ROOM UNDER SIDING.** Since you will need to slip roofing felt and flashing up under the siding above the cutout (steps 6 and 8), you'll need to remove any nails that might be in the way. Gently pry away the siding, and check with a putty knife or flat pry bar for nails. You may be able to pull them out. If not, use a reciprocating saw to cut through them.

6 **PROTECT THE SHEATHING.** Cut a piece of roofing felt (tar paper) or building paper 6 inches longer than the length of the cutout. Slip the felt up under the siding and slide it up at least 6 inches and over 3 inches on either side. Make sure the felt lies flat on the sheathing, and staple it in place.

7 **PREPARE THE FLASHING.** Use Z-shape ledger flashing (page 64) made of aluminum or vinyl. Cut it to the length of the cutout. If you need more than one piece, plan to overlap pieces by 6 inches or so. Where the flashing fits around the threshold it may need to be cut out with tin snips.

Measuring Shortcut

If you have a very long ledger, it may be difficult to stretch your tape measure along its entire length. Try this trick: At one of the layout lines, create a slot in the ledger with a chisel (left). Slip the tip of the tape measure into the slot, and continue measuring and marking (below).

8 **INSTALL THE FLASHING.** In most cases, the flashing can be simply slipped up into place. Tap the siding back into place to temporarily secure the flashing until you install the ledger—there is usually no need to use nails to hold the flashing, and nails would provide a point of entry for water anyway.

9 **SET THE LEDGER.** Cut the ledger to length. Working with a helper, set the ledger in place so that the flashing covers its top edge. Check for level and drive nails or screws to hold it temporarily in place.

10 **LAY OUT FOR JOISTS.** Draw the layout lines for the joists before you drive the final lag screw fasteners, so the lag heads won't be in the way. See page 71 for layout methods.

11 **STEP DOWN A LEVEL.** If the deck steps down, you will need to install a second ledger one step down—6½ to 7½ inches is ideal.

TIME SAVER

If the header joist at the outside end of the deck will be the same length as the ledger it runs parallel to (minus 1½ inches, on each end, as described on page 84), now is a good time to mark it with layout lines. Place it on top of the ledger with the crown down (not up; you will flip it over later), and mark it with the same lines as the header.

Anchoring a Ledger

Regardless of the type of siding the ledger is attached to, most codes require that a ledger be attached with thick ($3/8$ inch or $1/2$ inch) lag screws driven into house framing—usually, the rim joist that runs around the house, typically located just under the door threshold. Thick bolts and lag screws are required by codes because they have great shear strength—that is, they resist breaking when downward pressure is applied to them. Special ledger screws are not as thick, but they are as strong—and they're easier to drive. Some building departments accept their use. For regular or ledger lag screws, consider renting a pneumatic driver. A stronger connection relies on carriage bolts that run through the ledger, the house sheathing, and the rim joist, with nuts and washers attached in the basement or crawl space. In some installations both lag screws and bolts are used.

The size and spacing of the bolts or lag screws should be spelled out in your building code. If not, install pairs of $1/2$-inch bolts:

- EVERY 16 INCHES on decks with joist spans of up to 10 feet
- EVERY 10 INCHES for joist spans of up to 14 feet
- EVERY 8 INCHES for longer joist spans

Position the bolts about 2 inches from the bottom and top edges of the ledger.

Drill test holes to determine how long the fasteners need to be. A lag screw should penetrate through the $1\frac{1}{2}$-inch-thick ledger and the house's siding and sheathing and nearly all the way through the rim joist. A carriage bolt should extend about $1\frac{1}{2}$ inches past the rim joist.

The ledger attached to this house is not as wide as the deck it helps support.

Seal the Edges

Once the ledger and flashing have been installed, caulk all places where moisture could possibly seep in. Apply generous beads of exterior silicone, latex/silicone, butyl, or other caulk with excellent water-repelling and sticking properties.

Secure the Flashing

At the corners, tap the flashing with a hammer to fold it over the ledger. This will ensure that water cannot seep under the flashing at the edges.

SAFETY TIP

If the floors in your house are framed with something other than solid wood, such as a manufactured joist system, you will probably need to take extra steps to secure the ledger. Or you may opt for a freestanding deck (page 83). Discuss your options with your local building department or a construction professional.

Extra-Strong Ledger Hardware

For the ultimate in ledger security, use special ledger-attaching brackets like those shown at right. In this arrangement, the ledger is attached not only with bolts driven through the rim joist, but also to the house's joists via the bracket.

Attaching a Ledger to Masonry

When it comes to attaching a deck to masonry, you cannot be too careful. Consult with your building department for the approved way to attach to brick, block, or concrete in your area. If the deck is high, attaching to brick alone may not be considered strong enough; you may need to drive long bolts into the house. Or, build a freestanding deck with no ledger.

1 DRILL A PILOT HOLE. Support the ledger temporarily with 2 × 4s or scrap lumber—make sure it is level and snugly tucked under the flashing. Use a wood bit to drill just through the board; avoid hitting the masonry, which can ruin the bit.

2 DRILL THROUGH MASONRY. Switch to a masonry bit and perhaps a hammer drill in order to bore a hole in the masonry. Drilling through brick or concrete block may go quickly, while drilling through solid concrete can be slow work (for concrete, a hammer drill is a must). Exert moderate pressure only. Every couple of inches, pull out the bit to clear dust out of the hole. Stop if the bit or drill starts to overheat, and allow things to cool off. If the bit starts to bore slowly, it's time for a new one.

3 INSERT THE FASTENER. Once the hole is deep enough, insert a sleeve or wedge anchor made for use with masonry. Tap the fastener until it is flush with the wood surface; make sure the board is snug against the masonry wall.

4 DRIVE THE LAG SCREW. Use a ratchet and socket to screw in a lag screw sized to match the fastener.

Attaching a Ledger to Stucco

You may be permitted to simply snug the ledger against the stucco and apply a generous bead of high-quality caulk to the top and edges. However, many codes require that you set the ledger into the stucco. The process is similar to setting a ledger into cut-out siding (pages 103–105), but cutting and prying out the stucco is more difficult.

1 **CUT OUT A SECTION.** Measure and mark for the cutout as you would with wood siding (pages 100, 103). To cut through stucco, equip a circular saw with a masonry-cutting blade. Set the blade to cut through the stucco and wire mesh only; it can be $\frac{1}{2}$ inch to $1\frac{1}{2}$ inches thick. You may need to make several passes, and you may need to change blades if the first one wears down.

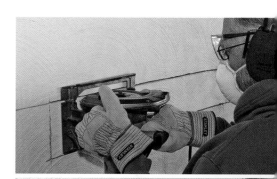

2 **PRY AWAY.** Gently pry the stucco and wire away from the wall. Work carefully to avoid cracking the stucco that you do not want to remove. Feel behind the remaining stucco with a putty knife or flat pry bar for nails that are less than 6 inches above the opening; cut them with a reciprocating saw (page 104).

3 **PROTECT THE SHEATHING.** Slip in roofing felt that is at least 6 inches wider than the opening, then add flashing, as you would with a wood-sided wall (page 104). Attach the ledger.

Working with Stucco

A classic stucco wall has roofing felt attached to sheathing, wire mesh attached over the felt, and two or three coats of stucco slathered onto the mesh. In some cases, though, stucco may have been applied directly over masonry or siding, boosting the thickness of the material you need to remove to more than 2 inches. Consult with your inspector or a professional carpenter. If you have old stucco that is very hard and difficult to cut, you may be better off building a freestanding deck with no ledger.

framing

THE DECK FRAME—ITS SKELETON—IS COMPOSED
OF POSTS, BEAMS, AND JOISTS. BY FOLLOWING
THE TECHNIQUES SHOWN ON THE FOLLOWING
PAGES, YOU CAN QUICKLY BUILD A FRAME THAT
IS STRONG AND DURABLE. YOU'LL ALSO FIND
TECHNIQUES FOR FRAMING ANGLES AND CURVES.

FRAMING OPTIONS

HOW YOU FRAME A DECK DEPENDS IN NO SMALL PART on whether the posts are above or below ground. The next 18 pages cover both situations, as well as some of the most common framing variations. Later in the chapter you'll learn how to build angles and curves, work around trees and boulders that break the plane of the decking, and construct a low-to-the-ground deck. Before you choose any framing method, though, confirm that it meets local codes and will satisfy your inspector.

Inground Posts

If your posts will be partially buried in the ground, you can build your deck's framing "box"—the outside joists, the header, and a header near the house if there is no ledger—using temporary supports. You can also build and temporarily attach the beams that support the joists. Once you've built your box, double-check that the holes are in the right locations for the posts, then pour concrete in the bottoms of the holes. After the concrete has cured, cut the posts to fit and attach them to the undersides of the beams. For more about this method, see pages 118–125.

Building with temporary supports is actually not as difficult as it looks. You will need to work with at least one strong-backed helper, so that one person can hold pieces in place while the other checks for level and attaches the temporary supports. And if the frame gets out of square or level during construction, it can be easily adjusted as you work.

Aboveground Posts

If the posts will rest on concrete footings that rise above grade, you'll attach the posts (left taller than they need to be) onto the footings using post anchors. Determine the correct height for the posts, use a level (laser levels work well) to mark the posts, and cut them. Next, install the beam(s) on top of the posts, and perhaps temporary braces. Now you can install the joists. For more about this method, see pages 126–129.

Once you have set a beam on top of posts the resulting structure will be unstable, so if you installed temporary bracing, you'll be glad you did. You can also straighten posts as you install the joists, if necessary.

When to Cut the Joists

For a rectangular deck or a rectangular section of a larger deck, many builders simply cut all the joists to the same length and install them. However, if the ledger is not straight (which will be the case if the house wall is wavy), then the joists' ends—and the header joist that attaches to them—will follow the ledger's contours. It's also easy to make mistakes while measuring and cutting a number of joists. To avoid these pitfalls, install joists uncut. Once they are all attached to the ledger (or the header near the house, in the case of a freestanding deck), use a chalk line to mark along the tops of the joists, mark each joist for a square cut, and cut the joists to length.

Posts and Beams

These days, most builders make beams by simply nailing or screwing two 2× stock together. The beam either rests on top of posts (pages 128–129) or a post is notched and the beam rests on top and is bolted to the side (pages 123–124). Other options include a side-by-side beam, in which a 2× is bolted or screwed to each side of the post (right). If you use this method, you can attach cleats to the post under each beam piece for added strength. Another way to support side-by-side beams is to set the beam pieces in notches cut in each side of a post, but this is feasible only if the posts are at least 6 × 6s.

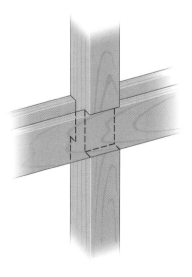

NOTCHED POST

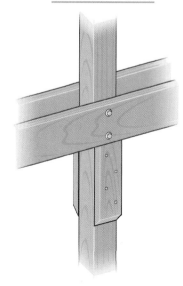

CLEAT SUPPORTS

Multiple Levels

Level changes can boost the visual appeal of a deck. On larger decks, they can be used to carve out use areas for dining or lounging. On smaller decks, they can create the illusion of more space. To support different levels, you could build separate abutting decks at different levels, but it is more efficient and cost-effective to use a single foundation to support adjacent levels. The transition between levels should feel like a standard step, which has a rise of $5\frac{1}{2}$ to $7\frac{1}{2}$ inches. A level change that's outside this range could be a tripping hazard.

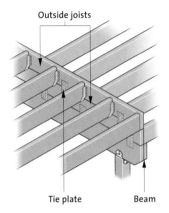

Outside joists

Tie plate   Beam

Shared beam. This technique uses a single beam to support two deck levels. The outside joist for the upper level sits directly on top of the lower outside joist, and the two are joined with tie plates. You can also build this style of level change by attaching the lower joists to the side of the beam with joist hangers and securing the upper joists to the top of the beam. With 2×6 or 2×8 joists, the shared-beam technique creates a comfortable step between levels.

Shared posts. If your deck will include a difference in height between two levels that's large enough to require stairs, then shared posts are a good solution. The upper beam rests on top of the posts.

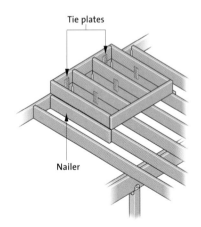

Tie plates

Nailer

Stacked deck. A simple way to create a small raised area is to construct a separate deck frame and set it on top of the regular frame. Use tie plates to hold the top frame in place, and attach nailers to the joists on both sides of the upper level to provide nailing surfaces for the decking.

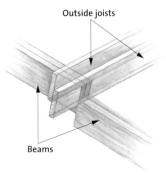

Outside joists

Beams

Different beams. In some situations you will have to support each level with a different beam (this method is shown on page 120). You will also attach the lower level's outside joist to the upper level's outside joist, but don't rely on this connection for strength; the beams will supply the real support.

Framing for a Spa

A hot tub or spa can impact the design of your deck's design and framing in several significant ways. Spas are heavy, so they require a serious amount of support. This support is generally provided by one of two methods: by placing the spa on its own concrete pad or by reinforcing the deck's framing. Most people find it more comfortable to enter and exit a spa whose rim is about 16 inches above the level of the deck rather than one that is flush with the decking. However, a spa that rests at deck level allows for sitting on the deck while dangling feet in the water. Your deck's frame may also be affected by the spa's plumbing and electrical lines. And when you are designing your deck, you may want to give some extra thought to privacy and shading around the spa. Whatever you do, make sure you understand the spa manufacturer's instructions before you begin building.

Framing around a spa. On a low deck, it is usually best to rest the spa or hot tub on a reinforced concrete pad. Check with the manufacturer and with your local building department for specifications on the size of the pad required, and pour the concrete before you begin framing the deck. With this approach, the deck frame surrounds the spa but does not support it. If the spa's rim will be level with the decking, plan the height of the deck very carefully. The framing must come close enough to the spa so that decking will not overhang joists by more than an inch or two, depending on the type of decking you are using.

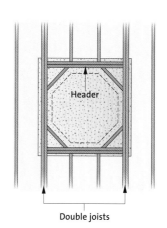

Double joists

Framing to support a spa. If you prefer to set the spa on top of the deck surface, you will need to substantially beef up the framing and the foundations below it. The frame must be able to support the weight of the spa filled with water and people. The framing plan at right provides an idea of the additional support that will be needed. Check with the manufacturer for more detailed recommendations.

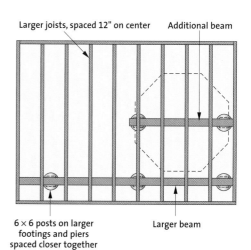

Larger joists, spaced 12" on center   Additional beam

6 × 6 posts on larger footings and piers spaced closer together   Larger beam

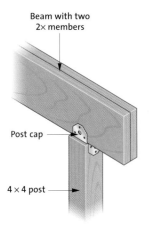

Beam with two
2× members

Post cap

4 × 4 post

DOUBLE BEAM

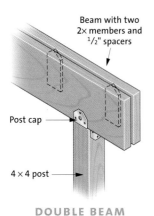

Beam with two
2× members and
1/2" spacers

Post cap

4 × 4 post

**DOUBLE BEAM
WITH SPACERS**

Beam with three
2× members

Post
cap

6 × 6 post

TRIPLE BEAM

BEAMS

A BEAM, ALSO CALLED A GIRDER, SPANS FROM POST TO POST AND SUPPORTS THE JOISTS. In most cases, joists rest on top of the beam, but if a deck is low you can save height by tying the joists into the beam via joist hangers. Modest-size decks are typically built with a single beam, but larger decks may require two or more. Consult local codes for approved ways to build and mount a beam. Regardless of the beam style, you can be sure the beam will be heavy, so have a helper or two available when you need to lift a beam into place.

Types of Beams

Older decks were often built using beams made of solid 4× lumber. If you can find good boards at this dimension, and if the piece will not be too heavy, this may be the easiest way to construct your deck. It can be difficult, however, to find boards of this size that do not have large cracks or twists. Both problems tend to worsen over time, and there is no way to fix a crack or straighten a twisted beam.

Constructing a beam by laminating two or more pieces of 2× lumber together is not difficult, and the result is a beam that is stronger and more stable than a single piece. Most commonly, a deck beam is made simply by fastening two boards together, as shown on the next page. Pressure-treated lumber is rot-resistant enough so that most inspectors do not worry about water seeping between boards. However, some builders like to protect the joint between the two pieces by applying a bead of caulk, or by applying a strip of adhesive flashing to the top of the beam.

A beam made of two 2× boards is 3 inches thick, while a 4 × 4 post is $3^1/_2$ inches thick. Most builders and inspectors do not see that as a problem, as long as the post is pressure treated. However, some builders construct the beam with $^1/_2$-inch spacers (made of pressure-treated plywood) sandwiched between the boards, to allow water to drain between the boards.

Beams are often attached to posts by angle-driving screws or nails through the beam and into the post. If you do this, drill pilot holes first, to avoid cracking the beam. A post cap makes a surer connection and may be required by local codes.

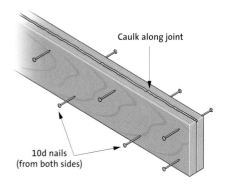

Caulk along joint

10d nails
(from both sides)

Building a Beam

In most cases, it is best to build a beam that is longer than needed; you can easily cut it to length later after the joists are installed, although you should trim any out-of-square or cracked ends.

Structural lumber nearly always has a visible crown, or arch, as shown above. Locate and mark the crown for each piece, and place one board on top of the other with the crowns facing up. That way, when the deck load bears down on the crown, the board will level out. You can usually see where the crown is by sighting down the edges of the board.

Always build with framing boards crown side up.

Building a beam is best done with two people. Position the top piece with its edges exactly matching the edges of the bottom piece. Drive a pair of 12d nails or 1½-inch screws every 8 inches or so. Start at one end and work toward the other end. Your helper may need to bend the top board from time to time so that the boards' edges are perfectly aligned in the place where you are driving fasteners.

If your boards are shorter than the distance your final beam must span, you can get the extra length you need by splicing (below, left). You can use multiple splices in a single beam, but be sure to offset them so that the splice on one side is at least 3 feet away from the splice on the other side. Some inspectors require splices to occur on top of a post, so that the board on each side is supported by the post. However, many builders do not worry about this; as long as you drive plenty of nails, the spliced area will be plenty strong.

Side-by-Side Beams

Build and install a beam like this one after the posts are in place. Use an angle square to draw lines all around the post at the correct height. Drive deck screws to hold the pieces temporarily in place, and check that their top edges are level with each other. Then drill holes and drive lag screws or carriage bolts.

FRAMING WITH SUPPORTS

IT IS POSSIBLE TO CONSTRUCT ALL THE FRAMING—INCLUDING BEAMS AND JOISTS—prior to installing foundations and inground posts. One virtue of this method is that you can easily adjust the positions of footings and posts as you go. It can also save time, since you don't have to wait for the footing concrete to cure before building the framing—and the inspector can check out the framing and the footings in one visit.

Once completed, the framing box should be square, level, parallel to the house, and correctly positioned over the footing holes.

Building a Framing Box

From your plan drawings you should be able to determine the lengths of all the framing pieces. (Where one piece butts into another, be sure to include the $1\frac{1}{2}$-inch thickness of the second piece.) The example shown on the next six pages includes some angles and a level change; your deck may be simpler.

TIME SAVER

If your deck is small and rectangular, you can quickly check for square by placing a sheet of plywood on top of the frame. Just make sure you are using two factory edges, which are perfectly square to each other.

The first board. Work with at least one helper; you may need two assistants for longer boards. Start at one end of the ledger, and continue until you have created a box of outside joists terminating at the other end of the ledger. With your helper holding the first board fairly square and level, attach it to the ledger with a joist hanger (pages 134–135). Use 2 × 4s or scraps of joist material for temporary supports. Rest each support on a small piece of wood so the support doesn't sink into the ground. Adjust the outside joist so it is level and square, and drive nails or screws through the temporary support and into the outside joist.

Angled joist. If your deck will have 45-degree angles, check your chop saw or circular saw for accuracy: Cut two pieces at 22½ degrees, and hold them together. If they do not form a 45-degree angle, adjust your saw and retest until you get it right. Join angled pieces by drilling pilot holes and driving three or more nails or screws. Another method is to build a rectangle first, and then cut off the corners later. See page 131 for this technique.

Continue framing. When building a framing box, continually check as you go. Check each board for square and level when you install it. After you have installed a few boards, go back and double-check previous boards, and make adjustments as needed. Drive at least two nails or screws into each joint. Install enough temporary supports so that the box is fairly stable; usually, a board longer than 6 feet should have two supports. Still, the structure will be somewhat fragile, so take care not to bump it out of position.

Check overall level. Once you've framed more than half the box, check that you are close to level with the other end of the ledger. You may need to go back and make adjustments.

Check measurements. As you frame, also make sure that the header is parallel to the house and the outside joists are parallel to each other. And whenever you complete a portion of the framing box that passes near a footing hole, take a minute to check that the hole is correctly positioned. You may need to enlarge the hole, a task that is easier to carry out at this stage when there are relatively few boards in the way.

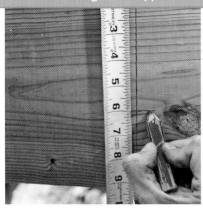

Framing a Level Change

In the example on these pages, ledger boards have been installed at two different levels. The framing for the deck's lower and upper sections—posts, beams, joists—will be level with their respective ledgers. Build the upper section first, following directions on pages 118–119. To begin the lower section, mark the upper section's outside joist to indicate the top of the lower section's framing (above, left). Make this mark in several places, or snap a chalk line, so you can align the lower-level joist along its length. Hold the board against the layout lines and drive nails or screws to fasten the lower-level joist to the upper-level joist (above, right). For more about level changes, see page 114.

Bracing a Beam

Temporarily brace beams by hanging them from the outside joists. Later you will support the beams with posts. Either build a two-part beam on the ground (pages 116–117) and then install it, or install each beam piece separately (next page).

To temporarily brace a beam, position a scrap piece of joist material or other substantial board to the side of the outside joist, and drive six or more nails or screws through the scrap and into the joist. Lift the beam into place, snug against the underside of the joists, and drive fasteners through the scrap and into the beam.

Where a beam will not be directly supported by a post, special fastening hardware is sometimes called for—your local building department may tell you exactly which pieces of hardware to get. In the example below, a metal strap ties the beam to the upper outside joist. Lag screws firmly attach the upper- and lower-section joists to each other—your building department may even specify the sizes and spacing of the screws. Two shallow notches chiseled on the top of the joist ensure that the strap will not create high spots that would raise the decking by $\frac{1}{8}$ inch or so.

Installing Interior Joists

A simple box made of outside joists and a header will be wobbly; adding a few interior joists can make the structure quite a bit more firm, and will allow you to straighten out a wavy header, which is a common problem. Lay out for positions of the joists (page 71). Double-check to be sure the joists will be parallel with the outside joists. Cut joists to length, and temporarily attach them. Remember that the header joist will likely not be straight, so if you measure for joist length near the middle of the header, you may well get an inaccurate figure. Instead, measure near the outside joists. Check that the interior joists are parallel to the outside ones, then attach with joist hangers.

PRO TIP

Before you fasten a beam, make sure that it will be suspended over the centers of the footing holes. In most cases, it will not matter if you move the beam over an inch or two from its planned location—better to align the beam with the hole.

Building a Beam in Place

In many situations, you can install the beam one piece at a time, saving your back from the weight of a heavier double beam. Make sure the two pieces are the same width, with similar crowns. Install each piece crown side up, taking care that the tops are exactly aligned, then fasten them together. In this example, a screw has been partially drilled into the top of one beam so that it can be leveraged with a claw hammer into alignment as it is fastened.

Finishing the Box

Continue adding pieces until you reach the last piece, which attaches to the ledger. Cut it according to the specs on your drawing; avoid measuring between the ledger and the second-to-last piece, which would probably give you an inaccurate measurement, because the framing box is likely out of square. In most cases, the last piece will be the same length as the first piece on the other side.

If the last piece is too long or short by more than a few inches, go back and double-check the rest of the framing box for square and parallel to the house. Often a slight adjustment at the first or second board will lead to a large difference at the last piece. Install the last piece with a joist hanger. In the example shown, the last piece is angled, so an angled joist hanger is used.

Give the overall box a final check. Measure the diagonals of a rectangle; they should be the same dimension. Use the 3-4-5 method to check corners for square, and see that the header is parallel to the house. Place a level in the centers of all the boards. If a section is out of plumb, you may need to remove a temporary support, re-level, and reattach the support.

Get Inspected, Pour Concrete

Your inspector may want to see the footing holes before you pour the concrete, or after you pour, or both. He also may want to inspect the framing box, the completed framing, or both. Mix and pour concrete following directions on pages 94–95 and 98.

Installing Inground Posts

Wait for the concrete to cure before you install posts. Some builders pour concrete in the afternoon and install posts the next morning. To be safe, allow at least 24 hours if you use high-strength (or "high early") concrete; curing may take longer in a humid climate or if the hole is damp. The concrete should feel completely firm when you tap it with a 4 × 4 or a hand tamper.

1 **MEASURE FOR POST LENGTH.** Once you are sure that the framing is level all around, measure the distance from the top of the concrete to the underside of the beam. Add 1/8 inch to allow the wood to compress with the weight of the deck.

2 **MARK THE POST.** If the post is 6 × 6, it is typical to notch it so that the beam can run through it. Make a notch that allows the full thickness of the beam to rest on top of the post. The upper part of the notched section (which will bolt to the side of the beam) should be about 1/4 inch below the top of the beam.

3 **CUT WITH A CIRCULAR SAW.** Check that the circular saw cuts square (pages 72–73). Set the blade to cut the thickness of the beam, and make the right-angle cut. Then set the blade to full depth, and cut the other lines on each side.

4 **COMPLETE THE CUT.** Use a handsaw or a reciprocating saw to finish the cut. Remove the cutout, and use a hammer and chisel to clean things up.

continued ▶▶

When Notching Is Not Practical

If a post is installed under the junction of two beams meeting at an angle, a notched beam cannot fully support both beam pieces. In such cases, cut the post to length and install it under the beams. Secure the connection using a post cap or mending plate (page 128); your building department may tell you which hardware to use.

5 **PLACE THE POST.** Slip the post into the hole. Have a helper raise the framing a tad while you place the post's notch under the beam. If the post is a little short, place shims under the beam. Use shims made of composite material, which will not compress or rust.

6 **CHECK FOR PLUMB.** The post should be plumb in both directions, and its notch should fit snugly around the beam. To adjust its position, have your helper lift up on the beam while you nudge the post into plumb with a 2 × 4.

7 **DRILL HOLES.** Drive screws or nails to snug the post against the beam. Drill pilot holes for lag screws or bolts. In the example shown, counterbore holes are also drilled, to permit shorter screws to fully penetrate the beam's thickness.

8 **DRIVE SCREWS.** Use a ratchet and socket to fasten the lag screws.

Fill, Tamp, Mound, and Stomp

You can wait until the framing is finished before filling the holes, but it will probably be easier to do it before the interior joists are installed. Once all the posts are installed and you are sure the entire structure is square and level, shovel about 16 inches of soil into the hole (above, left). Use a 2 × 4 to tamp the soil fairly firm, then repeat until you reach the top of the hole. Mound the soil up around the post, so rainwater will flow away from the post. Tamp with a 2 × 4 and stomp with your foot to make a tightly compacted mound (above, center). If your soil is sandy, you may need to lightly dampen the soil, then tamp. Pry away all the temporary supports (above, right). Now you're ready to frame the interior joists (instructions for this deck continue on page 130).

PRO TIP

Some codes require a sealer to be applied to the cut ends of the post. Consult with your inspector or a local builder; in many areas, pressure-treated lumber is considered good enough by itself.

Whether your posts are inground or above, you can enhance their appearance by covering them with decorative facing and trim.

ABOVEGROUND POSTS

FOR THOSE WHO INSTALLED FOOT-INGS THAT RISE AN INCH OR SO ABOVE GRADE (pages 96–99), here's where we pick up your story. Allow the concrete to cure for a day or so. While you wait, build your beams (pages 116–117), and leave them a bit longer than needed—you can cut them to fit later. Then install the post bases as specified by your building department. Use a string line to ensure that all the post bases have been adjusted so that they line up in a row. If the footings will be visible (i.e., not hidden behind skirting), cut away the exposed cardboard tube form, for appearance's sake.

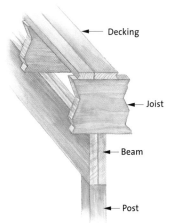

Decking

Joist

Beam

Post

In most designs, deck posts are cut to the finished height of the deck, minus the decking thickness, the width of the joists, and the width of the beam. Before you mark the posts for cutting, double-check the widths of the boards you will use for joists and beams. Widths can vary by as much as ¼ inch from board to board.

Installing and Cutting Posts

Most commonly, an aboveground post rests directly under a beam. See page 113 for other configurations. If you use 6 × 6 or 4 × 6 posts, you can notch them, as shown on page 123. Just be sure that the notch permits the entire thickness of the beam to rest atop the post.

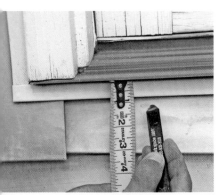

1 **MARK THE FRAMING HEIGHT.** If you have already installed a ledger (pages 103–109), then the top of the ledger is the framing height. If there will be no ledger (as shown on these pages), make a mark on the house indicating the top of the framing. In most cases, the decking should be either 1 or 2 inches below the door threshold (so snow and rain can't easily enter the house), or 5½ to 7½ inches below the threshold (so it feels like a regular step). The top of the framing will be lower still by the thickness of the decking.

2 **ATTACH THE POSTS.** Cut the posts longer than needed. Check that the post bottoms, which rest on the anchors, are cut square. Slip a post into an anchor and have a helper hold it level while you drive nails or screws through the holes in the anchor, and into the post.

3 **LEVEL WITH A LASER.** A laser level offers a quick way to get accurate measurements of the posts. Attach the laser to an outside post that has a "view" of all the other posts. Aim it at the framing height mark on the house (or at the top of the ledger, if you have one) and level it out. Swivel the laser until it points to another post. As long as the laser unit is attached correctly, its horizontal beam will be perfectly level with the top of the framing.

4 **MARK THE POST HEIGHT.** Hold a tape measure, pointing down, against the post and aim the laser at it. In the example shown, the posts need to be cut 15 inches below the top of the framing to allow for 2 × 8 joists and 4 × 8 beams, which are $7^{1}/_{2}$ inches wide. Position the tape so that the laser's red dot is at the tape's 15-inch mark—now you know where to cut.

5 **CUT THE POSTS TO HEIGHT.** Use an angle square to draw lines all around each post. Have a helper grasp the top of the post while you cut one side with a circular saw. When you cut the other side, have your helper lift up on the post as you reach the end of the cut; otherwise, the saw blade may bind.

Level Without a Laser

Some builders swear by a water level, which has a hose that you move from post to post. Others prefer a line level, which hangs on a string. But the simplest way for many do-it-yourselfers is to set a carpenter's level atop a straight board.

Installing Beams Onto Posts

On these two pages we show methods that use mending plates and post caps, but a variety of connectors can be used. Attach the beam to the posts using the hardware recommended or required by your building department.

A beam is a lot of weight to work with, especially if it is long and the boards are heavy from pressure treatment. In addition, the beams-and-posts arrangement can be unstable until you install the outside joists (steps 4–6). Have a few strong-backed and willing helpers on hand. If the weight is difficult and you don't feel in control, get another helper.

1 **SET BEAMS ON POSTS.** Raise the beam up and carefully lower it onto the posts. The posts will not be perfectly plumb, so don't be alarmed if the beam does not rest on the centers of all the posts. Remove your hands slowly, making sure that the structure is fairly stable.

2 **DRIVE SCREWS.** Assuming you cut it longer than it needs to be, set the beam so it overhangs the posts on either side. Unless you have installed post caps (page 123), drill pilot holes and drive angled screws or nails to attach the beam to each post. Have a helper check the post for plumb as you work.

3 **ATTACH A MENDING PLATE.** A mending plate, also called a nailing plate, has a grid of barbs that sink into the wood, so it attaches without nails or screws. Just keep pounding with a hammer, using medium-strength blows, until the plate lies flat against both the post and the beam. At each joint, attach a plate on both sides.

4 **SQUARE OUTSIDE JOISTS; MARK BEAM FOR CUTTING.**
Position the outside joists on top of the beams and temporarily screw them in place. Use the 3-4-5 method to check each outside joist for square; also check that they are the same distance apart at both ends. Once you are sure of the outside joist positions, mark the beams for cutting and move the joists temporarily out of the way.

5 **CUT THE BEAM.** Use an angle square to draw lines on each side of the beam, then cut each side with a circular saw. You could use a reciprocating saw, but the cut will probably not be straight.

6 **ATTACH THE JOISTS TO THE BEAM.** Attach joists to the ledger (or to the header running along the house) with joist hangers, then check the nearest post for plumb, drill pilot holes, and drive angled nails or screws to attach the outside joists to the beam. You will notice right away that the structure is quite a bit more stable.

JOISTS

JOISTS ARE THE FRAMING MEMBERS USED TO SUPPORT THE DECKING. Their size, span, fasteners, and spacing are determined by codes (page 45). The instructions on the next several pages apply to all decks, no matter which style of footing or beam they employ.

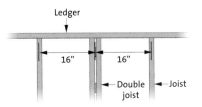

Joist spacing is commonly given as "on center" (o.c.), which means the spacing is measured from the center of one joist to the center of the next. The most common joist spacings are 12, 16, and 24 inches. Spacing can be less than specified—as is often the case between an end joist and the next joist—but it cannot be greater.

Where joists tie into a ledger or beam at the same height, joist hangers are used. Where joists rest atop and overhang a beam, they are attached by toenailing or with metal fasteners known as hurricane or seismic ties.

Choose joist stock carefully. Look for straight boards, and plan to cut off any cracked ends. Always install joists with the crown side up. Depending on the framing method you choose, you may cut all the joists to length before installing them, or you may cut them to length after they are installed (page 136).

Framing Around Corners

A deck that turns the corner of a house can provide a different view, open up a microclimate, and create privacy. Decide how you want the decking to look, because this will affect the framing. Parallel and diagonal decking usually requires no special joist framing. If the decking will be perpendicular, you will need a doubled joist where the two directions meet. Mitered decking also calls for a doubled joist; in this case each joist must be cut at 45 degrees at each end. Examine your plan carefully to be sure that every decking board will rest on a framing piece near its end.

PLAN AHEAD

Some railing designs—especially those using composite materials—require that the posts be installed inside the framing. You may need to install extra joists or blocking pieces as well; see page 151.

PARALLEL DECKING

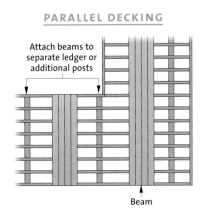

PERPENDICULAR DECKING

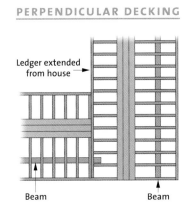

MITERED DECKING

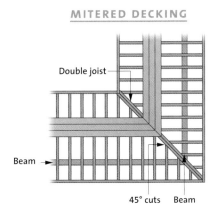

Framing for Angles

Angles are an easy way to add visual interest to your deck. You can use any angle you choose, but 45-degree angles are the least complicated. Plan ahead for this detail, cantilevering the joists enough that the beam will not interfere with the angled corner. If the angled corner will run more than 2 feet beyond the beam, you may need to insert an additional beam.

If you are certain of your skills and measurements, you can cut and install the angled pieces of the outside framing box first, then cut inside joists to fit (as shown on pages 118–119). A safer method for a do-it-yourselfer is to build the framing as though it were a rectangle, then cut off the corner. To add a small 45-degree corner (above, right), construct a rectangular frame. Set your circular saw at a $22\frac{1}{2}$-degree bevel and cut the outside and header joists plumb. Cut a short filler piece with a $22\frac{1}{2}$-degree bevel on each end, and attach.

A larger angled corner requires cutting one or more joists. In the example at right, the outside joist and header are cut at $22\frac{1}{2}$-degree bevels. A chalk line is snapped across the top of the joists to mark them for cutting at 45-degree bevels. Cut a filler piece to fit, and fasten it to the outside joist and the header. Fasten to the interior joists using 45-degree joist hangers.

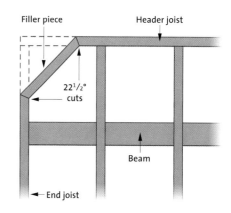

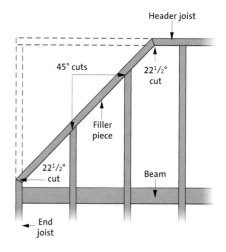

Bracing Options

If a deck has 4×4 posts more than 4 feet high or 6×6 posts more than 8 feet high, bracing may be required by local codes. The most common type of bracing forms a Y shape between the post and the beam. The simplest Y bracing has a 2×4 screwed or bolted to each side of the post and the beam (right). Many people prefer the look of solid 4×4 braces (far right). Lag screws secure the 4×4 braces at either end.

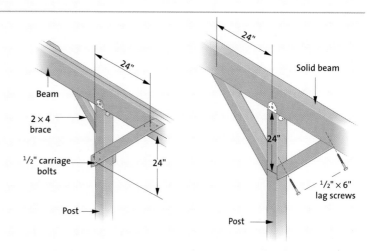

Laying Out for Joists

Hook a tape measure to the outside edge of an outside joist and pull along the ledger (or the header near the house, if there is no ledger). Make marks $^3/_4$ inch on either side of the on-center dimension. For instance, for 16-inch spacing, make marks at $15^1/_4$ and $16^3/_4$; $31^1/_4$ and $32^3/_4$; etc. Use an angle square to draw plumb lines at each of the marks. The distance between the two lines is $1^1/_2$ inches—the thickness of a joist.

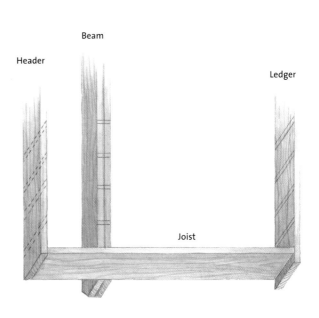

Mark the Beam and Header

To keep the joists running straight and parallel, you should draw layout lines on the header and beam (above). Perhaps the most common mistake in framing is to misalign the ledger's lines with those on the header or the beam. So work carefully, double-check your measurements, and then triple-check by measuring the joists after you have installed a few.

TIME SAVER

Hold the header on top of the ledger, upside down (with the crown side down), and draw lines that match those on the ledger. You need to hold the ledger upside down because it will face the opposite direction when it's placed in position.

Cut Now or Later?

Sight along your ledger, or stretch a string, to check it for straightness. If it waves no more than, say, $^1/_4$ inch, and if you are certain of your measuring skills, you can cut all the joists to length before installing them. However, many builders prefer to cut the joists later, after they have been installed onto joist hangers. If you have no ledger, or if the ledger waves, or if you are uncertain of your skills, follow the method shown on page 136 for cutting the joists to length.

Square the End, Check the Crown

Whichever method you use, be sure that the end that attaches to the ledger is square and free of cracks. Some builders cut all the ends square as a matter of course, while others cut only those that are out of square or cracked. Use an angle square to draw a line, check that your circular saw's blade is square (page 72), and cut.

You should also sight along each joist to see if it has a crown—a slight bulge in the middle. Mark an arrow indicating the direction of the crown, and install joists crown side up.

Decorative Cuts for Beams

If the beam will be visible, trim it at an angle for a neater appearance (right). Start the angle cut at least halfway down the width of the beam, so you do not weaken it. The small deck below would probably not have suffered if its visible beam had not been trimmed, but the angle is consistent with the deck's mitered design.

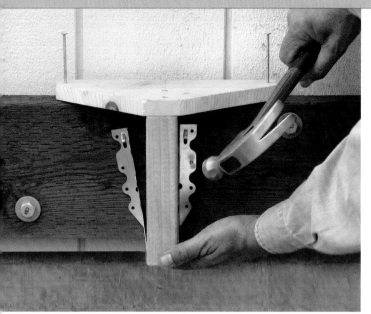

Attaching Joists with Hangers

In most cases, joists are attached with joist hangers at the house only; at the other end, it is usual to drive nails or screws through the header and into the joist ends. Builders use a variety of methods for installing joists with hangers; we show several on these pages.

Making and Using Jigs

Joists should be installed so their top edges are perfectly flush with the tops of the ledger and header; otherwise, the decking could be wavy, or even difficult to install. If your joists are all consistent in width (pieces can vary by as much as 1/4 inch), you can build a jig like the one shown below left. Be sure the length of the jig's 2 × 4 is exactly the same as the width of your joists. Align the 2 × 4 with the layout line on the ledger, push the joist hanger up against the underside of the 2 × 4, and drive joist hanger nails into the ledger. Now you can insert the joist into the hanger.

If, however, your joists vary in width, making a jig useless, attach a temporary strip of wood to the top of each joist (below, right). The strip should protrude about 1 inch so that it rests on the top of the ledger. When you set the joist in place, the strip will hold the joist at the right height. Now you can attach the hanger.

10d nail

12"

Plywood or 1× lumber

Length matches depth of joists

2 × 4

Thickness matches joist stock

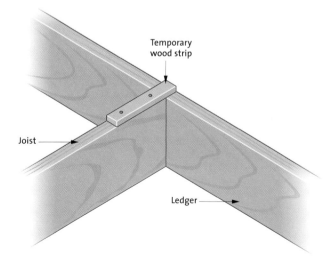

Temporary wood strip

Joist

Ledger

The Standard Method

Installing joists alone is difficult work. A single helper makes the task relatively easy and will prevent misaligned joists.

1 **ATTACH WITH TOENAILS.** Have a helper hold the joist against the layout lines on the ledger, and angle-drive nails or screws to hold the joist in place. If you use screws, drill pilot holes first. The fastener heads should sink completely into the wood so that they do not interfere with the joist hanger.

2 **TUCK THE HANGER UP.** Slide a hanger up under the joist— tap it with the head of a hammer to make sure it is tight against the joist's underside. Push one side of the hanger tight against the side of the joist.

3 **TAP THE TAB.** Hammer a tab near the top of the hanger into the ledger to hold the hanger in place.

4 **DRIVE THE NAILS.** Drive joist-hanger nails or screws into every hole. Some hangers have angled holes, so you can drive longer fasteners through the joist and into the ledger. Repeat on the other side.

The On-Joist-First Method

If you do not have a power nailer, it will be tough to temporarily toenail the joist in place (see step 1, above) because the joist will wobble and move out of alignment as you pound. So try this technique: Before you lift the joist into position, attach a hanger to its end. Position the hanger about $1/8$ inch from the end of the joist, then partially drive nails through the hanger's angled holes, until they just barely poke out the board's end. Now hold the joist-with-hanger in place against the ledger and finish driving the angled nails. Once the joist is toenailed, you can drive the other nails.

Attaching Joists to the Header and Beams

Once the joists are installed at the house, they need to be aligned and anchored at the header, as well as to the tops of the beams.

Cutting Joists to Length

If you cut your joists to length before attaching them to joist hangers, skip these steps. However, cutting joists after they have been installed at the house ensures that their ends will line up, which will prevent a wavy header.

1 **MARK THE LENGTHS.** Measure out from the ledger along each outside joist and mark the desired length. (Remember that the header's thickness will add $1\frac{1}{2}$ inches of framing length.) Snap a chalk line between these marks across the tops of the joists. You may need to snap twice to ensure a visible line on all of the joists.

2 **DRAW CUT LINES.** Use an angle square to draw vertical lines down from the chalk line on each of the joists.

3 **CUT THE JOISTS.** Use a circular saw to cut the lines. You could cut from the bottom up, but many people find it easier to stand on a board laid on the joists and cut down. That way the blade won't bind, and the weight of the saw works to your advantage. Be sure to cut to the same side of the line for all the joists (the rule of thumb is to cut just outside the line).

4 **ATTACH THE HEADER.** Cut the header to length, and mark it with layout lines that mirror those on the ledger (page 132). Have a helper or two hold it in place, so its top is flush with the tops of the joists. Drive nails or screws to fasten the ledger to the joists.

Straighten As You Go

As you attach the joists to the header and beams, you will likely find that some boards align and level easily while others need persuading. Take your time to ensure that the top of the header is flush with the tops of every joist.

Pry. If a joist end is higher than the header, use a 2 × 4 to pry the header up. If the joist is lower than the header, have a helper pull down on the header, or use a pry bar to leverage the joist up.

Chisel grooves. Discrepancies of ¼ inch or so can usually be resolved by prying; the weight of the deck will level things in time. However, if a joist end is significantly higher than the others (usually because the joist is wider), it can cause a wave in the decking. The solution is to push the joist to the side and chisel out a groove in the marks you've made on the beam (above, left). Shift the joist back into place (above, right) and check the alignment; you may need to chisel deeper.

Anchor to the Beam

Some building departments are happy if you attach the joists to the beam with angle-driven nails or screws (page 62). Others require you to use anchoring hardware, often called hurricane ties or seismic ties, as shown at right.

FRAMING VARIATIONS

FEW DECKS CALL FOR FRAMING THAT IS COMPLETELY STRAIGHTFORWARD. Most have some little tweak that will require extra attention. Here are a few of the most common framing variations.

Special Joist Hangers

You can buy a joist hanger to suit almost any situation and piece of lumber. For instance, beam hangers are wide enough to hold 4× lumber; some straps (page 120) can be adapted to carry a variety of beam or joist sizes. If you encounter a situation with no clear solution, contact your inspector for the hardware piece that will make a strong, and legal, connection.

Clipped hanger. Where an outside joist meets the header, there is no nailing surface on one side of the header for a standard joist hanger. You could buy a clip, but it is common practice to make your own. Use tin snips to cut a joist hanger to create an angle bracket, as shown at left.

Angled hanger. The angled beam hanger at left carries a doubled joist at a 45-degree angle. You can buy hangers at other angles, or even hangers that are adjustable.

Framing Around Obstacles

Remove or relocate as many obstacles, such as spigots and downspouts, as you can (page 102). Where an obstacle cannot be removed, the solution may be to box around it. Be sure that you will have adequate access after the deck is built. For instance, the spigot shown below will be reachable from under the deck. In a situation like this, you may choose to install a shutoff valve inside the house; that way, you can leave the outside spigot turned on, and control the water without crawling under the deck.

In the example shown, a short header (also known as blocking) runs parallel to the ledger from joist to joist, and an interior joist is attached to the blocking. The short header must be fairly close to the house, so that the decking pieces that will miss the ledger will not overhang by too much.

Making Openings

The most common reason for an opening is a tree. Build a basic rectangle, then cut angled framing pieces to fit, allowing room for trunk growth. Decking can then be cut to fit fairly snugly around the trunk.

For a rectangular opening, first double the joists on the two sides. Then insert header joists on the other two sides, using two pieces of joist stock. Use joist hangers or angle brackets at all connections. Attach joists to the headers, maintaining your regular on-center spacing. Cut and install the decking so that it overhangs the framing by 1 to 4 inches, depending on the strength of the decking.

To round the opening, cut and install diagonal joists across the corners. Cut and install decking so that it covers as much of the opening as possible, then mark and cut a circle in the decking.

If your deck will cover a water faucet or an electrical receptacle, you may need to build a small access panel. Attach 2 × 4 cleats to facing joists, $3^{1}/_{2}$ inches below the top edges of the joists. Build a frame with 2 × 4s, about $^{1}/_{2}$ inch narrower than the space between the joists. Cut and attach decking pieces to the frame, then drill two finger holes.

Installing Blocking

Some building codes require the use of blocking (also called bracing) between joists. Blocking can strengthen a deck, especially if the joists span 10 feet or more. Blocking also minimizes warping of joists. Cut blocking pieces out of joist stock; they will be $1^{1}/_{2}$ inches shorter than your on-center spacing. Snap a chalk line across the tops of joists, then install blocking on alternating sides of the line. Drive three nails or screws into each joint. If the blocking is so tight that it moves the joists out of alignment, you may need to trim some of the pieces $^{1}/_{4}$ inch or so.

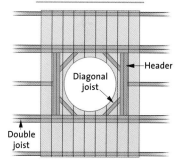

ROUND OPENING

Header

Diagonal joist

Double joist

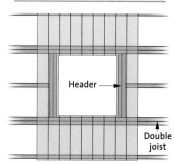

RECTANGULAR OPENING

Header

Double joist

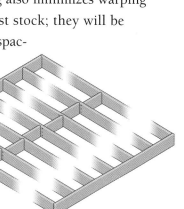

BLOCKING

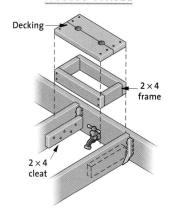

ACCESS PANEL

Decking

2 × 4 frame

2 × 4 cleat

FRAMING A CURVE

ANOTHER WAY TO PERSONALIZE YOUR DECK is to bend some of its straight lines. Constructing a curved deck does take more work than most rectangular decks, but it does not require special tools or skills.

The rules for sizing and spacing footings, piers, and posts are the same for a curved deck as for a rectangular one. Framing and decking applications are also similar. But if the deck needs a railing, the workload can increase substantially. Before committing yourself to a curved deck with a railing, take a look at the information on the following pages, and make sure you have a thorough plan for your railing before you begin construction.

PRO TIP

If the joists in a curved section need to be cut at angles that exceed the range of your circular saw, use a reciprocating saw or a handsaw.

Rounding a Corner

If you want to round one or two corners on an otherwise rectangular deck, the framing procedure is the same as for a large angled corner (page 131). Cantilever the joists well beyond a standard beam, cut the joists at an angle, as shown at left, and add an angled rim joist. To cut the decking, drive a nail temporarily into the decking, equidistant from each side. Tie string to the nail at one end and a pencil at the other and draw a line on the decking as shown at top. Cut the decking with a jigsaw.

Beam

22 1/2° cut

Joist

45° cuts

22 1/2° cut

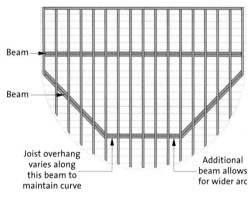

Beam

Beam

Joist overhang varies along this beam to maintain curve

Additional beam allows for wider arc

Framing for Large Curves

If your plan calls for a curved section that protrudes more than 2 feet past a beam, or if you want to round an entire side of the deck, you cannot support the deck with just one or two long straight beams. This is the biggest framing difference between a curved and a rectangular deck. Plan for additional beams to keep the joists from exceeding the allowable overhang. The shape of the added beam support should approximate the outline of the curved deck (see above), but the actual curve comes from the joists and the decking.

Marking Joists for a Curve

To lay out a large curve on joists, use one of the methods detailed here.

Begin by installing joists with plenty of overhang. For a circular curve, determine the radius you want and locate the center point. Place a temporary brace across the two joists nearest to the center point. Make a trammel (right) out of a straight 1 × 4. At the center point, drive a nail through one end of the trammel. Drill a hole in the other end where the trammel meets the planned curve. Place a pencil in the hole and mark the joists by pivoting the trammel.

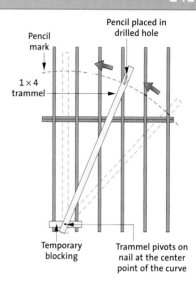

Pencil mark

Pencil placed in drilled hole

1 × 4 trammel

Temporary blocking

Trammel pivots on nail at the center point of the curve

If your curve will be elliptical, bend a long strip of flexible fascia material or synthetic decking across the tops of the joists (right), adjusting the position and arc until they're right. Attach the ends and middle of the strip to temporary braces attached vertically to the joists, then mark the cut line on the joists by tracing along the outside of the strip.

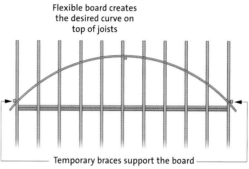

Flexible board creates the desired curve on top of joists

Temporary braces support the board

Framing the Curve

Now that you've marked the curve, you're ready to finish framing.

1 CUT JOISTS. With an angle square, extend the cut marks down both sides of each joist. Set your circular saw for the angle of the cut, then cut the joist as shown. Each joist will probably have to be cut at a different angle, requiring you to readjust the saw for each one. The angles of the cuts do not have to be perfect, but they should be fairly close.

2 INSTALL BLOCKING. Blocking between the joists will keep them from flexing as you bend the fascia (next step) and give you more surfaces to support the decking. Cut the blocking pieces one at a time—again, adjust your circular saw to produce different angles. Once a blocking piece fits fairly well, fasten it with nails or screws.

3 FACE WITH FASCIA. Composite decking or fascia material bends easily and is quick to install. You can also use strips of $1/4$- or $3/8$-inch exterior plywood. If you have a band saw or a table saw, cut thin strips out of the decking lumber. Use clamps to hold the fascia or strips in place, then drive at least two nails or screws into the end of each joist.

BUILDING A LOW DECK

A LOW DECK IS A NECESSITY IF THE FLOOR OF YOUR HOUSE IS CLOSE TO THE GROUND, but there are other reasons to keep decks low. A deck that is raised only inches above the ground has the feel of a patio. There's no need for a railing on a low deck, so it blends unobtrusively with the yard, and since a low deck is typically freestanding, you usually don't need to install a ledger.

Ways to Keep It Low

You can lower the height of a deck by using smaller-width joists and beams. However, this change may require you to reduce the beam and joist spans, which, in turn, may mean pouring more footings. Another strategy is to attach the joists to the side, rather than the top, of the beam.

Sometimes decks employ short posts to stay low, but posts that are less than 10 inches tall are prone to splitting, thanks to all the nails in their tops and bottoms. You can usually design your way around short posts altogether by increasing the beam width or by raising the height of concrete piers. Either way you'll need piers that are at precisely the same height, so make sure the tops of cardboard tube forms are level with each other before you pour concrete.

This low deck is just two steps up from the surrounding yard, so neighboring flowers grow above it.

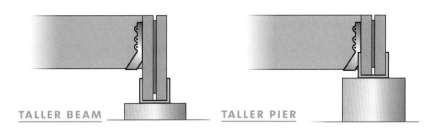

TALLER BEAM   TALLER PIER

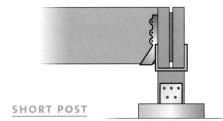

SHORT POST

DOUBLE-CHECK

A low deck is likely to come in contact with foliage, so make sure all lumber, including the decking, is rated for ground contact.

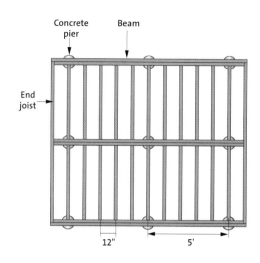

Constructing Without Posts

To build a low deck with no posts, plan to install at least two rows of equally tall piers (more for a larger deck) with identical beams installed along each row. Construct the beams of double 2× members. The inside board should be shorter by 1½ inches at both ends, to create a place for the end joist to fit (above, left). Attach the beam to the pier with a post cap, and the joists to the inside faces of each beam with joist hangers.

A Deck with No Footings

The small platform deck shown at right requires no poured concrete and does not even use precast piers. The foundation consists of two 4 × 6 timbers partially buried belowground. Timbers used this way must be pressure treated and rated for ground contact. Joists rest on top of the timbers.

Dig two parallel trenches that are about 6 inches deep for the timbers, then add about 4 inches of sand to each trench. Set the timbers on the sand as shown below right and make sure they are perfectly parallel. Level the timbers by adding or removing sand, then fill in the trenches by adding sand to the sides of the timbers.

Mark a joist layout on each timber. Install the joists on top of the timbers with two 12d toenails or two 2½-inch deck screws driven at an angle through each side into the beam. Trim the joist ends, if necessary, and attach the header joists. Install the decking.

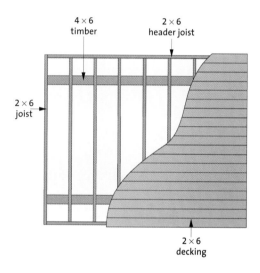

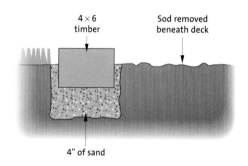

A Low Deck with Posts

You can also frame a low deck using in-ground posts and side-by-side beams. Just be sure that all the lumber is rated for ground contact.

USING PRECAST PIERS

PRECAST CONCRETE PIERS MAKE IT POSSIBLE TO BUILD A DECK without digging and pouring footings. You'll need to install quite a few piers, but they are not difficult to set. Several types of precast piers are available. Those shown here are shaped to firmly hold either 2 × 6 joists or 4 × 4 posts.

A deck built on precast piers must be freestanding; do not attach it to the house. The reason for this is that the deck needs to be free to move—to float. In an area with freezing temperatures, a deck can rise and fall as much as an inch when the ground freezes and thaws. Even in areas without frost, piers may settle a bit, causing the deck to lower slightly over time. Check with your building department to make sure this type of construction is allowed in your area. If it is, you may not need a permit for a deck that is modest in size, low to the ground, and unattached. In a typical deck of this type, joists are placed on 24-inch centers—close enough so you can install 2 × 6 decking. The piers must be spaced no farther than 5 feet apart.

This rectangular deck is built on piers that simply rest on firm soil. The posts below the left side of the deck are a bit longer than those on the near side to account for the site's gentle slope.

Using a level and a straight board, you can quickly mark posts for cutting.

When constructing without posts, the trick is to get all the piers level with each other.

A Low Deck on a Flat Site

If the yard is level and the deck will be low to the ground, you will not need posts. However, the piers must all be level with one another.

Excavate all sod and organic material from beneath each pier, digging just deep enough to reach bare dirt. Check that the area is roughly level, using a carpenter's level set atop a long straight board. Plan the locations of the piers, and set piers in place at the four outside corners. Place the four outside joists in the piers and check them for square, then for level. Adjust pier heights as needed by removing or adding soil. Drive screws or nails to fasten the outside joists to each other.

With the outside frame installed, cut the interior joists to fit. Set each joist in place, supported by piers as needed. Adjust the height of the piers so each supports its joist firmly, then fasten the joists. Once the framing is completed, install the decking (pages 150–159).

A Raised Deck on a Sloping Site

If the site is sloped, use joists or string lines to position all the piers. Cut posts longer than they need to be and set one in each pier. Set a carpenter's level atop a long straight board and mark all the outside posts at the appropriate height. Cut the posts with a circular saw (pages 72–73). Set the joists on top of the cut posts and anchor them using hurricane or seismic ties. Then hold the inside joists in position to mark the inside posts for cutting. Cut the posts and attach the joists.

decking

WHETHER YOUR DECKING IS MADE
OF WOOD OR SYNTHETIC MATERIALS,
YOUR DECKING PATTERN BASIC OR
COMPLEX, THIS CHAPTER OFFERS
DETAILED INSTRUCTIONS FOR
ACHIEVING A HANDSOME SURFACE.

DECKING PATTERNS

DECKING THAT FOLLOWS A SIMPLE PARALLEL PATTERN is easy to install and inherently attractive—for many, when it comes to decking patterns, the simpler the better. Installing decking boards whose pattern deviates from parallel lines is bit more complicated, but the result is unique and eye-catching. In most cases, patterns cost a bit more in time and materials, but building them does not require fine carpentry skills. Regardless of the pattern you choose, make sure the ends of all decking boards are supported by joists—patterns typically require additional framing.

Keeping It Simple

Most decks are constructed with decking that runs parallel to the house, and for good reason. This style is the quickest to install and has understated good looks. The decking is installed over the conventional arrangement of joists running perpendicular to the ledger.

Most decking boards are $5\frac{1}{2}$ inches wide. For a pinstriped look, consider installing decking boards of alternating widths. Perpendicular decking essentially rotates the deck's entire frame 90 degrees. Since decks are typically longer along the house than away from the house, this orientation often makes it possible to install decking boards without butt joints. It also makes it easier to shovel snow off the finished deck.

Decking that runs at a 45-degree angle to the house is one of the most popular patterns (pages 152–157). It requires that you measure the joist spacing (that is, the decking span) along the diagonal run of the decking. This often means that the joists must be spaced closer together, or that you need to use thicker decking. Since each board length differs, and both ends must be cut at an angle, diagonal decking takes more time to install.

PARALLEL TO THE HOUSE

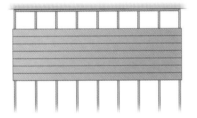

PARALLEL, PINSTRIPE

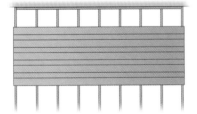

PERPENDICULAR TO THE HOUSE

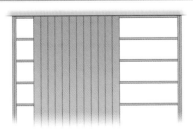

DIAGONAL

Getting Tricky

Complex decking patterns require careful planning—installation details will vary from deck to deck. Regardless of the design, observe two principles: The ends of every piece of decking must be supported by framing, and no piece of decking should exceed its allowable span.

A V-shape pattern requires special framing and a center strip (page 166) constructed out of two joists with a 4 × 4 or a flat-laid 2 × 4 between them. Center strips usually run down the center of decks (pages 166–169), but they can be placed wherever you bring the ends of your boards together to create a V.

A herringbone pattern is less demanding to lay than it looks, but it does require careful planning. Once the framing is correctly installed with doubled joists, you can square-cut many of the decking boards to the same length. Other pieces are square-cut at one end and can be left uncut at the other end, then trimmed all at once using a chalk line cut (page 156).

A diamond pattern is downright difficult because many miter-cut pieces must join together precisely. You will also need to install two rows of blocking (page 139).

The mitered deck shown below is just one example of a decking pattern that uses a border. Synthetic decking is particularly suited to these sorts of patterns (pages 166–169).

V-SHAPE

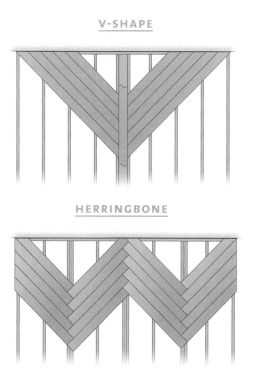

DIAMOND

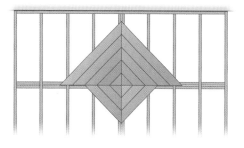

HERRINGBONE

MITERED BORDER

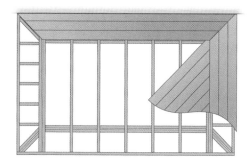

PREPARE FOR DECKING

ONCE YOUR BASIC JOISTS ARE INSTALLED (pages 130–139), take time to prepare for the decking. Inspect the framing to make sure the framing will support the ends of all decking boards; to double-check that all joists are level with each other; to install any posts that need to be attached inside the framing; and to choose the decking fasteners that are best suited to your boards.

Add Extra Framing

Ideally, every decking board end should be supported by a full $1\frac{1}{2}$ inches of joist thickness, though it is usually within code for two butted-together boards to share a single joist (giving each only $\frac{3}{4}$ inch of joist support). Where you will have butt joints, you can beef up the support by nailing a 2 × 4 alongside the joist, giving you 3 inches of support. If you do this, be sure the 2 × 4's top aligns perfectly with the joist's. At left is an example of framing for a center strip, which is used in patterns with angled butt joints. Other decking patterns require additional support pieces (pages 148–149).

Level the Joists

If the tops of the joists are not level, the decking boards either will follow their irregular contour or will not fasten completely down onto one or more of the joists. Check the joists for level with a straightedge or a tautly pulled string. A rise or fall of $\frac{1}{8}$ inch over a run of 16 inches will not be very noticeable; even $\frac{1}{4}$ inch over that span is probably acceptable. But where joists are closely spaced, as in the special framing at left, the joists should be very close to level. Use a plane, a power planer as shown, or even a circular saw to level things out. If a joist is high near a beam, you can usually bring it down by chiseling the beam (page 137).

To achieve a level decking surface like this, all the joists and blocking must be at the same height.

Install Railing or Bench Posts

Some railing designs—especially those that use synthetic materials—require posts that are installed inside the framing. Naturally, such posts must be installed and attached before you lay the decking. For tips on installing posts inside the framing, see page 203.

Choose Your Deck Fasteners

A deck surface is typically peppered with hundreds, even thousands, of fastener heads. Wood decking can be attached with nails or screws; synthetic decking must be installed with screws. As long as you choose nails or screws made for your type of decking, you can rest assured that they will do a good job of holding the decking in place. How will they look? That depends largely on how they are attached.

Galvanized nail heads are round and shiny, and will give a deck a classic look. But driving nails by hand is difficult work, and not as easy as you might think—you must drive every nail perfectly flush, without denting the decking boards. Hand-nail your deck only if you are very confident of your hammering skills.

A power nailer will drive nails into wood decking below the surface, leaving small holes (right, top). However, in time, and after staining and finishing, the holes will partially fill in and won't be very noticeable. That makes power-nailing both easy and attractive.

Screws are the only option for securing synthetic decking, but some screws produce little mounds, or mushrooms, in the decking surface when driven (right, second from top). To virtually eliminate these mushrooms, pound them with a hammer (right, second from bottom).

Self-tapping screws, made specifically for use with synthetic decking, actually cut counter-bore holes that are just the right size for the screw heads. That's why you end up with visible screw heads, but no mushrooms (right, bottom).

For an even neater appearance, use hidden fasteners, as shown on pages 162–163.

DECKING TECHNIQUES

THE NEXT SIX PAGES SHOW BASIC DECKING TECHNIQUES. The deck shown here uses ⁵/₄ cedar decking that's at a 45-degree angle to the house and attached with a power nailer; the posts will be installed after the decking. For instructions on synthetic decking, which is installed with screws and usually has in-framing rail posts, see pages 158–159.

Getting Started

This deck has a 45-degree-angled portion at its outside edge, so it makes sense to start on the outside and work toward the house. If there is no angle like this, it is best to start with the middle piece, as shown on page 158.

Gang-cut a number of boards at 45 degrees (left) so you can efficiently place them. In most cases, the other ends can wait to be cut until you make a chalk line cut (page 156). If your decking comes in various lengths, you will need to sort through the pieces and arrange them to keep waste to a minimum. Make sure each piece will overhang the framing far enough—in this case, the thickness of the fascia (³/₄ inch) plus 1 inch (page 157). If your decking is made out of 2 × 6s or 2 × 4s, it can overhang by up to 2 inches.

For decking that will run parallel to the house, start with the piece closest to the house. Cut it to length, since you will not be able to cut it with a circular saw when you make the chalk line cut. Attach it about ¹/₂ inch away from the siding, and use a string line to ensure that it is straight.

Driving Nails and Screws into Wood

Before you hand-drive nails into decking, practice on scraps until you are adept at avoiding miss-hits, which create frown- or smile-shaped indentations. To play it safe, you may want to use a nailset when delivering the last blow, so that the nail finishes flush with the top of the decking.

If you drive screws with a standard drill, consider using an attachment (left) that will allow you to adjust the screw depth. Be careful, though; on soft woods such as redwood and cedar, this tool may create circular indentations. Experiment with scrap pieces until you are proficient at driving fasteners without marring the wood.

Racking and Attaching

The job of attaching the decking to the joists will go quicker if you "rack" the boards—that is, lay out 10 or so rows of decking boards across the joists so you'll have easy access to them as you work. This is especially helpful if you have to deal with butt joints, which you can prearrange by row to ensure that they are staggered. Make sure all butt-joint boards meet cleanly and are free of splits. If they don't, cut flawed ends before you start nailing. If the decking is angled, you can rack boards that are progressively longer or shorter, as the pattern demands.

   Check the first piece to make sure it's straight, then drive only as many fasteners as are needed to secure it. Align the next piece by pushing it tight against the first, or by using nails or a spacing tool (right) to maintain a consistent gap, and attach the second piece in the same way as the first. Later, when all the boards are attached, you can finish nailing down the decking to produce reasonably straight rows of fasteners.

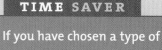

TIME SAVER

If you have chosen a type of decking that will not shrink, use a spacing tool (below) to create drainage gaps between decking boards. If you attach the spacer to the end of a board, it can easily be inserted and removed by a helper standing on the deck, as shown on page 159.

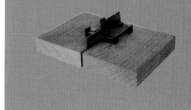

Straightening Deck Boards

If one board is attached bent, it will be difficult to straighten out subsequent boards. In most cases, you can straighten a crooked board simply by pulling on it with your hand as it's attached (below, left). If that doesn't work, knock the sharp end of a chisel or pry bar into the joist at an angle as shown (below, middle), then pull the board toward you. If you are building a large deck and have a lot of crooked boards to deal with, it might be best to invest in a specialized deck-straightening tool (below, right).

Continue to Lay Decking

You can lay decking by yourself, but the work will go more smoothly with a helper. While one person is racking (above, left), making cuts, and helping straighten boards, the other can be driving fasteners. With a helper, it's easier to plan ahead for the chalk line cut (page 156). Make sure all boards overhang the joists far enough, and when you come to a corner, mark the board for the overhang in the new direction (above, middle). Where chalk line cuts are not practical, you may need to cut some boards to the exact length ahead of time (above, right).

As You Approach the End

The last board you attach should be parallel with the first, but regardless of how careful you are, it is common for boards to go out of alignment. So when you reach the last 4 feet of decking, measure boards at their ends and in the middle (right). If the decking is not running parallel, slowly take out the angle over the course of six or seven boards—the gaps between the boards will be slightly uneven, but not very noticeable. If the outside joist is not parallel to the decking, you can cut and attach two angled pieces against its side (below, right). You will eventually cover these pieces with fascia (page 157).

TIME SAVER

If you are using a cordless drill, buy an extra battery and set up a battery charger in a convenient location. That way, one battery can always be charging while the other is being used.

Notching Techniques

If your posts have been installed inside the framing (page 151), you will have plenty of notching to do. In some cases, the notch must be cut precisely; if there will be a piece of molding, you may not need such precision (page 211). In general, it is easier to cut the notch first, then cut the board to length. You may need to add 2 × 4 nailers to one or more sides of a post to provide a nailing surface all around the post. The joint between decking and post can be left open for water to drain through, or it can be caulked to keep water out.

Straight notch. Where the decking is parallel to the face of the post, set the board in place against the post (right, top) and measure for the depth of the cut—subtract the width of the gap (if any) that you want between the boards. Mark the cutout, then cut the notch with a jigsaw (right). Cut a little to the outside of the lines so that the notch will not be too tight, and continually blow away sawdust so you can see the cut line. Then drill pilot holes and drive fasteners.

Angled notch. Where the decking is at a 45-degree angle to the post, things get trickier. If possible, plan to install molding around the bases of your posts, so the cuts don't have to be precise.

1 **MARK THE CORNER.** Hold the decking board against the corner of the post, and mark where the post's corner meets the board.

2 **MEASURE OVER.** Measure the distance between the post corner and the previous (already installed) decking board, and subtract the width of the gap (if any).

3 **MARK FOR THE CORNER OF THE POST.** On the board, measure and mark this distance from the edge of the board that is away from the post. Draw a square line from the first mark (step 1). Where the two lines meet is the corner of the post.

4 **DRAW THE OUTLINE.** Use an angle square to draw the outline of the cut. If the lines are greater than 3½ inches long (the thickness of a 4 × 4 post), you will need to draw more lines. In the example shown here, the board will need to be lifted up and slid down the post.

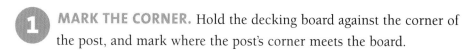

Finish Fastening

No one expects decking fastener heads to form perfectly parallel rows, but your deck will look better if the rows are more straight than crooked. Once all decking boards are secured, go back and drive all the fasteners, usually two per joint. You may choose to snap chalk lines as guides for the rows, but be sure to use blue chalk, which washes away—red chalk is permanent.

The Chalk Line Cut

Using the marks you made indicating the correct overhang (page 154), have a helper pull out the string from a chalk line, taking care not to let the line drop on the decking and lose its chalk. Pull the string taut and press it down on the overhang marks. Lift up the line and let it go, thus snapping a line on the boards. If the line is not visible on all boards, repeat.

Cut decking boards at the chalk line with a circular saw. If you have reasonably good carpentry skills and can get in a comfortable position while you work, you can cut along the chalk line free-hand. If you are unsure of your skills, or if you want a precisely straight line, tack a straight board alongside the line to act as a guide for the saw.

Frame for a Step-Up

To build a small stepped-up section, simply construct the framing directly on top of the decking. If you use 2 × 6 framing (which is typically 5$\frac{1}{2}$ inches wide) and $\frac{5}{4}$ decking (which is 1 inch thick), you will have a 6$\frac{1}{2}$-inch rise— a comfortable height for a step. In the deck shown here, the stepped-up section is flush with the deck's upper level. To frame for a larger elevation change, see page 120.

Sanding or Routing

Smooth sharp decking corners using a hand sander or a router. Practice on scrap pieces first, especially if the decking is a soft material like cedar.

Fascia

You could leave the header and outside joists visible, but it looks better to cover them with fascia. On a wood deck, the usual choice is 1× material, the same width as the joist and the same species as the decking. On a composite deck, you could use a piece of decking or two, or the manufacturer may offer thin fascia material specially made for the purpose. If you are installing skirting (pages 218–219), it is sometimes best to install the skirting at the same time as the fascia.

In most cases attaching fascia is as easy as cutting it to length, holding it snug against the underside of the decking, and driving fasteners. Builders often miter-cut the fascia at the corners (right) for a professional look. Do this only if you have an accurate power miter saw and good carpentry skills. Wood that you intend to miter-cut at the corners should be kiln dried (or at least "S-dry") or it will almost certainly shrink and/or warp and create an ugly gap in a year or so. A safer course is to simply straight-cut the fascia boards and butt them together at the ends. The resulting joint will be a bit rustic, but if the boards shrink or warp the gap will not be as apparent.

Breadboard Edging

If the decking has been cut straight, you can trim it with breadboard edging, typically made of either 2 × 2s or pieces of decking rip-cut to 1½ inches or so. Apply edging only to the side of the decking where you made the chalk line cut. Miter-cut the board at the end, and fasten it with a nail or screw driven into each decking board.

MONEY SAVER

When making a chalk line cut, you can usually let the waste side of the board drop if it's 2 feet or shorter. However, if the waste side is longer, its weight may cause the board to crack before you finish the cut. Have a helper gently support the piece while you cut, but don't lift up or the saw can bind.

SYNTHETIC SURFACES

SYNTHETIC DECKING, BE IT PURE VINYL OR A COMPOSITE OF WOOD AND PLASTIC, is usually cut and fastened much like wood, except screws must be used for fastening rather than nails. You can follow the basic guidelines for installing decking shown on pages 152–157. Synthetic decking varies in strength depending on its composition, so follow the manufacturer's instructions for the span between joists. If you will be installing a composite railing system, railing posts will likely need to be attached inside the framing, so be prepared to cut plenty of notches in the decking (page 155).

The instructions on these pages apply to most types of solid composites; see page 160 for other types of synthetic decking. Attach decking to joists using composite decking screws or a hidden fastener system, as recommended by the decking manufacturer. To review the difference between regular decking screws, which produce mushrooms, and self-tapping screws, which leave exposed screw heads, see page 151.

A stand-up screw gun, as shown on the next page, makes short work of the task of laying the decking and is easy on your back. A hand-held drill will work, too, but if it starts to feel hot, take a break to let it cool down or you may fry the motor.

Aligning the Pieces

The decking shown on these pages is laid at a 45-degree angle to the house and the framing is rectangular. That means the builder won't have to worry about the last piece being parallel to either the framing or the house (page 154).

Gang-cut the ends of a number of pieces at 45 degrees. Begin with a piece near the middle of the deck. Use a string line to check it for straightness, then drive a screw alongside the string into every joist, so you will have a firm frame of reference for subsequent boards.

If you need to make a butt joint, it is sometimes easiest to partially fasten the decking, then mark the board for cutting in the middle of the joist. Raise the board up a bit while cutting it so you don't cut into the joist.

Screwing It Down

Arm yourself with a screw gun set at the correct depth and the process of installing the decking can really fly. Experiment on scrap pieces to make sure the screws will be set either flush with the surface (if you want them exposed) or sunk about $1/4$ inch (if you will pound the mushrooms to cover the screw heads).

Have a helper insert the spacer and kick the decking board against it while you drive a screw into a nearby joist (above). Bending boards into position is never a problem with synthetic decking.

Every eight boards or so, check alignment with a taut string or your eyeball to make sure the decking is straight. If it isn't, install the next board against a taut string.

Avoid the Bends

Because decking boards are both long and flexible, it is best to have two people carry them. As you work with the material, take extra care to keep it straight.

Finishing

With some types of decking, you may choose to simply sand or rout the edges. Other types are designed to accept edging strips, which create a neater look. Miter-cut the edging at the corners (with synthetic material, you don't have to worry about shrinking or warping). Attach the edging with a small nail driven into the ends of the decking boards (left, top).

If a piece of synthetic decking is scratched, you can usually make the mark go away using a heat gun (left, bottom). There is little danger of melting the "wood grain" beyond recognition, but the board will be hot, so be careful.

Webbed Decking

Hollow-core, or webbed, synthetic decking is available in both rectangular and tongue-and-groove profiles. Fasteners must be driven into specific places in each board; if you drive a screw into the center of a wide hollow area, the decking will indent. Some products have a groove to show you just where to drive the screws. The ends of some boards are designed to be covered with matching caps; others call for edging strips (page 159).

Tongue-and-Groove

Tongue-and-groove composite decking is installed a lot like hardwood flooring. Screws are driven through the groove, which is then covered with the tongue of the next board.

1 **INSTALL THE STARTER STRIP.** Attach the starter strip at one end of the deck by driving screws into an outside joist. Use a string line to make sure the starter strip is straight throughout its length.

2 **INSTALL THE DECKING.** Slide the tongue of the first full board into the groove of the starter strip. The dimensions of the tongue and groove create a $\frac{1}{4}$-inch gap between the boards at the decking surface. Drive screws through the tongue of the board and into the joist. Continue driving screws and sliding tongues into the grooves of previously installed boards.

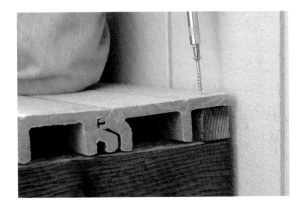

3 **INSTALL THE LAST BOARD.** If a full board fits comfortably in the last row, install it as usual. If you have to rip-cut the last board to fit, you may need to install a 1-inch-thick support piece, as shown. (You can rip this out of $\frac{5}{4}$ pressure-treated decking.) Allow a $\frac{1}{4}$-inch gap between the decking and the house. In this example, fascia boards will cover the edges of the decking and the joist below.

Modular Decking

Most decks are made of wood or synthetic materials that are cut to fit. However, there are a few modular products on the market that allow you to build decks with stonelike surfaces, or to purchase wood decking in preassembled sections.

Pavers. Some paving products are designed to be attached to standard wood deck framing. In the system shown at right, a waterproof barrier is placed over thick beam-like joists spaced 24 inches on center, followed by large webbed fiberglass panels holding faux-stone concrete pavers, which are set on the panels using adhesive. These pavers are reinforced so they can span across joists.

Duckboards. Modular squares made of decking material often go by the name of duckboards. You can make your own by assembling lengths of decking on top of 2 × 3s. Informal duckboards like these can be strewn across a lawn to serve as a path, or they can be laid side by side on a gravel bed to form a deck surface.

Manufactured duckboards, like those shown at right, are available in a variety of sizes, shapes, and colors. If your local home improvement center does not carry a wide enough selection, type "modular decking" into an Internet search engine for a list of manufacturers. Most duckboards are made of long-lasting hardwood that is stained and finished. They snap together easily by means of plastic clips.

You can install manufactured duckboards so that all boards face the same direction, or alternate the orientation for a more patterned look. The surface the duckboards sit on should be fairly smooth, and should slope away from the house so water can drain away. Though modular, the units can be cut to fit using a circular saw or power miter saw. Where they go around a post or other obstruction, you may choose to apply trim (right, bottom). Once installed, duckboards should be given an extra coat or two of sealer.

HIDDEN FASTENERS

IF YOU WOULD RATHER NOT SEE ROWS OF NAIL OR SCREW HEADS on your deck surface, consider one of the hidden fastener systems described on the next four pages. Any of these systems, which attach either to the edges or the bottoms of decking boards, will give you a better-looking deck surface, but all cost more than surface fasteners and require more time and effort. Make sure the system you choose is compatible with your decking. In addition, wood decking can shrink, and excessive shrinkage can weaken the bonds of many hidden fastener systems, so it is critical to use decking that is as dry as possible. If your decking has butt joints and you are planning to use deck clips, you'll need to double the width of the joists at the joints, since you cannot install more than one deck clip on a joist.

Hidden fasteners make for an unblemished work surface.

Tap-and-Screw Fasteners

These 1½-inch-wide metal deck clips have fairly long barbs that grab the edges of decking boards on each side. The clip itself gets screwed to the joist. A variety of clip types are made by the same manufacturer; be sure to choose the one made for your decking—for instance, cedar or other softwoods, hardwoods, or composites. The first decking board will need to be attached conventionally, with screws or nails driven into the face of the board (see page 164 for a way to hide the fastener heads).

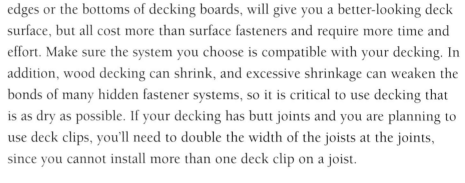

1 DRIVE THE CLIP. Slip the special installation block over the clip, align it directly over a joist, and drive the clip into the side of the decking with a hammer.

2 ATTACH TO THE JOIST. Drive a decking screw at an angle through the clip and into the joist. Attach all the clips before you install the next decking board.

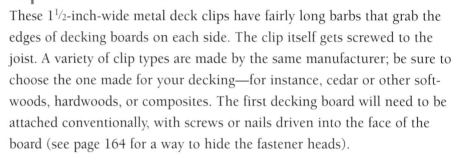

3 POUND IN THE NEXT BOARD. Place the subsequent board on the joists, next to the clips. If the piece has been cut to fit precisely, hold it carefully in place, making sure it is parallel with the previous board. Place a 2 × 4, long enough to span three joists, next to the board. Standing on the decking board to make sure it is lying flat on the joists, pound the 2 × 4 with a sledgehammer to drive the decking into the clip. Repeat for the remaining boards.

Clip-and-Toenail

Less expensive clips like these also attach to the sides of decking boards and provide a uniform gap between boards. However, they do not actually fasten the decking to the joists; they rely on nails or screws driven at an angle through the deck board. Use this clip only if you are certain the board will not shrink. Fasten the first board by angle-drilling pilot holes and then driving screws or nails into the joists.

1 **FASTEN THE CLIP.** Determine which side of each board you want to show, and be sure to install the clips on the underside of the decking boards. Place a board where it will go, and tip it up on edge. About 2 inches from each joist, drive a nail or screw to fasten a deck clip to the edge that will butt against the previous board.

2 **POSITION THE BOARD.** Push the board into place, slipping its clips under the previous board. If necessary, tap the board into position using a hammer and a scrap of lumber to keep from marring the board.

3 **FASTEN THE BOARD.** Once the board is aligned, drill angled pilot holes and drive screws or nails to fasten the board to each joist. Toe-fastening will likely move a crooked board over only ¼ inch; if you have a larger gap, use the straightening techniques shown on page 153.

Continuous Brackets

This system is labor intensive—you'll drive lots of screws. Both galvanized and stainless-steel brackets are available, with screws to accommodate either 2× or ⁵⁄₄ decking. To prevent corrosion, choose brackets and fasteners that are compatible with both the joists and the decking (page 55). Test on scrap pieces to make sure the screws are long enough to grab tightly, but not so long that they might poke up through the decking.

1 **ATTACH BRACKETS TO JOISTS.** Fasten brackets along the full length of each joist, alternating sides. Use tin snips to cut the pieces to length.

2 **ATTACH BRACKETS TO THE DECKING.** It is easiest to drive screws up through the brackets and into the decking if you work from below the deck. If you have to work from above, be sure to equip your drill with a screwdriver attachment that has a magnetic sleeve. Place the screw on the bit and carefully reach under the board, keeping the screw firmly in place on the bit. Kneel on the board as you drive the screw upward.

To install a center strip and picture frame pieces with invisible fasteners, you will likely need to add extra joists or blocking pieces.

Biscuit Fasteners

The system featured on these pages uses polypropylene biscuits and stainless-steel screws. Installation requires cutting slots into both sides of the decking boards at each joist location, a task for which you will need a biscuit joiner (if your decking is pregrooved, you can skip this step; see opposite page). This particular product can be used with wood or synthetic decking.

Since the biscuits can slide in their grooves, the joists below them could move from side to side, or "float." To prevent this, apply deck adhesive between decking and joists, as described in step 6, or face-drive a screw every 6 feet or so into every joist, as shown in step 1.

1 **DRILL AND FACE-SCREW THE FIRST PIECE.** At each joist, drill a ⅛-inch pilot hole and a ⅜-inch countersink hole. You can do this with two separate bits, or use a combination bit. Drive a #7 screw down into the joist.

2 **PLUG THE HOLE.** Squirt in some exterior wood glue, and tap in a ⅜-inch wood plug. Use a hand saw or a belt sander to remove the top of the plug. Sand smooth with a hand sander.

3 CUT THE SLOTS. Use a biscuit joiner centered over the joists to cut slots in the first board. For subsequent boards, cut slots on both sides. If you are installing composite decking, make the slots oversize, to allow the decking to expand.

4 ADD BISCUITS. Insert a biscuit into each slot on the already-installed board. Test to be sure the next board will slide in all the way. The biscuits will maintain $1/8$-inch gaps between decking boards.

5 DRIVE SCREWS. Drill an angled $1/2$-inch pilot hole for each screw. The biscuit's hole is angled to help guide the drill bit. Drive screws through the holes. Avoid overtightening the screws; a screw head should be snug against the biscuit, but should not cause it to flex downward. You probably want to have two drills on hand so you don't have to constantly switch from drill bit to screwdriver bit.

6 INSTALL THE NEXT BOARD. Apply a bead of decking adhesive to the tops of the joists. Carefully set the next board down on the adhesive, so you won't have to slide the board more than an inch or two (which would weaken the adhesive bond). Use a rubber or plastic mallet to tap the board snugly against the biscuit. If a board needs to be straightened, use the techniques shown on page 153.

Pregrooved Decking

Decking with grooves running along the edges makes it easy to install biscuit-type hidden fasteners. Some Brazilian hardwoods such as Ipé are grooved this way, and can be installed with small clips since the wood will barely shrink or expand (inset). Some synthetic decking products also have grooves, while others have tongues, which are secured in place by specially designed clips (right).

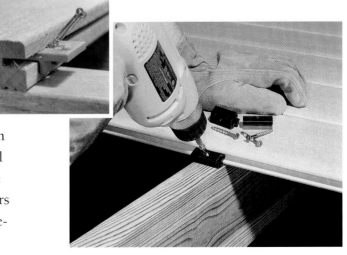

A CUSTOM V-SHAPE

SYNTHETIC DECKING COMES IN A VARIETY OF CLEARLY DISTINGUISHED COLORS, making it easy to create geometric designs. On such decks, the framing is built with the decking design in mind. The deck on the next four pages has a band running around the perimeter of the deck, sometimes called a picture frame, and a center strip where the decking comes together at 45-degrees to form a V. The deck is octagonal in shape, making the picture frame a bit more of a challenge.

Framing

Composite and vinyl decking is flexible, so the ends of all boards must be well supported, with at least $1\frac{1}{2}$ inches of framing material to rest on. In this example, a $6\frac{1}{2}$-inch-wide center framing piece runs through the middle of the regular framing to support the angled decking boards that will butt up to the center strip. Around the deck's perimeter, 2 × 6 blocking pieces (which fit between the joists) are attached to the outside joists, making a 7-inch-wide surface to support the picture frame and the decking that butts into it.

1 LAY OUT THE HEADERS. Here, the two header joists are temporarily nailed together so they can be marked at the same time. (If you have a ledger, temporarily attach the outside joist to it.) The joist layout starts in the middle of the headers rather than at either end to ensure that the center framing piece is really in the center. Find the center of the header, then measure $3\frac{1}{4}$ inches to either side—this leaves room for the center framing piece, which will consist of a $3\frac{1}{2}$-inch-wide 4 × 4 with $1\frac{1}{2}$-inch-wide 2× joists on each side. In this case, on-center spacing for the joists is 12 inches, beginning at the center of the 4 × 4.

2 LAY OUT THE JOISTS. Mark the positions of all the joists on the headers. Stand back and give it a visual once-over to make sure you have made no obvious mistakes.

3 MAKE A CENTER FRAMING PIECE. Assemble a center framing member to support the center strip and the rest of the decking. Use boards that are straight and warp-free. A 4 × 4 (as shown) is stable and easier to work with than a flat-laid 2 × 4, but a 2 × 4 would function just as well.

4 **FRAME.** Install the joists as you would normally. In this case, a rectangular deck was built first; then the angles were cut and built (page 131). Use a string line to confirm that the header joists are perfectly straight.

5 **ATTACH THE CENTER PIECE.** It is important that the center framing piece be very straight. Use a string line to check for straightness while you drive fasteners to attach it to the beams.

6 **INSTALL BLOCKING.** All around the perimeter, install cut-to-fit 2 × 6 blocking pieces between the joists. This can be painstaking work when you get to the corners, but a precisely adjusted power miter saw can make it a rewarding project.

7 **FIND THE 45-DEGREE ANGLE.** Chalk a line running down the exact middle of the center framing piece. Use the 3-4-5 method (page 71). Then, starting where the center chalk line meets the outside of the header, measure along the center framing piece and mark a point about halfway across the deck. From the same point on the header, measure and mark the same distance in both directions.

8 **CHALK THE 45-DEGREE ANGLE.** Snap chalk lines between the two marks on the header and the mark on the center framing piece. If you measured correctly, these lines will be at exactly 90 degrees to each other.

Decking

Cut and attach synthetic decking as described on pages 158–159. The design has many boards precisely angle-cut so they meet tightly, but most of the cuts will be done with a chalk line, so it is not as difficult as it may appear.

1 **ATTACH THE FIRST TWO PIECES.** Use a power miter saw to gang-cut a number of decking boards at 45 degrees. Lay the first two boards in place, precisely aligned with the chalk lines (step 8, page 167), and fasten them securely.

2 **INSTALL THE ANGLED DECKING.** Attach the rest of the decking, so it meets in the middle. The boards do not have to overhang the framing; they only have to be long enough so they will meet the picture frame (see step 11, opposite).

3 **MARK THE FRAME'S WIDTH.** Use an angle square and a tape measure to mark the decking boards for the width of the picture frame pieces. (In this case, the picture frame will over-hang the framing by the thickness of a decking board; see step 12, opposite.)

4 **MARK WITH CHALK LINES.** Snap chalk lines between the marks to indicate the inside edge of the picture frame.

5 **CUT THE LINES.** Set a circular saw's blade to cut just barely below the thickness of the decking, so you don't cut a deep line in the framing. Cut the lines freehand if you feel confident of your skills, or use a guide board as shown in step 8, opposite.

6 **MEASURE FOR THE CENTER STRIP.** In this case, the decking will be rip-cut to make room for the center strip. At each end of the deck, center a piece of strip material over the center line, and mark either side for the width of the cut.

7 **SNAP LINES AND INSTALL A GUIDE.** Snap chalk lines for cuts on either side of the center line. Place a scrap of center strip material between the lines to get an idea whether you should cut to the inside or outside of the chalk lines. The strip should fit with a $\frac{1}{8}$-inch gap on either side to allow for expansion. Use a guide for the circular saw (you will have to reposition the guide for the second cut).

8 **CUT THE LINES.** If you use a piece of decking for the guide (as shown), support it every few feet by standing on it, or by partially driving nails into it. Otherwise, it could flex and cause your line to wave.

9 **INSTALL THE CENTER STRIP.** Clean out the area between the cut lines. Cut center strip pieces to length, and install with gaps on either side. Here, a simple spacer guide is made of an angle bracket.

10 **CUT AND INSTALL THE PICTURE FRAME.** On an octagonal deck, the picture frame pieces are cut at $22\frac{1}{2}$ degrees. Cut some scrap pieces to test the angle; you may need to adjust the saw. Wherever possible, hold a piece in place to mark it for cutting, rather than using a tape measure.

11 **FINE-TUNE.** If two pieces do not come together tightly, hold them in place and use an angle square or a straight edge to mark one piece for cutting to a slightly different angle.

12 **INSTALL THE FASCIA.** Here, a banded fascia look is achieved by installing a dark-colored lower piece and a light-colored upper piece.

stairs

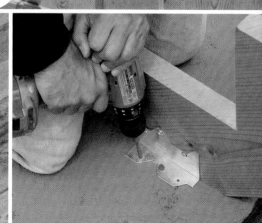

BUILDING THE STAIRS THAT LEAD TO YOUR DECK, CONNECT IT TO YOUR HOME, OR BRIDGE LEVELS IS AN EXACTING, BUT CERTAINLY NOT IMPOSSIBLE, UNDERTAKING. IN THIS CHAPTER WE SHOW YOU A NUMBER OF STAIR DESIGNS, AS WELL AS TWO TYPES OF LANDING PADS TO GIVE YOUR STAIRS A FIRM FOUNDATION.

PLANNING STAIRS

UNLESS YOUR DECK IS SET ON THE GROUND, IT WILL MOST LIKELY NEED SOME TYPE OF STAIRS. Basic stair building is not especially difficult, but building stairs that are safe and legal does require careful attention to detail.

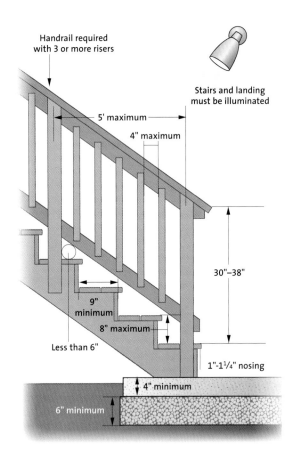

Handrail required
with 3 or more risers

Stairs and landing
must be illuminated

5' maximum

4" maximum

30"–38"

9"
minimum

8" maximum

Less than 6"

1"-1¼" nosing

4" minimum

6" minimum

Stair Codes and Safety

The vertical distance from one stair tread to the next is called the rise. Codes usually allow a maximum rise of 8 inches or so, but a rise of 6 to 7½ inches is more desirable. The rise must be consistent from one step to the next, differing by no more than ⅜ inch. In particular, the first and the last steps must have the same rise as the others.

The tread depth is called the run. Codes may require a 9-inch minimum for the run, but 11 to 12 inches is better. Working within code requirements, choose a rise and run that work well together (pages 180–181). Steps with a shorter rise are more comfortable to use with a deeper run; those with a taller rise are better with a shorter run. If treads are 11 to 12 inches deep, make the rise 6½ to 7½ inches; if treads are 15 to 16 inches deep, a 5½- to 6-inch rise is best.

Stairs are usually required to be at least 36 inches wide. If you want two people to pass each other on the stairs comfortably, make the stairway at least 48 inches wide.

Stairs with three or more steps should have a railing on at least one side. The railing height must be 30 to 38 inches above the front edge of each tread. Railing posts must be spaced no more than 5 feet apart, and balusters cannot be more than 4 inches apart. Deck stairs are frequently built without risers (that is, boards filling the rise at the back of the tread), but codes often require them, and many people think stairs look much better with risers. In most cases, the stringers should be attached to a concrete or masonry pad at their bottoms.

Some codes require a graspable handrail (page 209) for stairs that have three or more steps. You can buy hardwood railing stock and attach it with standard railing brackets; be sure to seal the wood well against the elements. Or, construct a handrail yourself using 2 × 3 lumber and a router.

How It's Put Together

A standard stairway is made with stringers, which are notch-cut or equipped with brackets to support the treads on which you walk. Risers may fill the vertical space between treads. Stringers must be firmly attached to the deck at the top, often with angle brackets, and to the landing pad at the bottom. If there is no landing pad, stringers may be attached to rail posts instead.

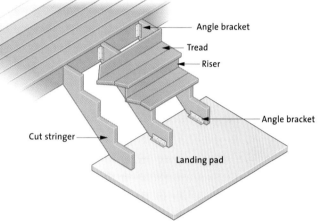

Angle bracket

Tread

Riser

Angle bracket

Cut stringer

Landing pad

Stringer Options

Stringers, also called carriages, are the basic framing components of stairs. Typically made out of 2 × 12s, stringers are often cut with notches to create level surfaces for treads and plumb surfaces for risers (bottom, right). This produces a strong stairway and also provides a vertical nailing surface for risers. Adding a trim board to the stringer (bottom, middle) enhances the strength as well as the appearance of a stairway. Stringers can also be made of solid boards with metal brackets attached (bottom, left). These are the easiest to build, but they can be used only on short, narrow stairs or where risers are not required. In some designs, solid stringers are installed on either side, and cut stringers are placed in between.

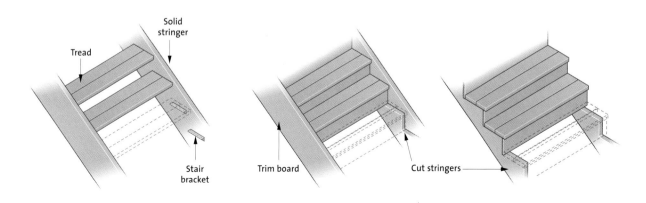

Solid stringer

Tread

Stair bracket

Trim board

Cut stringers

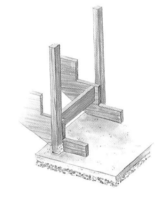

2 × 4 cleat

Hangerboard attached to cleats to support stringers

Attaching at the Top

If the stringer is attached to the joist just below the decking, then the first "step" will actually not step down, but will simply cantilever out. If you want to start with a step down (which is the more common arrangement and is shown at right), the stringer's top (where the top tread will rest) must be one riser's height below the top of the joist (assuming that the treads are the same thickness as the decking; if the treads are thicker, adjust the stringer's height accordingly).

If you position the first tread one step down, the stringer will not rest against much of the joist. In that case, support the stringer by adding a hangerboard. In most cases, a 2 × 6 or 2 × 8 hangerboard will be wide enough to support the ends of the stringers. Attach 2 × 4 cleats to the inside of the joist, each about 8 inches long and spaced about 16 inches apart. Then fasten the hangerboard to the cleats.

The Bottom Rail Post

The rail post at the bottom of a set of stairs should be attached to the stringer, but if that is the only means of fastening, it may become loose and wobbly after a year or two. One way to add strength is to set the post in a hole, 3 to 4 feet deep, and fill the hole with concrete (right, above). Another method is to install the post inside the stringer, and attach it to a piece of 2 × 6 that runs from one stringer to the next (right). Attach the stringer's bottom to a post anchor that is anchored to the concrete pad (page 99).

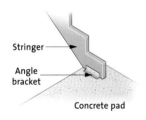

Stringer

Angle bracket

Concrete pad

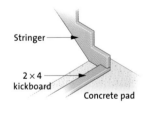

Stringer

2 × 4 kickboard

Concrete pad

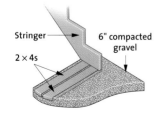

Stringer

6" compacted gravel

2 × 4s

Landing Pads

A landing pad provides a firm surface for the first step up, as well as an anchor for the stringers. You can make a solid landing pad by pouring concrete (pages 176–177) or laying pavers in a firm gravel-and-sand bed (pages 178–179). If you are a meticulous planner, it's possible to pour a concrete pad while you are working on the footings and piers, but it is safer to wait until the decking is installed.

The bottoms of the stringers are often attached to the landing pad with angle brackets. However, they can be cut to fit over a 2 × 4 kickboard fastened to the pad. For short stairs, a landing pad of compacted gravel may do; attach two 2 × 4s across the bottoms of the stringers to distribute the load.

A landing pad is not necessary in all situations. Deck stairs are sometimes built right on top of the ground. If you do this, be sure that all lumber that comes within a few inches of the ground is labeled "ground contact." Lumber that is rated "above ground" may rot.

An octagonal landing pushes the boundaries of a standard, rectangular one.

Solid stringers made of 4× lumber are a handsome counterpoint to steel-cable railing.

Choosing a Style

Stairs serve a utilitarian purpose, but they can also add to the visual appeal of a deck. They can be prominent and grand, or minimal and understated. Stairs may serve simply as a path from the deck to the yard, or they can provide a comfortable, informal seating area between deck levels. One of the most visible parts of a stairway is the railing, which usually repeats the design of the deck's railing.

Wraparound steps create a graceful transition between two deck levels.

Lights for Safety

Even if local codes do not require it, consider adding stairway lighting as a safety measure. Riser lights (right) will make it easier to see your way up and down the stairs at night. Rope lights placed under the stair railing's top piece can also illuminate your path.

CONCRETE LANDING PAD

FOR A SMALL LANDING PAD, IT IS USUALLY BEST TO MIX BAGS OF CONCRETE in a wheelbarrow (pages 94–95). Choose concrete that is high strength and has fiber reinforcement to prevent cracking.

1 **BUILD THE FORM.** Remove all sod and roots larger than ½ inch thick. Dig and scrape an area that is about 7 inches deeper than the top of the pad. Use a 2 × 4 or a hand tamper to tamp the ground firm. Build a temporary form of 2 × 4s. Support the form with stakes driven into the ground every 2 to 3 feet. If you want a curved corner, nail a piece of flexible material to the inside of the form and support it with stakes too. Drive the stakes below the tops of the form, and drive nails or screws through the stakes and into the form boards. The form should feel solid when you kick it outward. Check that the pad is sloped slightly away from the house, so water can run off.

2 **SPREAD AND TAMP GRAVEL.** Pour compactible gravel (sometimes called hardcore) so it is level with the bottom of the form boards. Tamp firm with a 2 × 4 or a hand tamper.

3 **POUR THE CONCRETE.** Mix the concrete in a wheelbarrow and pour it into the formed area. Wear rubber boots, as shown, or stand on the outside of the formed area.

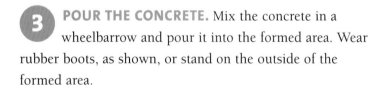

4 **SPREAD THE CONCRETE.** Use a shovel to distribute the concrete evenly around the area, so it is slightly above the top of the form boards.

5 **SCREED.** Use a screed guide—a straight 2 × 4 will do—to level the concrete at the height of the form boards. Work the screed back and forth in a sawing motion as you pull it across the form. It sometimes helps to work the screed up and down to remove air pockets and to bring water to the surface. Fill any low spots, then screed again.

6 **SMOOTH WITH A MAGNESIUM FLOAT.** As soon as the surface is free of puddles, use a magnesium float to smooth the surface. You can use a wood float, but most do-it-yourselfers find a magnesium float easier to control. If possible, kneel outside the formed area; otherwise, use two kneeling pads, as shown. Start floating at the far corner and work back so that you do not kneel on newly floated concrete. Hold the tool so that the leading edge is slightly raised, and press down gently as you move it in long, sweeping strokes.

7 **EDGE.** Run an edging tool along the outside edges of the pad. Use back-and-forth sawing motions at first, then long strokes to achieve a neatly rounded edge at all points.

8 **BRUSH FINISH AND CURE.** Using a soft-bristled broom, pull the broom toward you—never push it—to produce a lightly textured surface. If the bristles don't dig in and produce the surface you like, wet the broom. Avoid overlapping strokes; make them right next to each other. The more slowly concrete cures, the stronger it will be. Keep the finished concrete moist for at least several days. Cover the entire pad with plastic or spray it with a fine mist twice a day (or more often if the air is dry). After a day, pry away the forms.

Calculating Concrete Needs

A 60-pound bag of mix produces $1/2$ cubic foot of concrete; a 90–pound bag yields $2/3$ cubic feet. To figure how many bags you need, first multiply the area in feet times the thickness in inches, then divide the result by 12 to get the number of cubic feet. For example, if a pad is 6 × 4 feet, its area is 24 square feet. If the pad is 4 inches thick, then 24 × 4 = 96, and 96 ÷ 12 = 8 cubic feet. Adding about 10 percent for waste gives you 9 cubic feet of concrete mix, which means you will need 18 60-pound bags or 14 90-pound bags.

BRICK LANDING PAD

A PAD MADE OF BRICKS SET ON A BED OF WELL-TAMPED GRAVEL AND SAND will be nearly as solid as a concrete pad. Unlike with the forms used to make a concrete pad, the boards surrounding a brick pad will be permanent, so anchor them firmly.

Make a screed guide (left) from a 2 × 4 and a section of plywood. The 2 × 4 should be 3 feet longer than the area to be screeded so you can use its ends for handles. The plywood should be 1 inch shorter than the area to be screeded and as wide as the thickness of the bricks (less ¼ inch) plus the width of the 2 × 4.

1 **BUILD THE FORM; ADD GRAVEL AND SAND.** Remove all sod and organic material, and dig away the soil to a depth of about 7 inches. Install a form made of 2 × 4s (page 176); see that it slopes slightly away from the house. Shovel in compactible gravel that comes up 1 to 2 inches below the top of the forms. Tamp the gravel firm. Cover the gravel with landscaping fabric, then pour coarse sand (sometimes called torpedo sand) into the formed area. Use a rake or shovel to spread it so it is slightly higher than its final level. The sand should be a little damp; if it dries out, spray it with a mist of water.

2 **SCREED THE SAND.** If the screed is longer than 5 feet, perform this step with a helper. Starting at one end, move the screed across the formed area to smooth the sand. Then set a brick on top of the sand to be sure it is at the correct height. It may help to "saw" back and forth as you push or pull the screed across the sand. Fill any voids, moisten the sand if needed, and repeat until surface is uniform.

Going Padless

A landing pad is not necessary in all situations. Deck stairs are sometimes built right on top of the ground. If you do this, be sure that all lumber that comes within a few inches of the ground is labeled "ground contact." Lumber that is rated "above ground" may rot.

3 **RUN A GUIDELINE.** To prepare for laying bricks, stretch a length of mason's line across the patio to serve as a height guide. Pull the line taut so that it does not sag. Attach it with a nail or screw or wrap the line around a temporary stake.

4 **LAY THE BRICKS.** Starting in a corner, set several bricks to abut the edging. Use a level to confirm that the bricks are at the desired height. Set each brick straight down onto the bed, gently scraping the side of the edging or an already-laid brick as you lower it; if you slide a brick more than $1/2$ inch or so, you will create waves in the sand and the surface will not be level.

5 **BED THE BRICKS.** After you have set 10 or 12 bricks, place a beater board—a flat 2 × 6 that is about 2 feet long—on top of them and tap it with a hammer or mallet. If a brick is noticeably higher, tap it directly with the mallet.

6 **MOVE THE EDGING TO MINIMIZE CUTTING.** Install bricks until you're near the end of the landing pad, then move the edging to abut them. Push the edging up against the bricks and drive stakes and screws to secure it. Use a handsaw or a reciprocating saw to cut the adjacent piece of edging flush.

7 **FILL THE JOINTS.** Once all the bricks have been installed, pour fine sand over them and use a soft-bristled broom to sweep the sand into the joints. Tamp the surface lightly by walking around on it, then fill the joints with sand again.

STAIR DIMENSIONS

REGARDLESS OF HOW YOU BUILD YOUR STAIRS, you must first calculate the dimensions. In the terminology of stair building, the rise is the vertical distance, or height, and the run is the horizontal distance.

Finding the total rise. The total rise is the vertical distance the stairs must travel from the landing pad to the decking surface. The measurement should be taken directly over the landing pad. Use a level or a straight 2 by 4 to extend the deck surface over the pad, then measure the total rise.

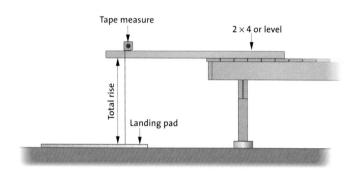

Tape measure
2 × 4 or level
Total rise
Landing pad

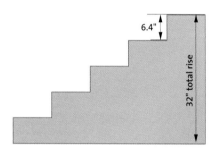

6.4"
32" total rise

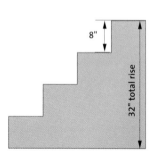

8"
32" total rise

Figuring the unit rise. The next step is to calculate the unit rise (the vertical distance from one tread to the next); see the diagrams at left. Let's assume that the total rise is 32 inches. Divide that figure by 7, or whatever your ideal unit rise is. The result, rounded to the nearest whole number, will give you the ideal number of risers (five, in this example). Now divide the total rise (32) by the number of risers (5) to determine the actual unit rise (6.4 inches). If you consider a rise of less than $6\frac{1}{2}$ inches too short, reduce the number of risers to four, which will result in a unit rise of 8 inches—pretty steep, but typically within code.

If you have no landing pad and the yard is not level, estimate how many steps you will need, and measure that many unit runs out from the deck. Use a level and tape measure to measure down to the yard from that point, to find the total rise. After you do your calculations, you may need to change the number of steps; if so, measure again.

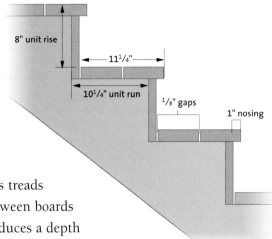

Figuring the run. The illustration at right shows treads made with two 2 × 6s, allowing a ¹/₈-inch gap between boards and a 1-inch nosing, or overhang. While this produces a depth of 11¹/₄ inches from the nosing to the riser, the actual unit run, which is the figure used to lay out the stringers, is 10¹/₄ inches.

Calculating the lumber size. Short deck stairs can often be made with 2 × 10 stringers, but many builders routinely use 2 × 12s. The critical determination is the minimal width left in the board after the notches have been cut. If this width will be less than 4 inches (see illustration, page 182), you should use wider boards for the stringers.

To determine the length of the boards you will need for stringers, use a framing square and a tape measure and assume that 1 inch represents 1 foot. On many framing squares, one edge of the square is marked in twelfths of an inch to facilitate this calculation. Figure the total rise and total run in terms of feet and inches, then mark the total run on the long side of the square and the total rise on the short side. The distance between the marks will determine the minimum length of the boards you will need.

In the example shown at right, the total run is 51¹/₄ inches (five treads × 10¹/₄ inches each) or 4 feet 3¹/₄ inches, and so one end of a tape measure is placed at about the 4¹/₄-inch mark on the left side of the square. The total rise is 43¹/₂ inches (6 risers × 7¹/₄ inches each), or 3 feet 7¹/₂ inches, and so the other end of the tape is set just beyond the 3¹/₂-inch mark on the right side. The distance between these two marks is about 5⁵/₈ inches, which means a board at least 5 feet 8 inches long is needed for each stringer.

NOTCHED STRINGERS

THE NEXT FIVE PAGES SHOW HOW TO BUILD A STAIRWAY WITH NOTCHED STRINGERS, which is the most common method. For alternative techniques, see pages 187–189. This example includes the installation of a hangerboard (step 4), which means the top of the stringer will be one step below the surface of the decking. If you prefer the top step to be level with the deck, then the stringer must be cut one step longer. Also note that in the example shown on these pages, an old set of concrete stairs was left in place—there is no need to remove a structure like this, as long as it will not get in the way of the stringers.

Stair gauge set at unit rise

Stair gauge set at unit run

Plumb cut line

Add amount of decking overhang

4" minimum

Reduce by thickness of tread

Level cut line

1 MARK FOR THE STRINGER CUTS. Position the board for the first stringer across a pair of sawhorses. Place the framing square along the crown side of the stringer with the corner resting on the board and the pieces of tape (as shown) or stair gauges (which can be purchased at home improvement centers or lumberyards) against the edge. Leave enough room to make the bottom riser. Run a pencil along the outside of the square. Slide the framing square along the board until it meets the previous mark perfectly, align the pieces of tape or the gauges, and mark again. Continue marking all the riser and tread cuts.

2 CUT WITH A CIRCULAR SAW. Double-check your measurements, visualizing the stringer in its place (the illustration above will help). Make sure you have allowed for the thicknesses of the treads; the bottom riser should be one tread's thickness shorter than the other risers. Cut the bottom and top, and check the stringer by placing it against the deck. When you're certain of the layout, cut the notches with a circular saw.

3 **FINISH THE CUTS.** Use a jigsaw, handsaw, or reciprocating saw to finish the cuts. Hold the blade perpendicular to the board, so you do not overcut. The triangular pieces will fall out. Note that the stringer's "teeth" will be fragile until the treads and perhaps risers are installed (page 186), so handle the stringer with care. If a tooth breaks off, you can reattach it by drilling pilot holes and driving screws.

4 **INSTALL A HANGERBOARD.** The vertical edge at the top of the stringer must be completely supported by a joist, or by a hangerboard, or both. To install a hangerboard, either power-drive nails or drive screws; do not nail by hand. Attach vertical 2 × 4 cleats every 16 inches or so to the back of the joist; then attach the hangerboard to the cleats.

5 **CHECK THE FIT.** Temporarily install the first stringer, and check it for accuracy. Make sure all the steps will be equal in rise and run, and see that all the treads are at least close to level.

continued ▶▶

Finding the Top of a Stringer

If your deck boards are the same thickness as your treads, you can simply measure down one unit rise from the top of the joist to determine the location of the stringer's top. If, however, the stair treads are thicker than the decking, as is the case if you have $5/4$ decking and 2× treads, measure down an additional $1/2$ inch (or whatever the difference is between the decking and tread thicknesses). Otherwise, the last step leading to the decking will not have the same rise as the ones below it, which could cause someone to trip.

6 **CUT THE OTHER STRINGERS.** Once you are certain that the first stringer is correct, use it as a template to mark for cutting the other stringers. Set the cut stringer on top of a stringer board, making sure that the new stringer will have its crown side up. Check that the edges are perfectly aligned, and mark the new piece by tracing with a pencil.

7 **ATTACH THE STRINGERS.** Once the stringers are cut, install the first one onto the joist or the hangerboard by driving screws or by power-driving nails (do not hand-drive nails) through the back of the joist and/or hangerboard and into the stringer. Drive three fasteners into the top of each stringer.

8 **MEASURE FOR THE OTHER OUTSIDE STRINGER'S HEIGHT.** Unless the landing pad is level, check for the height of the other stringers' bottom steps. (In the example shown, the stairs will rest on an out-of-level concrete pad at the bottom.) Hold a carpenter's level on top of the first stringer's bottom tread, and measure up from the pad to find the new stringer's bottom step height.

PRO TIP

If you are absolutely certain of all the stringer dimensions, you can attach the stringers to the hangerboard first, then attach the entire structure to the deck.

9 **TRIM STRINGERS AS NEEDED.** Use a circular saw to cut a stringer bottom to the dimensions determined in step 8.

10 **MEASURE FOR MIDDLE STRINGER HEIGHTS.** Once you have installed the outside stringers, place a straightedge on top of them, and measure up to find the bottom stair height for the interior stringer.

continued ▶▶

A landing can be modest and utilitarian or accommodating enough for two chairs.

Attaching Methods

Check with your building department to learn how they want you to attach the stringers. Use a framing square to make sure each stringer is square to the deck. It may help to attach a temporary brace to the bottom front of each stringer, to hold them in place while you attach them.

At the top, the usual method is to first back-drive nails or screws through the joist or hangerboard, then attach angle brackets (which may be made by clipping joist hangers, as shown on page 138). For the bottom, one method attaches an angle bracket to the stringer by drilling pilot holes and driving screws. To attach the brackets to concrete or masonry using masonry screws, first drill pilot holes using the masonry bit that comes with the screws; then drive the screws. See page 174 for other ways to attach stringers to the landing pad.

11 **INSTALL THE RISERS.** If you will be installing risers, attach them before you attach the treads. Depending on your unit rise, you may need to rip-cut the risers to fit. If so, cut them about 1/4 inch narrower than the rise to accommodate any stringer imperfections. The bottom riser needs to be cut narrower than the others by the thickness of a tread. Riser top edges should be flush with the tops of the stringers, but the bottoms do not need to fit tightly, since they will be covered by the treads. Drill pilot holes and drive two nails or screws at each joint.

12 **ATTACH THE TREADS.** Cut the treads to length. For drainage, leave a 1/8-inch gap between the riser and the rear of the tread, and if you are using two boards for each tread, leave a comparable gap between them. Allow each tread to overhang the riser below by at least 1 inch. Secure the treads with screws or nails driven down through the tread and into each stringer. Also drive one or two screws or nails at an angle down through the tread and into the riser.

DESIGN TIP

In the example on these pages, the treads and risers are installed flush to the sides of the stringers to provide an even surface for the side trim pieces (step 13). If the edges of your treads and risers will not be covered, install risers so they run past the stringers by 3/4 inch, and the treads so they overhang the stringers by 1 1/2 inches. This produces a neat appearance, and you don't have to be a master carpenter to get all the pieces to align with the stringers.

13 **COVER THE SIDES.** You can easily trim the sides of the stringers if they are solid, or if the treads are cut flush. To add skirting, see pages 228–229.

Adjustable Stair Brackets

Bracket-based stair systems are available at decking-supply stores and online; some home improvement centers may have them as well. You will use 2× lumber for both the treads and the stringers. The risers effectively act as joists, so you can build a stairway up to 7 feet wide with no interior stringers.

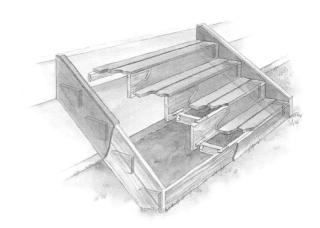

If you want to match the look of a synthetic deck, use 2× lumber for the structure, as shown here, then cover the lumber with synthetic decking or thin trim pieces. Note: You will need to cover the stringer boards with the synthetic material before you install the brackets.

Use calculations on pages 180–181 to determine the rises and runs, the length of the stringers, and the number of stairs. Use two 2 × 6s for each stringer, 2 × 8s for risers, and 2 × 12s for treads.

1 **ATTACH THE BRACKETS.** Set two 2 × 6 stringer boards side by side on a flat surface. Adjust the spacers to the desired rise-run dimensions of the stairs, and use them to space the brackets. The spacers will also provide the correct gap between the stringer boards. Attach the brackets by driving one screw into each of the stringer pieces; do not tighten the screws all the way.

2 **ROTATE THE BRACKETS AND TRIM THE STRINGERS.** Remove the spacers, and slide one stringer board past the other to rotate the brackets. Use a framing square to check that you have the correct riser height. Drive more screws to attach all brackets except the top and bottom ones. Use a framing square to mark the stringer boards for cutting. Rotate the top and bottom brackets out of the way, and cut with a circular saw. Align and attach the top and bottom brackets.

3 **INSTALL TREADS AND RISERS.** You can preassemble the entire unit and then install it onto the deck and landing, or you can build it in place. Drive screws from the underside to attach the risers to the brackets, then attach the treads in the same way. (It is also possible to attach from the top of the stairs, though with this method the screw heads will be visible.) Attach the top stringer to the deck with a 2 × 4 cleat, and attach the stringers to the landing pad as well.

OTHER STAIR OPTIONS

IF YOUR PARTICULAR SITUATION CAN-NOT BE ADDRESSED WITH STANDARD STAIRS, you will need to design and build to suit. Consult closely with your inspector to be sure that the design conforms to codes, and follow the span chart on page 45 to ensure that the structure will be strong. Here are some common variations on the basic stairway.

Deep Stairs

Stairs with treads that are extra-deep call for special framing, because a notched 2 × 12 stringer may have its structural width reduced to less than 4 inches (see the illustration on page 182). You may need to support the stringers with a beam that has its own posts and footings. Or, you may be able to beef up the stringer with a 2 × 4 or 2 × 6 brace screwed alongside, as shown at left.

Framing for One or Two Steps

A single step can sometimes be simply framed as shown at left, with an outside joist that rests on the ground. Because the outside joist is supported all along its length, it should be strong enough to support the step. Or in-ground posts can be installed every 4 feet or so inside the frame, and the outside joist can be attached to the posts.

Building a Landing

If your deck is high, you may need to add a landing midway up the staircase. In fact, you may have no choice in the matter, as building codes often limit the total span of stringers to 16 feet. Stairs with a landing also look better than stairs with long, straight stringers, and adding a landing allows you to change directions with the stairs.

A landing is really just a step expanded into a mini-deck. Determine the total rise of your staircase, and calculate a suitable rise and run for each step. Then decide which step should be the landing. It needs to be big enough that the upper stringers can rest on it (see illustration), and it should be supported by four posts resting on concrete footings and piers and joined by joists. Install interior joists, spaced just the same as in a regular deck. Install a hangerboard to support the tops of the lower stringers. The bottoms of the upper stringers get attached to the landing's decking, as shown below.

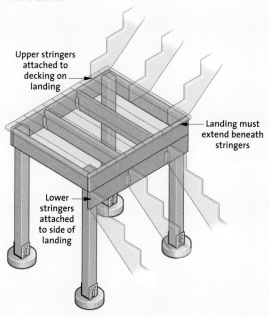

Upper stringers attached to decking on landing

Landing must extend beneath stringers

Lower stringers attached to side of landing

Wraparound Stairs

Stairs that turn a corner present special challenges, especially when it comes to supporting the treads at the corners. If you build with stringers only, the corner stringers will have to be longer, both in overall length and in individual run lengths; figuring this out is difficult. The alternate solution shown above is to run flat-laid $2 \times 8s$ between equal-length stringers at the corners. The treads overhang the framing a bit more at the corners than elsewhere, but as long as they are 2×s, they will be strong enough to handle the overhang.

railings

THE RAILING IS PROBABLY THE FIRST THING PEOPLE WILL NOTICE WHEN YOU SHOW THEM YOUR NEW DECK. IT ALSO HAPPENS TO BE AN IMPORTANT SAFETY FEATURE. IN THIS CHAPTER YOU'LL LEARN HOW TO BUILD STRONG AND ATTRACTIVE RAILINGS OUT OF WOOD AND SYNTHETIC MATERIALS, AS WELL AS HOW TO CHOOSE FROM ALTERNATIVE DESIGNS, INCLUDING STEEL AND ACRYLIC.

CODES AND SAFETY

A RAILING IS FREQUENTLY THE MOST VISIBLE PART OF A DECK. It's also the part that keeps you and the people on your deck safe. Local building codes regarding deck railings range from fairly lenient to tightly restrictive. Even if your code tends toward the former, do not take that as an excuse to cut corners when building a railing.

A railing may not be required unless your deck surface is 30 inches or more above the ground. That said, 30 inches is a long way to fall. More safety-conscious codes lower the requirement to 24 or even 15 inches.

Railings are often designed to withstand 200 pounds of downward or outward force, so that a person falling against a railing will not crash through it. On wood railings, notched posts (pages 204–205) are commonly installed and are appropriate for a deck that is not too high. Unnotched posts, preferably installed inside the framing, are stronger. If a deck is so high that a fall would cause serious injury, check out the stronger post brackets on the next page.

The minimum height of a railing is usually 36 inches, though many people prefer their railings to be higher. Railing height may be limited by restrictions on the length of the 2 × 2 balusters; adding a middle rail will allow you to use longer balusters and thus create a higher railing. Spacing between all components of the railing should not be greater than 4 inches (some codes allow 6 inches). This rule is designed to prevent a child's head from getting stuck between balusters.

Codes may also stipulate the type and sizes of fasteners to be used. Bolts are stronger than screws, and hardware fastening pieces are usually stronger than nails or screws by themselves. Setting rails into notches cut in a post can increase the strength of the railing, but only if the joints are tight and the lumber is dry (otherwise it will shrink and loosen).

Strong railings are especially important when a deck is high, or when seating on a deck is situated so that chairs are close to the edge.

If a deck is low, its railing can be more casual—in this case, benches have taken the place of railings entirely.

COMMON CODE REQUIREMENTS FOR RAILINGS

Must withstand 200-pound load

2 × 4 top rail

4 × 4 post (some codes prohibit notching)

36" minimum

2 × 4 bottom rail

2× blocking at post locations

6' maximum

34" maximum

2 × 4 balusters

4" (or 6") sphere cannot pass through any opening

Railing required if deck surface is 15"–30" or more above ground

Post Brackets for Greatest Strength

Special post brackets like this one make it virtually impossible for a post to come loose—the only way it can fail is if the post actually cracks in two. If the post is inside the framing, install brackets alongside intersecting joists or a joist and a piece of blocking (below, left). If the post is outside the framing, beef up the inside face of the header with a "sister" piece, then attach brackets so that the deck's joists are secured to the sister piece and the header (below).

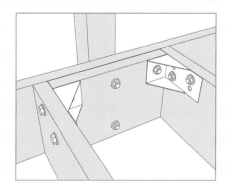

RAILING STYLES

ALMOST ALL DECK RAILINGS HAVE THE SAME BASIC COMPONENTS—posts, rails, and balusters. But there are myriad variations on this basic theme. Don't be afraid to try something a little different; for a modest investment in time and materials, you can build a railing that is a cut above the ordinary.

Railings are typically built from the same wood or synthetic material as the decking, but that is not a rule. Railings that contrast with the decking can be stunning. If you have a great view, alternative materials like metal, cable, or acrylic will obstruct the vista less than a traditional wood railing with closely spaced balusters.

ABOVE: Stainless-steel rails and cables create a railing with clean lines and provide good visibility.

DESIGN TIP

Railings are usually installed with a gap between the decking and the bottom railing, which makes it easier to sweep debris off the deck. When balusters extend all the way down to the decking, there will be dozens of places where dirt can collect.

A curved wood railing like this calls for special skills and tools, so it is best left to a pro.

Custom-cut balusters like these are expensive but easy to install.

Acrylic panels are strong without impeding the view.

ABOVE: The spaces between these balusters are varied to produce a pattern; a circle interrupts the pattern for maximum design effect.

LEFT: This metal railing is encased by wood posts and rails.

RAILING PRODUCTS

LUMBERYARDS AND HOME IMPROVE-MENT CENTERS SELL THE MATERIALS to make many of the most common designs for wood railings (pages 200–201). However, railings are easy to customize, which probably explains why there are so many products on the market designed to enliven their look and beef up their strength. Some of these products can be purchased at retail outlets; others can be ordered online. Here are just a few of the many options.

Turned balusters, also called milled balusters, lend an air of elegance to a railing. Buy them cut to the desired length. The only negative is that you will need to stain and finish them from time to time, which can be a time-consuming job.

Sometimes called newel caps, post caps attach quickly to the top of posts and add a graceful finishing touch. Post caps are most commonly used on a railing with ladder-type construction (page 109), where the top of the post is exposed. However, caps can also be installed on top of a cap rail, giving the illusion that the post pokes up through the rail. Post caps can be made of wood, metal, or vinyl.

You can purchase 4 × 8 or 3 × 6 sheets of lattice made of pressure-treated wood, untreated cedar, or vinyl at most home improvement centers and lumberyards. These can be cut to fit between the top and bottom rails and the posts. To install lattice panels, sandwich them between 1 × 2s. Buy wood lattice whose individual pieces are at least ³/₈ inch thick.

Balusters made of metal with a powder finish are easy to maintain. You will likely need to drill holes in the top and bottom rails (page 213) or buy rails with predrilled holes.

Lattice products like the one at left are more expensive, but stronger and easier to maintain than ones cut from 4 × 8 sheets. Choose from a variety of patterns and cut them to fit between your posts. This product includes its own top and bottom rails.

Standard 4 × 4 posts are rather plain-looking, and they sometimes develop unsightly cracks. A post sleeve slips over the post, is easy to attach, and gives your railing a furniturelike appearance. Some sleeves have light fixtures on top—for those, you may need to cut a vertical groove in the post for the electrical cable.

Outside-attached metal balusters are easy to install because they are simply screwed onto the top and bottom rails.

In addition to acrylic panels like those shown on pages 159, 195, and 198, consider balusters made of tempered glass. Some are made of straight rectangles while others have curved shapes; some are clear while others are tinted. Whatever you choose, make sure they are strong enough to meet local codes.

Like post caps, post lights attach to the tops of posts. Make sure you have planned how you will run the wiring before you purchase post lights.

NON-WOOD RAILINGS

AT HOME IMPROVEMENT CENTERS YOU WILL FIND AN ASSORTMENT OF RAILING SYSTEMS manufactured of the same materials as composite or vinyl decking. A composite railing system comes with all the parts you need to build a railing that is both sturdy and attractive, and that will almost certainly satisfy code requirements.

Balusters may resemble straightforward 2 × 2s, or they may be turned for a more stately look. The cap rail may be flat and plain, or it may have a milled appearance that resembles an interior railing. Posts are also available in a range of designs. Post skirting pieces trim the bottoms of posts; use them to cover imperfect decking cuts.

A composite railing system is easy to assemble. Balusters and posts are precut to the correct length, so you need cut only the cap rail and the top and bottom rails. The balusters fit into channels in the top and bottom rails. See pages 210–211 for installation instructions.

Clear acrylic panels are strong enough to keep people from falling through, yet they can be cut with a knife, making installation a breeze.

This cable system, composed of stainless-steel components, produces a surprisingly firm railing. The parts must be custom ordered to fit your deck. After that, they can be installed by a do-it-yourselfer using basic carpentry tools, plus bolt cutters and a crimper.

Every other one of these wrought-iron balusters is crowned with a brass finial. Notice how the distance from the top of the finial to the bottom of the top rail is the same as the space between each baluster.

Powder-coated aluminum balusters combined with synthetic decking create a distinctive look that's easy to keep clean.

How It Fits Together

Composite pieces must fit into a manufactured slot, be supported from below, or be attached with screws and angle brackets supplied by the manufacturer. Be sure to purchase the correct brackets for each situation. Some systems use simple angle brackets that are partially hidden when installed (top). Other brackets are decorative and meant to be seen. At right (below) is a skirting piece, which slides into place to cover all four sides of the post's bottom.

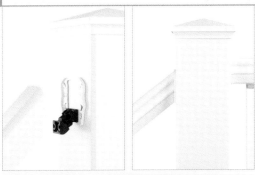

WOOD RAILING DESIGNS

PERHAPS THE MOST TYPICAL DESIGN FOR A WOOD RAILING IS THE LADDER STYLE; instructions for assembling this type of railing are on page 209. These pages show a ladder-style railing, as well as a few other designs. You can also design your own railing, incorporating portions of one or more of these designs.

Once the posts are installed, railing sections can be built. A ladder-style railing (below, left) is constructed on a flat surface like a ladder, then turned sideways and inserted between the posts. The top and bottom rails and the balusters are all made of 2 × 2s and are fastened with screws. The cap rail is installed on top.

The advantages of a design like the one below right are that it's easy to install, it saves lumber, and it looks handsome. The disadvantages include the need to cut the decking flush with the outside joists (or their fascia) rather than allow decking boards to overhang, which requires precise carpentry skills. In addition, the absence of a gap between the decking and bottom rail makes it harder to sweep debris off the deck.

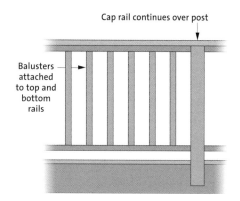

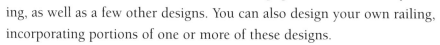

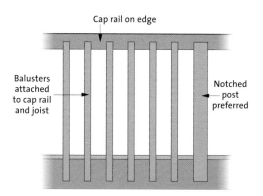

Cap rail continues over post

Balusters attached to top and bottom rails

Cap rail on edge

Balusters attached to cap rail and joist

Notched post preferred

A two-tier railing has a horizontal void between the railing section and the cap rail. Make sure this horizontal space is no wider than the maximum gap allowed by your building department (page 192). A 2 × 6 cap rail with no underlying support should span no more than 3 feet between posts or it may sag. This cap rail is supported between the posts by end-laid decking pieces, which have been bent to follow the curve of the decking surface and railing.

You can buy turned balusters that match the rest of the railing, paint them in contrasting colors, or both, as seen at left. In this design, a wedge-shaped nailer on both the top and bottom rails helps keep the balusters solidly in place. The posts are essentially oversize balusters, with post caps at their tops and trim where the post meets the decking. A rounded cap rail in a contrasting color completes the railing's design.

If you want additional privacy, consider building a section of railing that is more like a fence. One option is to install lattice sheets that run from post to post and are taller than the rest of the railing, as seen at left. For a more solid, albeit wall-like, structure, this deck builder could have installed sheets of pressure-treated plywood first, then added the lattice.

Horizontal railings are perhaps the easiest to build, if local codes allow them. Once the posts are installed and checked for plumb, attach the rails—which can be 2 × 2, 2 × 4, 2 × 6, or 5/4 decking—to the sides of the posts in any configuration you like. In the example shown at right, the interim vertical braces between the posts lean at an angle away from the edge of the deck.

In Praise of 2 × 6 Cap Rails

Many railings are topped with a flat-laid 2 × 6, for two good reasons: (1) It makes a more usable surface for drinks and potted plants than a 2 × 4. (2) Because it overhangs the post and rails by 1 inch on each side, your work does not have to be precise, and imperfections are covered up.

RAILING POSTS

THE STRENGTH AND APPEARANCE OF THE RAILING DEPEND ON the connection of the posts to the deck frame. If the posts are plumb and evenly spaced, installing the rails and balusters will proceed smoothly. For most railing styles, it is best to attach all the posts before assembling the rest of the railing.

In some designs the railing posts are made from the tops of the foundation posts. These pages deal with posts that support only the railings.

Railing posts are usually made from 4 × 4s, but you can use 6 × 6s if you prefer a heftier appearance. Space the posts no more than 6 feet apart; a 4- or 5-foot spacing will create an even stronger railing. While working within these guidelines, make an effort to keep the posts equally spaced along each deck edge.

Posts should be bolted to the joists, not nailed or attached with decking screws. In some cases lag screws can be used. For these, drill pilot holes of the recommended size, so the screws will grab tightly without cracking the joist, which can happen if the pilot hole is too small. To create a trimmer profile, you can notch the railing posts to fit over the decking and joist (pages 204–205). However, because this practice weakens the post connection, it is prohibited by some building codes.

Perfectly plumb posts make possible a railing with clean lines.

BUILDING TIP

It is important that your balusters be evenly spaced between posts. To check your calculations, lay the posts on the deck where they will go, and measure the spaces between them. In some deck designs you can build one or more ladder-style railing sections first, and then use them as spacers when you mark for other post locations.

This short railing is low enough to double as an informal bench.

Anchoring to Joists and Blocking

Railing posts need to be attached to the header joist and/or the outside joists. There are several ways to do this. A simple connection to the header joist, if it is within several inches of a perpendicular joist, can create a strong attachment. However, if the post is attached to an outside joist—or to a header joist in a place where it is not near a perpendicular joist—it will wobble when you push on it. To build firm posts, install blocking in any of the ways shown in the illustrations at right. If access to the underside of the deck is difficult, install the blocking before you lay the decking.

Turning Corners

At an outside or inside corner, you may install one corner post or two posts on either side of the corner. Since corners are by their nature strong, either method will produce a firm railing.

If you choose to install two posts, the top and bottom rails can meet with miter joints as shown (right), or they can be butt-jointed. To measure, temporarily install one rail longer than it needs to be, and hold the other one, also longer than it needs to be, directly on top of or below the first rail; mark them both for cutting.

When installing a corner post, make sure it is aligned with the other posts in both directions so the railing will be parallel with both sides of the deck. If your railing is inside the framing, simply install it in the corner of the framing. You can also install a corner post on the outside of the joists, but only if the rest of the posts are notched. To make a corner post that installs outside the joist, cut a notch as shown at right. The notch should be the same depth as the notches on the other posts (pages 204–205) running in both directions.

STRONG POST CONNECTIONS

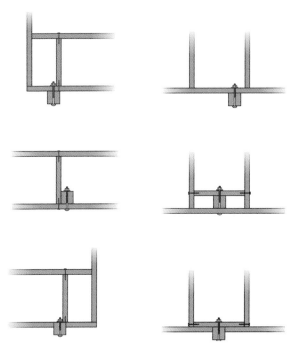

STRONG POST CONNECTIONS

TWO POSTS AT CORNER

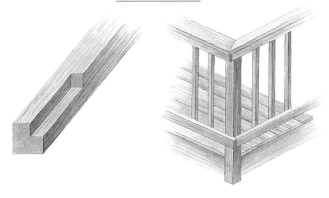

CORNER POST

Installing Notched Wood Posts

Notching a 4 × 4 post allows you to make the post more flush with the edge of the deck—the unnotched portion rests on top of the decking. Some people feel that notching significantly weakens a post. Others point out that after notching, the post still has strength greater than that of a 2 × 4, and it takes a great deal of pressure to snap a 2 × 4. See pages 202–203 for general instructions on attaching posts, and consider hardware such as the brackets shown on page 193.

1 **CUT THE POSTS AND MARK THEM FOR NOTCHING.** Cut all posts to the desired height above the decking, plus the thickness of the decking (1 inch for $^5/_4$ decking) and the width of the joists ($5^1/_4$ inches for 2 × 6 joists). From the bottom of each cut post, measure up the joist width plus the decking thickness, subtract $^1/_2$ inch, and make a mark across the post.

2 **CUT THE NOTCHES.** Set your circular saw to cut exactly $1^1/_2$ inches deep; test on scrap pieces to make sure you have this right. Make a series of closely spaced cuts between the line marked in step 1 and the post bottom. You can also make these cuts using a table saw or radial arm saw.

3 **REMOVE THE WOOD.** With a hammer, knock out the pieces of cut wood. Use a chisel to clean out the notch. Work carefully to create a notch that is squarely cut and the same depth throughout; avoid gouging out too much wood with the chisel.

4 **BEVEL THE EDGE.** The exposed bottom edge of the post will look better if it is beveled. Use a power miter saw or a circular saw with the blade tilted to make a 45-degree cut.

Attaching Posts

The procedure for attaching posts is similar whether they are notched or solid, or placed inside or outside the joists. Be sure to add any blocking that may be needed, as shown in the illustrations on page 203.

1 **NOTCH THE DECKING.** If the decking overhangs the joist, cut a notch so the post can rest against the side of the joist. For 4 × 4 posts, cut the notch 3½ inches wide. A jigsaw is the best tool for this job. When cutting along the joist, be sure to hold the blade just against the side of the joist.

2 **PLUMB POST AND DRILL HOLES.** Set each post in place with the top of the notched portion resting on the decking. Have a helper hold the post in place, or use clamps. Use a level or post level to ensure that the post is plumb. Drill a pilot hole for each bolt using a bit the same size as, or just slightly larger than, the bolt diameter. To minimize the chances of splitting the post, do not locate the top bolt directly over the bottom one; instead, set each off center just a bit, as shown in the next step.

3 **SECURE THE POST.** Slide carriage bolts through the pilot holes. Reach beneath the deck and behind the joist to place washers on the bolts, then tighten the nuts using a socket wrench or an adjustable wrench.

Fine-Tuning Posts

If the post is not plumb in the direction facing the deck, loosen the bolts and insert a galvanized washer or two, as shown at right, or use composite shims. Retighten the bolts and test for plumb.

If you are installing a post sleeve, you will need to notch it as well (far right). Cut the notch the same depth as the post, but measure from the inside of the sleeve rather than the outside.

INSTALLING RAILS

TOP AND BOTTOM RAILS INSTALLED ON EDGE ARE SUFFICIENT for installing the balusters (page 208), but you may prefer to add a cap rail, which provides a flat surface along the top of the railing.

The easiest way to install rails is to attach them on edge to the inside or outside faces of the posts. Unless your deck is particularly long, you can probably manage with a single board for each rail.

Installing rails between posts, as shown on these pages, is a more painstaking process. Rails can be attached with angle-driven screws or nails, or you can use special brackets (left). On these pages we show installing rails on end. When rails with balusters are to be installed flat (with the wide surface horizontal), it is usually best to assemble them ladder style, and perhaps set them in dadoes cut into the posts (page 209).

1 MEASURE THE BOTTOM RAILS. If you are installing rails between posts, the joints will be on prominent display. Choose lumber that is dry and stable to produce rails that fit snugly—if you have to do more than tap them into place, they are too tight. Cut with a power miter saw, or work carefully with a circular saw. Test on scrap pieces to be sure the saw is cutting accurately. On a deck with angles, the joints may not be perfect 45- or 22½-degree angles. With the board in place, mark it for the precise angle, as shown.

2 CUT THE RAILS. Cut the bottom rail first, then use it as a template for cutting the top rail, which is resting on the bottom rail in the photo at left to check its length. This will help you straighten out any out-of-plumb condition in the posts.

3 ATTACH THE RAILS. Use screws with small heads. You can also use nails, but they do not grab quite as well. Determine the correct heights for the rails, so the balusters will fit as you like them to. The top rail is often flush with the top of the posts, and the bottom rail should be a few inches above the decking; it is common practice to set the bottom rail on a 2 × 4 when installing, as shown. To attach, drill angled pilot holes (or faux pilot holes using a Phillips screwdriver bit, as shown on page 74) and drive screws in at least two places.

4 **CONTINUE INSTALLATION.** Most of the rails will be installed aligned in the same way. However, in some situations you may need to attach rails to the outside of the post when the others are on the inside, and vice versa.

5 **PREPARE THE RAIL CAP.** Use your best lumber for the rail cap; it will be the most visible board on the deck, and can serve as a small table for flowerpots and tableware. In this design, the rail cap is cut to fit between the posts; in other designs it rests on top of the posts and spans the length of the railing. Because it is so visually prominent, consider routing the edges, as shown. First cut the piece to length and test that the fit is snug. Use an ogee bit, as shown, or perhaps a round-over or chamfer bit. Practice on scrap pieces until the bit is at just the right depth and you are adept at creating professional-looking edges and corners. This is not difficult, but you must always keep the router's base pressed firmly flat on the board's surface.

6 **ATTACH THE RAIL CAP.** Whenever possible, attach from below, to avoid visible fastener heads. The screws should be long enough to drive through most of the cap rail's thickness, but not so long that they are in danger of poking through. It often works best to drive screws at angles up through the top rail.

Attaching an On-Top Rail Cap

Many railings are topped off with a flat-laid cap rail. Because it is so visible, use straight and clean boards, and choose dry lumber that is unlikely to shrink or warp. If possible, use long boards to avoid joints, which are apt to widen over time, and keep it well protected with sealer.

When cap rails meet at a corner, joining them with miter cuts will hide the end grain. Such miter joints, however, are notorious problem areas; consider a butt joint, which will look less finished at first but will not become unsightly if the wood warps. To make a miter joint more secure, it is a good idea to use a biscuit joiner (with a composite biscuit) and polyurethane glue. At the very least, carefully drill pilot holes and drive screws to hold the miter tightly together. If you need to make a butt joint on a long run, be sure to locate it over a post.

INSTALLING BALUSTERS

BALUSTERS CAN BE CUSTOMIZED TO GIVE YOUR DECK A DISTINCTIVE PROFILE, but more often they are made out of ordinary 2 × 2s installed vertically. You can buy precut 2 × 2s, perhaps with bevel cuts at one or both ends. If you want to save a few dollars, cut your own balusters from long 2 × 2s. The most efficient way to cut balusters is to use a power miter saw and construct a simple stop block, as shown at left. If you bevel-cut one or both of the baluster ends, the balusters will look nicer and shed water better. If the post bottoms will be attached to the outside of the deck, cut matching bevels on the posts and the balusters.

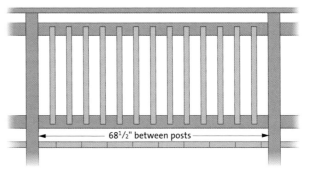

68$^{1}/_{2}$" between posts

Spacing Balusters

To ensure that your balusters are evenly spaced, make a spacer out of plywood or 1× lumber to match the desired space between rails. The spacer should be long enough to span from the top to the bottom rail. Start in the exact middle of the rail section and use a level to install the first baluster perfectly plumb. Have a helper hold the spacer while you drive nails or screws.

When you start in the middle of a rail section, it's likely the last spaces next to the posts will be somewhat narrower or wider than the others. If you crave symmetry, take the time to calculate baluster spacing.

Do the following math: Add the width of one baluster (1$^{1}/_{2}$ inches for a 2 × 2) to the maximum allowed spacing (typically 4 or 6 inches). Divide this total (5$^{1}/_{2}$ inches in most cases) into this measured distance between two posts (68$^{1}/_{2}$ inches in this example). Round up the result (12.45) to the next highest whole number (13) to find the number of balusters.

Now multiply the number of balusters (13) by the width of one (13 × 1$^{1}/_{2}$ inches = 19$^{1}/_{2}$ inches). Subtract that number from the distance between the posts (68$^{1}/_{2}$ − 19$^{1}/_{2}$ = 49) and divide the result by the total number of spacers, which is always one more than the number of balusters (49 ÷ 14 = 3$^{1}/_{2}$ inches). You now have your ideal spacing. Make a spacer that is $^{1}/_{16}$ inch narrower than that to allow for variations in boards.

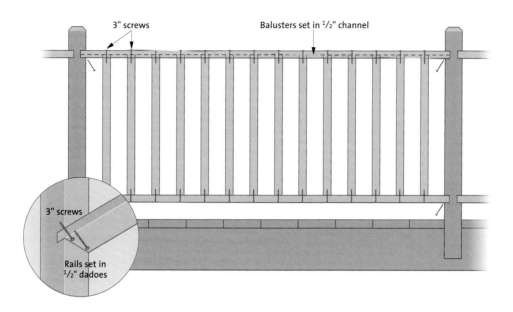

Ladder-Style Construction

A railing built ladder style has a well-crafted appearance. With this technique, the railings are assembled in full sections, as you might build a ladder, and the sections are attached as units between the posts. This type of railing takes time to build, and requires posts that are perfectly plumb.

To strengthen the assembly, you can set the rails into $\frac{1}{2}$-inch-deep dadoes cut into the posts, using the notching technique shown on page 204; make sure to cut the rails 1 inch longer than the space between the posts. It's easiest to cut the dadoes before the posts are installed. If you do not set the rails into dadoes, it's a good idea to set them on top of a short block of railing material that rests on the deck.

To keep the balusters from rotating in place, purchase a top rail with a $\frac{1}{2}$-inch-deep channel along the underside of the top rail just wide enough for the balusters to fit. Or attach a 1 × 2 nailer to the rail, so that the balusters can be fastened in a second direction.

When all the parts have been cut, assemble a railing section on the deck. Position the balusters with a spacer, as described on the previous page. Drill a pilot hole at each baluster location; then attach the baluster with 3-inch deck screws driven through the top and bottom rails into the center of the baluster.

Once the balusters have been attached to the rails, lift the railing section into place, sliding the rail ends into the post dadoes. Fasten the assembly by drilling pilot holes and driving small-headed deck screws at an angle through each rail into the post.

TECHNIQUE

Balusters are typically attached to the sides of rails, ideally with two fasteners per joint. If you are attaching balusters to rails from above and below, you may be able to drive one screw through the upper and lower rails into the end of the baluster, and another small-headed screw at an angle through the rails and into the baluster's side.

WORKING WITH SYNTHETICS

COMPOSITE OR VINYL RAILINGS ARE USUALLY QUICK TO INSTALL because they come with special brackets and spacing tools, and many of the parts are precut. The company that makes the synthetic railing system will supply instructions for assembly. Many systems follow the basic steps shown on these pages.

Install the posts after the framing is finished and before you lay the decking. With a synthetic railing system, you cannot equalize the spacing between balusters as described on page 208, so the gap between the balusters and posts may be different from the gaps between balusters.

1 **SLIDE ON POST SKIRTING.** Slip the post skirting over the post and slide it down to the deck, to act as trim for the post's base. You can attach it with small screws or nails, but that's not necessary.

2 **ATTACH CLIPS ONTO POST.** Insert rail brackets into the spacing tool supplied by the railing manufacturer. (This is often the same tool used for assembling railing sections; see step 4.) Place the tool on top of the skirting and snap it onto the post. Drive screws to attach the brackets to the post, then remove the spacing tool.

3 **MEASURE FOR RAILING SECTIONS.** Measure between the posts at the bottom rather than the top because the posts may be slightly out of plumb. You will straighten the posts when you install the railing section.

4 **ASSEMBLE A RAILING SECTION.** Working on a pair of boards laid across sawhorses or on the deck, use the spacer tool to make a railing section that is 6 inches or so longer than needed. Slip the balusters into the spacer's notches, snug the balusters against the grooves in the rails, and drive screws as needed.

5 **CUT RAILING SECTION TO LENGTH.** Mark the rails for cutting to length, so that the spacing between baluster and post will be equal on each side. Cut the top and bottom rails with a power miter saw or a circular saw, taking care to produce perfectly square cuts.

6 **INSERT THE RAILING SECTION.** Working with a helper, slip the railing section between the posts. You may need to bend one or more posts over slightly. The fit should be snug at all four points. Push down to seat the rails on top of the brackets; this will establish them at the right height and center them on the posts.

7 **ATTACH THE RAILS.** Check that the top and bottom rails are correctly aligned with the posts. Drive screws up through the brackets to attach them.

8 **SUPPORT WITH BOTTOM BLOCKS.** A synthetic railing section will sag unless you support it every few feet. Cut pieces of baluster material to fit snugly under the bottom rails near the posts (or use blocks provided). Attach the blocks with screws or power-driven nails.

9 **ADD POST CAPS.** The caps simply slip on. Like post skirting pieces, they can be attached with nails or screws, or you can just leave them in place. Another option is to attach them with a bit of construction adhesive.

STAIRS AND HYBRIDS

STAIR RAILINGS SHOULD RESEMBLE THE DECKING RAILING AS MUCH AS POSSIBLE, with matching balusters and rail shapes. For safety, stair railings should have a graspable handrail. Stairs that are built against the house may need only a single railing, but stairs in any other location usually need a railing on each side.

SHARED POST

SEPARATE POSTS

Stair Railings

You can use deck posts as the top posts on your stairs, but with some railing designs and in some stair locations it is preferable, or even necessary, to install separate posts for the deck and the stair railings. Start by installing posts longer than you need; then measure and cut them to height after they are in place.

Lay a board or railing piece across the treads as shown at left. See that it is parallel with the cut edges of the treads. Scribe with a pencil along the post to get the angle at which you will cut the rails. Mark the rail at both the top and the bottom post. Once you have cut the bottom rail, test to see that it is the right size for the top rail; if a post is not plumb and you cannot move it over, you may need to cut the top rail a slightly different length. Attach the rails by drilling angled pilot holes and driving screws. With most stairs, the bottom rail can be installed about 1 inch above the front edge of the treads; check your local code.

To determine the correct angle for cutting stair-rail balusters, use a T-bevel to capture the angle. Depending on the style of railing, you can build the railing section in advance and install it, or attach the rails first, then add the balusters.

If you have a rail cap that rests on top of the posts, you will need to cut the top of the bottom post at an angle. The easiest way to do this is to set one end of a straight board on the top post where the rail cap will rest, then draw a line under the board to mark the bottom post for cutting.

Hybrid Rails

Custom-installing metal balusters calls for no special skills, but you need to work methodically. For the balusters, use powder-coated metal tubing, or use another product that is strong and will resist corroding. Type **K** or **L** copper pipe is another option. Tubing with a ³⁄₄-inch outside diameter is best for the type of installation shown here; if you use wider tubing, you may need to install the rails laid flat rather than on end.

1 **DRILL THE HOLES.** Clamp the top and bottom rails together on edge. Calculate the baluster spacing as explained on page 208. Instead of making a spacer, however, mark an on-center layout for the balusters on the two rails. Unclamp the rails, and use a drill guide, as shown, to drill straight holes to a consistent ³⁄₄-inch depth. A forstner bit, though expensive, is recommended for this because it drills clean, splinter-free holes.

2 **ASSEMBLE THE RAILING.** Clean out the holes, and make sure the balusters all fit. Squirt a small amount of silicone caulk into each hole. Insert all balusters tightly into one rail, then fit the other rail over the baluster ends. With one rail clamped in place, use a hammer and a piece of wood to tap the other rail to ensure that all the balusters are fully seated.

3 **ATTACH THE RAILING SECTION.** Lift the section into place. Fasten the rails to the posts with brackets or with angle-driven screws. If you like, install a flat-laid 2 × 6 cap rail on top.

Handrails

Building codes often require that a handrail be graspable; choose one that can be grasped by children as well as adults. The most sensible width (or diameter) is from 1¹⁄₂ to 2 inches.

Most people can get a fairly good grip on a 2 × 4 or 2 × 6 laid on edge. Even better are handrails that allow the fingers to curl around them. These can be made by ripping a board to a 2-inch or smaller width, then fastening it to the top of a 2× handrail.

Another good choice is a standard round-topped handrail, attached to posts with metal brackets. This approach allows you to build a stair railing that looks exactly like the deck railing, and then attach the handrail.

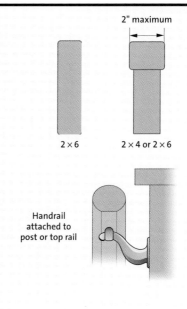

2" maximum

2 × 6

2 × 4 or 2 × 6

Handrail attached to post or top rail

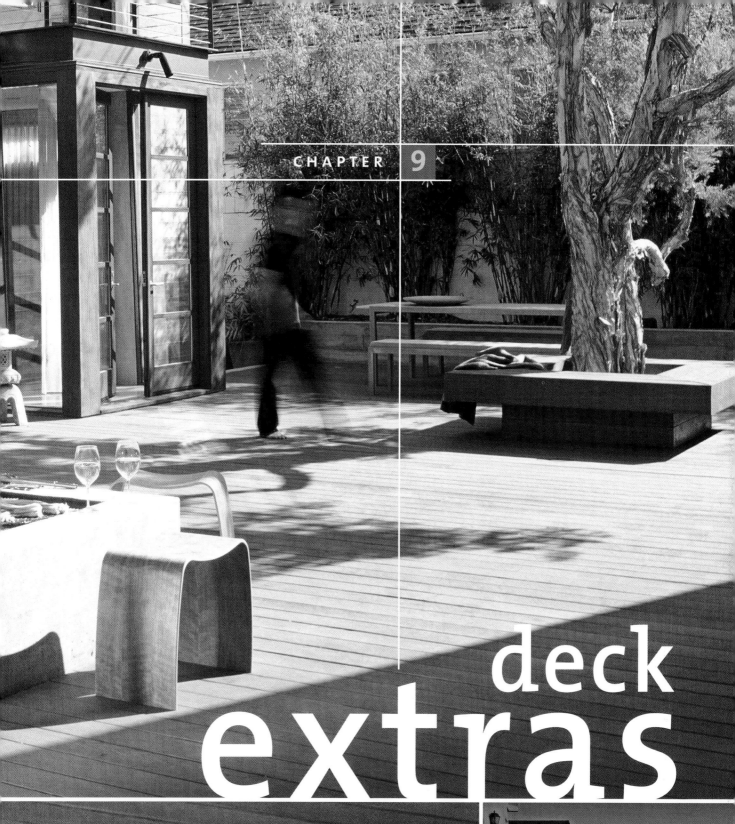

deck
extras

THE RIGHT ACCESSORIES CAN TRANSFORM AN ORDINARY
DECK INTO SOMETHING DOWNRIGHT WONDERFUL. MOST
DECKS WILL LOOK BETTER AND PROVIDE MORE COMFORT
IF THEY INCLUDE ONE OR MORE OF THE PROJECTS IN
THIS CHAPTER. A SHADY OVERHEAD MAKES THE DECK
MORE LIKE AN OUTDOOR ROOM. OTHER ENHANCEMENTS
INCLUDE PLANTERS, BENCHES, AND KITCHENS.

BENCHES

OUTDOOR PATIO FURNITURE IS THE EASIEST WAY TO PROVIDE SEATING on your deck, but you may want to augment purchased goods—and show off your craftsmanship—by building benches. Here we present two relatively easy projects. The first, installed on a deck, must be started before the decking is laid. The second, a free-standing bench, can be built anytime. Choose materials that match the deck or other elements in your yard. Use high-grade lumber that is not likely to shrink or warp.

A planter bench is easy to build; connect the seating to the planters, and add support as needed.

Built-In Bench

This simple but attractive bench is solidly supported by four 2 × 8 legs bolted to the joist framing. At 5 feet in length, it can comfortably seat three. If you plan to install 2 × 6 seat pieces, the supports should be no more than 48 inches apart; if you are using composite lumber or ⁵⁄₄ decking for the seats, you will need to install the supports even closer together. The basic design can be adapted to run either perpendicular or parallel to the joists. You can make a longer bench if it runs perpendicular to the joists; install additional supports spaced no more than 4 feet apart. However, lengthening the bench is not a good idea if all the weight rests on a single joist.

Before you lay the decking, construct the seat supports out of 2 × 8 lumber. Assemble the pieces by drilling pilot holes and driving deck screws. Install the supports so they are equidistant from the decking edge, and see that they are plumb. Attach the supports with deck screws. Install the decking, then attach the seat pieces.

60" maximum

2 × 6 seating

¼" gap

2 × 8 seat support

2 × 8 leg

48" maximum

16"–18"

Nailing cleat for decking

³⁄₈" × 5¹⁄₂" carriage bolts

Joist

BENCH PERPENDICULAR TO JOISTS

BENCH PARALLEL TO JOISTS

Slatted Seating

Another popular seating design uses numerous spaced slats that are 1½ inches wide. If the supports are less than 2½ feet apart, you can use 2 × 2s for the slats. Otherwise, use 2 × 4s set on edge. Space the pieces with strips of 1 × 2 (or 1 × 4) as shown. Or "self-space" the slats by installing 2× spacers. Assemble the seat on a flat surface. Drive two 2½-inch screws into each joint.

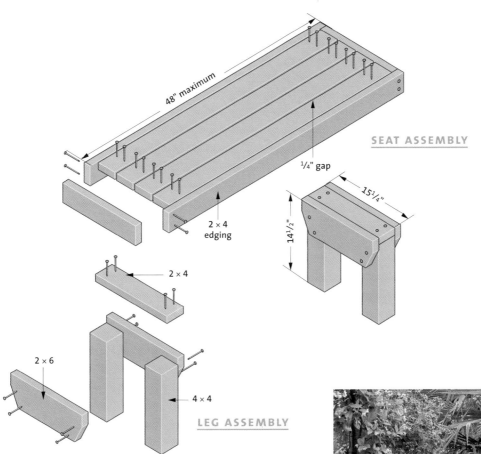

48" maximum

SEAT ASSEMBLY

¼" gap

2 × 4 edging

15¼"

14½"

2 × 4

2 × 6

4 × 4

LEG ASSEMBLY

Freestanding Bench

This bench is equally at home on a deck or a patio. The 4 × 4 legs make it stable. Take extra care to cut all the leg pieces precisely square, and clamp them together so they are aligned before you drill pilot holes and drive deck screws. Fasten the 2 × 4 seating pieces to the supports, then add the edging pieces.

A Custom Bench

THIS BENCH WAS DESIGNED FOR THE PATTERNED COMPOSITE DECK shown on pages 166–169. Benches like this are incorporated into the deck's overall design and built along with the structure and decking.

When building benches like this, you must continually check that posts, braces, and framing are correctly aligned with the deck edge and each other; that everything is plumb; and that all elements are level with each other. You may find yourself making minor adjustments as you go.

1 ATTACH THE POSTS. Cut all posts to the same length: the width of the joists, plus the thickness of the decking, plus the desired height of the bench (most people are comfortable with a 16- to 18-inch-high seat), minus the thickness of the seating pieces. Firmly attach the posts by cutting blocking pieces to fit snugly against them, and by driving screws or nails. Check for plumb as you work, and be sure the post bottoms are flush with the bottoms of the joists.

2 ARRANGING THE POSTS. Position the posts so they are the same distance from the edges of the framing and equidistant from each other. It may help to create a cardboard or plywood template of the seat and set it on top of the posts to make sure they are correctly spaced. If one post is off by a couple of inches, it usually doesn't matter; the framing can be adjusted, and it will not be visually obvious, provided the post is not centered under the bench.

3 ASSEMBLE THE FRAME PIECES. You could make a detailed drawing and calculate the exact size of each framing piece, but ironically, that is likely to produce mistakes. Instead, use the trial-and-error method. Bevel-cut the pieces (here, use 22$\frac{1}{2}$-degree bevels to create 45-degree

angles). Leave boards longer than they need to be, and lay them in place to mark for the final cuts. Construct a frame that follows the contours of the deck, as shown.

TIME SAVER

If you are building more than one bench, use the framing pieces cut for the first bench as templates for marking the pieces of the other benches.

4 **FINISH THE ASSEMBLY.** As you work, see that the front and back framing pieces are parallel with each other, and that pieces on opposite sides are the same length. Hold two pieces in place, one on top of the other, to mark for the final cuts. Attach the pieces by drilling pilot holes and driving 3-inch decking screws.

5 **ADD THE CROSS BRACES.** With the frame assembled and resting temporarily on the deck, cut cross braces to fit, and attach them to the framing so they are snug against each side of the posts.

6 **ATTACH THE FRAMING.** Raise the framing up flush with the tops of the posts. Check that it is fairly level in all directions, and drive screws to attach the cross braces to the posts.

7 **CLAD THE POSTS.** For appearance sake, cut pieces of decking or fascia material to fit snugly around the posts. Here, a table saw was used to bevel-cut the pieces and produce finished-looking corners. If this is difficult, simply butt-joint the fascia pieces, and have two of the pieces run past the others by $1/4$ inch or so to produce a rustic appearance.

8 **FINISH WITH DECKING AND TRIM.** Install decking boards, longer than they need to be, across the framing. Make chalk-line cuts to produce crisp edges. Cover the sides with trim or with more decking boards.

PLANTERS

A PLANTER IS BASICALLY A BOX MADE OF ROT-RESISTANT MATERIAL with drainage holes in the bottom. The outside of the planter can be dressed up any way you want.

There are two basic types of wood planters—those actually filled with soil and those used for holding flowerpots. A soil-filled planter must be extremely resistant to rot. To make one that will be durable, build a wood planter, then hire a sheet-metal shop (or gutter-supply company) to make a galvanized box to fit inside the planter. The bottom of a planter for flowerpots must be made of a very rot-resistant material, such as pressure-treated lumber, but the sides can be made of cedar or redwood.

Both types of planter must have ample drainage at the bottom. Either install bottom slats spaced about $1/4$ inch apart or drill a grid of $3/8$-inch holes. If the planter will be filled with soil, place a layer of gravel at least 3 inches deep in the bottom before you add the soil. If the planter will rest on the deck, raise it at least a half inch above the deck, and provide holes in the decking so the water can easily run through.

This planter's gray-stained shingles blend well with the decking and provide a neutral backdrop for colorful plants.

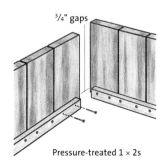

³/₄" gaps

Pressure-treated 1 × 2s

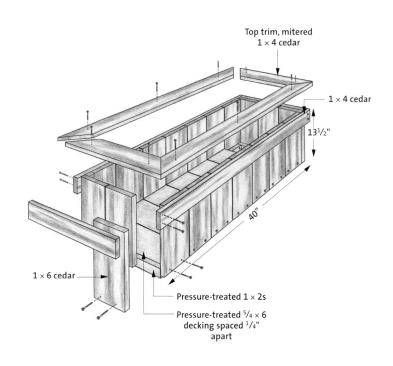

Top trim, mitered
1 × 4 cedar

1 × 4 cedar

13¹/₂"

40"

1 × 6 cedar

Pressure-treated 1 × 2s

Pressure-treated ⁵/₄ × 6 decking spaced ¹/₄" apart

All the visible boards in this planter are made of inexpensive 1× cedar fencing, which is rough on both sides. For a cleaner look, use regular smooth-sided 1× lumber or ⁵/₄ decking. Stainless-steel screws add a subtle touch of class without much additional expense, but regular deck screws are just as effective.

This classic bench/planter uses decking boards that are stained a bit darker than the surrounding decking.

1 **CUT AND SAND THE PIECES.** Cut the 1 × 6 vertical pieces. The planter shown has seven pieces on the sides and three on the ends, but you can change the shape and size by using more or fewer pieces. Round off the edges of the pieces with a sanding block, both to minimize splinters and to emphasize the planter's vertical lines.

2 **CONSTRUCT THE SIDES.** For each side, place the vertical pieces against each other with the finished sides down. Use a framing square to make sure they are aligned to form a rectangle. Cut a 1 × 2 cleat 3 inches shorter than the length of the assembled vertical pieces. Position the 1 × 2 so it hangs below the bottom of the vertical pieces by about $\frac{1}{4}$ inch, keeping the vertical pieces from resting on the deck. Leave a $\frac{3}{4}$-inch gap at either end of the 1 × 2. Apply polyurethane glue, drill pilot holes, and drive two $1\frac{1}{4}$-inch deck screws through the 1 × 2 and into the vertical pieces.

3 **ASSEMBLE THE SIDES AND FLOOR.** Hold two sides together so the shorter side covers the edge of the longer side. Using a framing square to ensure that the two pieces are at right angles, hold the pieces flush, and drill pilot holes. Apply glue and drive 2-inch screws. After all four sides are assembled, cut pressure-treated floor pieces to fit and set them on top of the 1 × 2 cleats. If the planter will hold flowerpots, space the floor pieces as much as 2 inches apart; if you will fill the planter with soil, leave only $\frac{1}{4}$-inch spaces. Check the planter for square, then drill pilot holes and drive 2-inch screws to attach the floor pieces to the 1 × 2 cleats. From the outside of the planter, drive 2-inch screws through the vertical pieces and into the floor pieces.

4 **TRIM THE TOP.** Rip-cut 3-inch-wide trim pieces. Measure and cut pieces to fit around the top of the planter. Attach them with 2-inch screws at the corners and then drive $1\frac{1}{4}$-inch screws from the inside of the vertical pieces. Miter-cut the top trim, as shown, or straight-cut the pieces. Attach the top trim using 2-inch screws.

OVERHEADS

IN ADDITION TO PROVIDING SHADE, AN OVERHEAD STRUCTURE (sometimes called a pergola or lanai) functions as a "space frame" that defines all or part of your deck. It may also provide a place for plants to climb or a ceiling from which to hang flowerpots, wind chimes, and other decorative objects.

Choose a design that harmonizes with your home and your deck. An overhead need not be built from the same materials as your house, but the new materials should not contrast jarringly. A formal setting probably calls for neatly spaced members and several coats of paint; with a more informal home it may work best to have an unpainted overhead and a few accessories.

When considering whether or not to build an overhead structure, check the sight lines from the house and from the deck. Make sure the new overhead will not make a room too dark or obstruct views.

Greek-style pillars like these can be bought from online sources; the decorative rafter ends can be cut with a jigsaw.

Installation Methods

An overhead can be freestanding or attached to the house at one end with a ledger. Posts can be set deep in holes just outside the deck's perimeter for added lateral strength or they may rest on post anchors that are attached to the deck. Use lumber that will resist rotting and warping. Wood that is still wet with treatment or high in moisture content may quickly twist when exposed to intense sunlight.

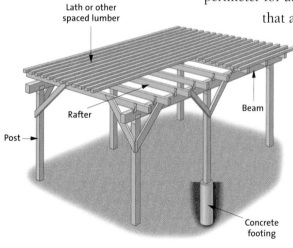

Lath or other spaced lumber

Rafter

Beam

Post

Concrete footing

FREESTANDING OVERHEAD

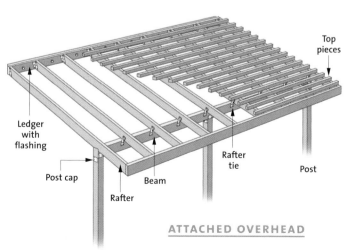

Top pieces

Ledger with flashing

Post cap

Rafter

Beam

Rafter tie

Post

ATTACHED OVERHEAD

Rafter and Beam Spans

Framing members do not need to be as strong as ones for a deck. That said, if rafters and beams span too long a distance, they will sag over time. The following are some recommended maximum spans for rafters and beams.

RAFTER SIZE	IF RAFTERS ARE SPACED	
	16" APART	24" APART
2 × 4	9'	8'
2 × 10	10'	8'
2 × 8	18'	16'

BEAM SIZE	IF BEAMS ARE SPACED	
	12' APART	16' APART
2 × 8	8'	6'
2 × 10	10'	8'
4 × 6	8'	6'
4 × 8	12'	10'
4 × 10	14'	12'

Note: A doubled 2× beam has the same strength as a 4× beam. For instance, a beam made with two 2 × 6s is equivalent to one 4 × 6.

Attaching a Ledger

If the overhead is attached to the house, begin construction by installing a ledger. An overhead ledger does not have to be as strong as a deck ledger (pages 100–109), but it should be firmly attached with long screws that are secured into the house's framing, not just the siding and sheathing.

On a one-story house, it is often best to attach the ledger just below the eaves. On a two-story house, you can usually tie into the house's band joist located between the floors, as shown at right. Find the band joist by measuring down from a second-story window.

Consult local codes to see if you need to cut out the siding for the ledger, or if you can simply attach it through the siding. The hold-away method (page 101) is another option.

Dressing It Up

Rafter and beam ends that overhang a structure are highly visible, so you may want to cut them into a decorative pattern. Experiment with designs, using a compass if the design calls for a curve or two. Once you've settled on a design, make a cardboard or plywood template, use it to trace the pattern onto the rafter or beam ends, then cut with a jigsaw.

You can also dress up post tops. The easiest way is to buy decorative post caps that screw in. Or use a circular saw to make beveled chamfer cuts.

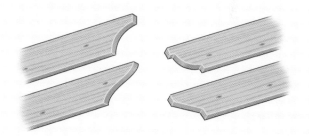

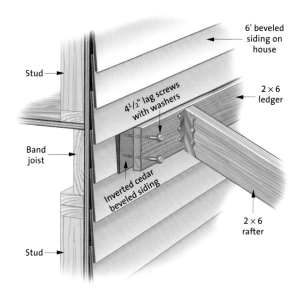

Stud

Band joist

Stud

$4\frac{1}{2}$" lag screws with washers

Inverted cedar beveled siding

6' beveled siding on house

2 × 6 ledger

2 × 6 rafter

Posts and Beams

Beams can either rest on top of the posts or be attached to their sides. Rafters can be set on top of two beams or be fastened to a ledger at one end (for example, with joist hangers). Top pieces, sometimes called laths, are usually evenly spaced and sized to provide the desired amount of shade.

Shade Strategies

Shade needs vary according to the time of day and the time of year, so spend some time developing a shade plan. If you want midday shade, run the top pieces of your overhead east to west; for more shade in the morning and early evening, run the pieces north to south. Of course, changing the orientation of the top pieces means changing the orientation of the beams and rafters as well.

Experiment with different materials and configurations by temporarily screwing some pieces on top of the rafters. Pay attention to the amount of shade they provide in both the morning and the afternoon. Top pieces laid on edge diffuse early-morning and late-afternoon sun but let in plenty of light at midday. The same pieces laid flat admit more sun in the early morning and late afternoon but block midday sun.

Overheads are most commonly topped with 1 × 2s, 2 × 2s, or other small-dimensioned lumber, but there are additional options. Shade cloths are available in a variety of densities to provide from 20 to 90 percent shade. Lattice panels, which install quickly, add a richly textured look and provide fairly even shade throughout the day. Be sure to support lattice panels every 16 inches to prevent sagging. Other possibilities include woven reed or bamboo shades, which can be rolled up when shade is not desired.

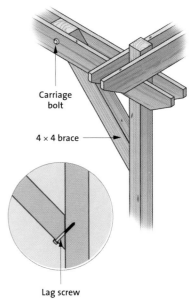

Carriage bolt

4 × 4 brace

Lag screw

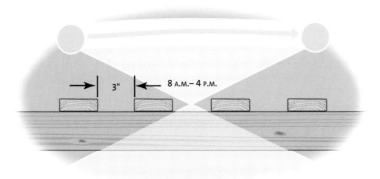

10 A.M.– 2 P.M.

3"

MIDDAY SUN

3"   8 A.M.– 4 P.M.

EARLY-MORNING AND LATE-AFTERNOON SUN

A Two-Post Arbor

This arbor begins with two 4 × 4 posts sandwiched between pairs of 2 × 4 beams. If you use the technique shown here, in which the beams are attached before the posts are set in their holes, you must make sure the tops of the posts are level with each other when you pour concrete. Another method is to set the posts first, cut one or both at the top so they are level, and then install the beams.

In the arbor shown, the beams are cut at a 45-degree angle on each end—the rafters are cut somewhat more decoratively. For other rafter-end designs, see page 222. Carriage bolts are used here to attach the beams because they have a neat appearance. If you don't mind how they look, four deck screws driven in at each joint would be strong enough.

1 **ASSEMBLE THE POSTS AND BEAMS.** Cut four beam pieces to the same size and shape. Clamp a pair of beams to each post and use a square to make sure they are square to the post and at the same height. Drill all the way through all three thicknesses. A larger countersunk hole, about ³⁄₈ inch deep, helps conceal each bolt's washer and nut. Use a ratchet-and-socket set to drive the nuts below the surface.

2 **SET THE POSTS AND RAFTERS.** Place the posts in post holes. Measure to make sure the beams are parallel with each other. Check the posts for plumb in both directions, and brace them temporarily but firmly (see next page). Cut two rafters to the same length and shape, and mark for the notches. Cut 1¹⁄₂-inch-deep notches (page 204). On the inside faces, where they will be least visible, angle-drive pilot holes and drive screws to attach the rafters to the beams.

3 **COMPLETE THE ARBOR.** Space 2 × 2 top pieces evenly on the rafters. Drive nails or screws down through the top pieces and into the rafters.

Attached Pergola

This design is straightforward, but two subtle features—paired rafters and decorated post tops—give it interest. Painted white, the crisp lines of the boards create a contemporary look. If the pergola were stained or allowed to turn gray, the effect would be more casual.

As shown, the overhead extends over two deck levels and part of the yard; the design could be easily adapted to form other shapes. Paired rafters are not structurally necessary, but they add a nice touch. Attaching blocks between rafter pairs allows for very solid connections without joist hangers.

Enlist the aid of at least one helper, and have two sturdy stepladders available. Soak all ends of boards in sealer before you install them. If you will be painting the structure, also prime all the pieces before installing them.

1 Use batter boards or triangulation to lay out the post positions (pages 84–89). Attach post anchors directly onto the decking surface or dig holes at least 3 feet deep. Check with your local building department to see if you need to dig below the frost line.

2 Cut the ledger and mark the rafter locations. Cut 2 × 4 nailing blocks and attach them by drilling pilot holes and driving deck screws. Firmly attach the ledger to the house (pages 100–109).

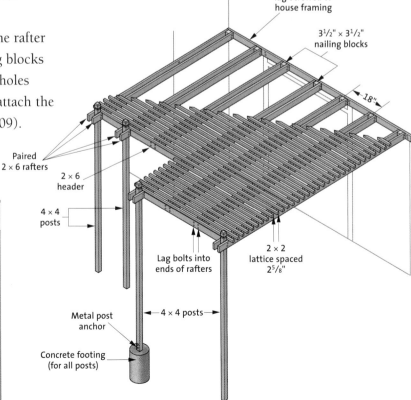

2 × 6 ledger lag-screwed to house framing

3½" × 3½" nailing blocks

18"

Paired 2 × 6 rafters

2 × 6 header

4 × 4 posts

Lag bolts into ends of rafters

2 × 2 lattice spaced 2⅝"

4 × 4 posts

Metal post anchor

Concrete footing (for all posts)

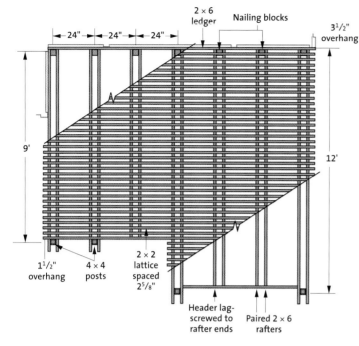

2 × 6 ledger Nailing blocks 3¹⁄₂" overhang

24" 24" 24"

9' 12'

1¹⁄₂" overhang 4 × 4 posts 2 × 2 lattice spaced 2⁵⁄₈"

Header lag-screwed to rafter ends Paired 2 × 6 rafters

6 Cut the headers to fit between the installed rafters. Attach each header to the rafters with deck screws (you will have to drive them at a slight angle).

7 Measure and cut the remaining rafters, which fit between the ledger and the headers. Attach them to the nailing blocks by drilling pilot holes and driving deck screws. At the other end, drive pilot holes through the header and into rafter ends, then drive 3-inch lag screws with washers.

8 Cut 2 × 2 top pieces to length, letting them overhang the rafters by 3¹⁄₂ inches on either side. Starting at the farthest point from the house, run a string line across the tops of the rafters to establish a straight line for the first top piece; install it by driving a 3-inch deck screw at each joint. Use a spacer board to maintain even spacing for the remaining top pieces. Every sixth piece or so, check for straightness with a new string line. As you near the house, measure the remaining space to make sure the boards will end up parallel to the house. You may need to make minor adjustments in the spacing of the final boards.

3 Position the posts in holes or on the deck. Temporarily brace each post so it is plumb in both directions, and double-check that the posts are square to each other. Using a laser level or a carpenter's level set atop a straight board, mark a point on each post that is level with the bottom of the ledger.

4 Cut the post tops 9¹⁄₂ inches above the marks. (You may find this easier to do if you remove them and set them on the deck.) Four inches down from the top of the post, use a square to draw a line around the post. Use a circular saw or a router to cut a ¹⁄₂ × 1¹⁄₂-inch groove around each post on the line. One inch down from the top, draw another line around the post. Set a circular saw to cut at a 45-degree angle and cut to the line to create a chamfered top.

5 Cut the rafters that attach to the posts; they should run past the posts by 3¹⁄₂ inches. At the ledger, attach the rafters to the nailing blocks by drilling pilot holes and driving deck screws. At the other end, attach the rafters to the posts with ⁵⁄₁₆ × 6¹⁄₂-inch carriage bolts, washers, and nuts.

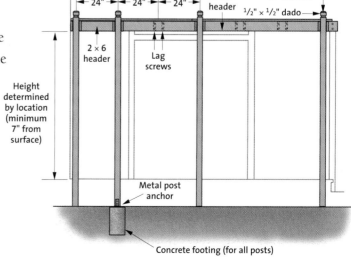

24" 24" 24" 2 × 6 header 45° chamfer ¹⁄₂" × ¹⁄₂" dado

2 × 6 header Lag screws

Height determined by location (minimum 7" from surface)

Metal post anchor

Concrete footing (for all posts)

SKIRTING

VISUALLY SPEAKING, THE WEAKEST ASPECT OF A DECK is the space between the bottom of the decking and the ground. If the view of the framing below your deck is not to your liking, cover it with skirting. The area can also be put to work as storage.

If the skirting is attached to the outside and header joists, it may take the place of the fascia (page 157). Or, a fascia board that is as wide as the joist may be applied over the skirting, for a layered look.

Here, skirting extends down a uniform 30 inches below the deck, where it is neatly trimmed. Bushes finish the job of covering up the deck's underside.

PLANNING TIP

Unless you live in a dry climate, be sure to allow for adequate air circulation under the deck; otherwise you may end up with musty odors and/or mosquitoes. Choose lattice, or install solid boards with spaces between them.

Framing

If a deck is less than 2 feet above the ground, you can simply attach vertical skirting boards to the outside and header joists. They will not be supported at the bottom, but will likely not need to be unless you expect them to be bumped against. If a deck is higher than 2 feet, or if you want to install another type of skirting, you must be able to attach the skirting to a solid framing member at the bottom as well as the top.

Most decks are not ready for skirting, because there is no continuous nailing surface for the top, sides, and bottom of the skirting. If the beam rests on top of the posts, you can run 2 × 4s from post to post a few inches above the ground, but that will provide framing for only one side. If the skirting will be on a plane with the outside and header joists, frame it as shown at right. Attach vertical 2 × 4s to the insides of the joists, then run and attach horizontals.

Materials

Solid vertical boards, perhaps made of the same material as the decking, are often perfect for skirting. Use a decking spacer to ensure ventilation. If you use synthetic boards, they can extend down to the ground; if you use wood, keep it at least an inch above grade.

Lattice, the most popular material for deck skirting, is inexpensive and easy to install. Choose wood lattice composed of pieces that are ³⁄₈ inch thick, for a total thickness of ³⁄₄ inch; thinner lattice is easily damaged. Vinyl lattice panels are the sturdiest and require little maintenance. For a finished look, attach horizontal 1 × 2 strips at the top and bottom of the panels.

You can also install horizontal skirting pieces. If you use house siding, you will need vertical framing pieces every 2 feet, or the siding will be easily bent. If you use 1× boards, the framing pieces can be spaced 3 or 4 feet apart.

Access Panels and Doors

You can make a door out of the same material as the skirting. Frame it simply with 2 × 4s as shown above. If the panel will only be removed occasionally, attach it to the framing with four screws. If you will use it often, add framing pieces on the sides and install hinges and a latch (left).

LIGHTING OPTIONS

ATTRACTIVE, WELL-PLACED LIGHTING WILL GIVE YOUR DECK a friendly ambience at night. Home improvement centers offer a wide selection of appealing light fixtures that provide either general or focused illumination. More options are available at deck specialty stores and online. Some deck builders make their own custom-designed lights, which may be housed in a post sleeve. A variety of possibilities is shown here.

Outside lighting also provides safety and security; when it's well planned, it can create a welcoming environment as well. Paths, steps, and doorways should be well lit for safety, but these lights need not detract from the mellow atmosphere that subdued illumination can provide. The following pages demonstrate how to plan and place lighting for best effect and how to install low-voltage lighting in a yard and on a deck.

Combining Lighting Types

The key to deck lighting is flexibility. For instance, strong lights that are controlled by motion detectors provide security against intruders and visibility to keep you from tripping when carrying in the groceries. But these lights are too glaring for entertaining. So install them with a switch that allows you to turn them off while you are dining; then install a separate system, using low-voltage lighting, that will offer just the right amount of illumination for social occasions.

Many of the lights that come in standard landscaping light kits can be easily attached to a deck's posts or fascia. However, there are products made specifically for attaching to wood structures, and these will probably look and perform better. A riser light is installed inside the riser of a step, where it shines down at just the right angle to illuminate the steps below. A wall-mounted decorative spotlight is easily screwed to any vertical surface such as a post. Some can be mounted overhead. For the best appearance, the wiring should be run through the wood. Finally, a post cap light is decorative as well as illuminating.

Lighting to Suit Your Needs

Outdoor lighting should be suited to specific tasks, yet should create a pleasing effect when all the lights are on.

Walks and steps. Walkways should be lit with low fixtures that point down and spread soft pools of light. Nestle the lights into plantings along the edge of a path to camouflage them. Steps can be lit by fixtures placed off to the side, into the step risers, or into retaining walls on either side of the steps. (Some codes require riser lights to be installed every two or three steps.)

Dining areas and living spaces. Use soft lighting around the dining table and for conversation areas—wherever indirect lighting will allow people to see who they're talking to without robbing the evening of its mood. Sconces, placed on the house wall, a railing post, or an overhead post, may be just right for these situations. Candlelit lanterns and hurricane lamps can also work. A food preparation area calls for brighter lighting— perhaps a downlight attached to an overhead or to the house.

Foliage. Lighting that highlights nearby features in your yard can create a stunning effect and also provide general illumination. To simulate dappled moonlight, place lights to shine up from the ground at the base of a large tree as well as a few lights that point down from its branches; this arrangement highlights foliage and creates shadows on the ground.

Decorative mini-lights used to outline trees and other features can lend sparkle to the landscaping around the deck. Small lights placed in flowerbeds, planters, and large flowerpots can create a similar effect on a smaller, more intimate scale.

LOW-VOLTAGE LIGHTING

MOST HOME IMPROVEMENT CENTERS CARRY A GOOD SELECTION of low-voltage lighting kits. Such kits contain everything you need, with lights that are attractive, reliable, and easy to install. Purchase a kit that has as many lights as you want. If you need to install more lights than your kit provides, purchase another kit rather than trying to add lights, which may put undue stress on the transformer/timer.

Running the Cable

The low-voltage wires carry only 12 volts of current, so you don't need an electrical permit. But you do need to plug into an outdoor electrical receptacle, which should be GFCI (ground fault circuit interrupter) protected. The receptacle should have an in-use cover to protect it from rain when the lights are plugged in. If you do not have

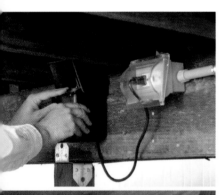

such a receptacle, have an electrician put one in. Mount the transformer/timer near the receptacle, in a spot where it is not likely to get bumped (left). As long as you can get there without too much difficulty, the underside of a deck is an ideal location for a lighting transformer. From this location wires can be run along the joists and either up through the decking or out through an end or header joist.

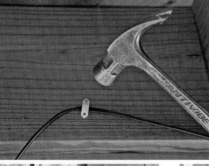

Most kits come with a transformer equipped with a programmable switch. Make sure the transformer has all the options you're looking for—for instance, the ability to set the lights on either a timer or a photo cell that turns lights on when it gets dark. The wiring can be run in a line, from one light to the next, or it can branch off from the transformer in two or three directions.

Use exterior-grade cable clips or wire staples to hold the cable firmly in place and keep it neatly tucked away (left). When running cable through a post, you may need to drill a hole or two. In the example at bottom left, the post has a groove and a hole; it will be covered later by a post sleeve.

Join the wires using the connectors provided. Some types simply snap together by hand or with pliers (right). Other types screw together. Attach the wires to the transformer and program the lights to turn on and off at certain times or to have them come on when it gets dark.

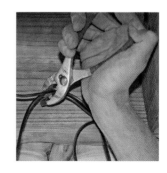

Installing Lights

Install a riser light (above, left) before you install the treads. Draw the outline of the hole using the manufacturer's template. Drill a hole near one corner, then cut the outlined shape using a jigsaw. Insert the light's box, make the connections, and screw on the cover. Test the light before you install the treads.

Many post lights (above, center) simply attach to the top of a post. After drilling the hole, run the cable down through it and screw the light fixture to the top of the post. A custom-fit weatherproof light can be made using a jelly jar (above, right). The light's housing can be made of metal or wood. Or a post sleeve can act as the housing (left).

Riser lights, sconces, and lights set atop poles are spaced throughout the deck to create a magical feeling at night.

OUTDOOR COUNTERS

THESE DAYS IT'S NOT UNUSUAL TO FIND SOME-THING CLOSE TO A FULL-SERVICE KITCHEN located outside the house. Outdoor kitchens may include not only grills and heating elements, but also re-frigerators, pizza ovens, sinks with running water, fireplaces, drawers and doors for storage, and even stereo systems. For a complete description of the possibilities, as well as installation instructions, see Sunset's *Barbecues & Outdoor Kitchens*.

The centerpiece of an outdoor kitchen is an outdoor counter. Many outdoor counters are made of heavy masonry—making them suitable for a patio but too heavy for a deck. However, you can build a fairly lightweight counter by framing it with wood or metal studs.

Before installing the counter, you will likely want to run electrical lines for a receptacle or two, and perhaps for lighting. Many counters have natural gas lines for the grill, though you can also use a propane tank inside the counter. If there will be a sink, you will need to pro-vide running water as well as a drain, which may tie into the house's drain or may simply run to a dry well (a large gravel-filled hole). When running any type of utility line, be sure to comply with local building codes. It's often a good idea to hire a professional plumber or electrician to rough in the lines.

After framing either of the counters shown on the next page, cover them with cement backerboard. You can cover the backerboard with stone or ceramic tiles, or you can apply a stucco finish to it. Leave openings for doors or even drawers to gain storage space. Metal doors, which may be stainless-steel or powder coated (typically black), can be purchased from outdoor kitchen supply stores or from online sources.

The countertop can also be covered with cement backerboard, onto which you can install tiles. Other options include a poured-in-place concrete coun-tertop, or slabs of granite, limestone, or bluestone.

BELOW: A blue-tinted countertop rests on a redwood frame.

BOTTOM: Indoor-style cabinetry can survive outdoors if it's kept well sealed.

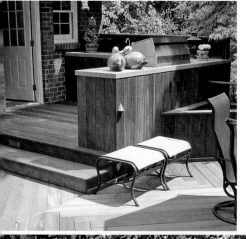

Framing with Wood

Use pressure-treated 2 × 4s or 2 × 3s for the framing. It is common to build the framing 34 inches high, so it will be 36 inches tall once a 2-inch-thick countertop is installed. When building, keep in mind that ½-inch-thick cement backerboard will be installed over the studs.

Build the front wall (above, right) on a flat surface. Carefully plan and build openings for the doors, the grill, and perhaps a refrigerator. Check for square as you go, and test to be sure the doors and appliances will fit. Drive two 3-inch deck screws into each joint.

Next, build the sidewalls and the rear wall. Have a helper hold them square to the front wall, and drive screws to attach the walls to each other. You will likely need to install 2 × 4 cross braces at the top, so that the top backerboard will be well supported. Cut pieces of ¾-inch pressure-treated plywood for the floor, and attach it with screws.

Framing with Metal Studs

Metal framing, also called steel framing, is fire resistant and lightweight. It is also inexpensive. You may be surprised at how easy it is to work with. Wear gloves to protect your hands from cuts.

There are two basic components: U-shape channels, also called runners, and the studs that fit into the channels. To make a straight cut, use tin snips on the two sides, then bend the metal back and forth several times to break it. To cut cross braces and other pieces that must have tabs that grab at each end, cut studs 3 inches longer than the opening, then snip each end in two places and bend back two side tabs. This will give you three tabs that can attach to an adjoining channel or wood stud.

Cut and assemble a rectangle of channels to form the bottom of the frame. Lay out the positions of the studs. To attach a stud, slip it into the channel and drive self-tapping metal framing screws. The frame will be unstable as you work, but it will firm up later when you apply the backerboard. Build the side and rear walls. Then build the front wall, with its openings for appliances and doors.

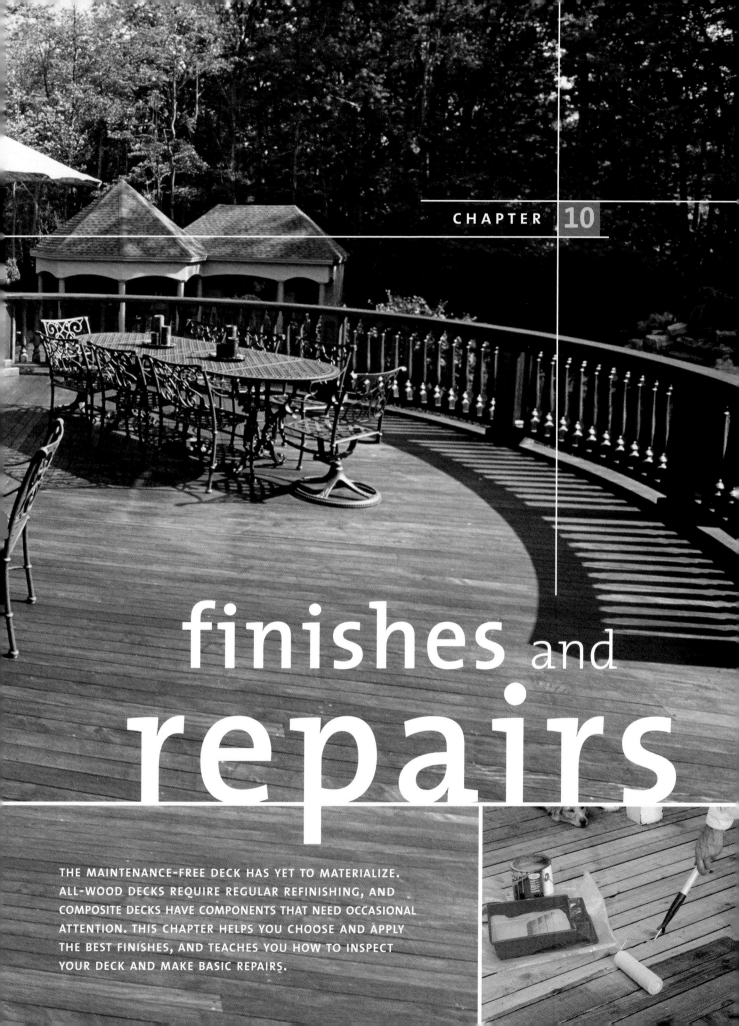

finishes and
repairs

THE MAINTENANCE-FREE DECK HAS YET TO MATERIALIZE.
ALL-WOOD DECKS REQUIRE REGULAR REFINISHING, AND
COMPOSITE DECKS HAVE COMPONENTS THAT NEED OCCASIONAL
ATTENTION. THIS CHAPTER HELPS YOU CHOOSE AND APPLY
THE BEST FINISHES, AND TEACHES YOU HOW TO INSPECT
YOUR DECK AND MAKE BASIC REPAIRS.

FINISHING A DECK

WOOD DECKS NEED A FINISH TO PROTECT THEM from sun, rain, mildew, and insect damage. In the paint department of home improvement centers you will find a variety of finishing products, some made specifically for decks and others that can be applied to exterior surfaces generally. Consult a sales associate to see which products are best suited to your deck.

As long as it is free of large cracks or serious rot, the dingiest decking can usually be made to look nearly new. Even old pressure-treated wood can be made to resemble finished cedar or redwood.

BEFORE

AFTER

Choosing Finishes

Broadly speaking, there are two categories of wood finishes. Penetrating finishes provide protection by soaking through the surface of the wood. Film-forming finishes create a protective coating on the wood's surface.

Penetrating finishes. Most products sold as deck finishes allow the surface of the wood to show through. Wood preservatives, water repellents, and pigmented deck stains are the major types of penetrating finishes.

Clear penetrating finishes (opposite top, left) are very popular. Readily available and affordable, they retain the natural color of the decking. But clear finishes are also the least durable and need to be reapplied every year. Many clear finishes contain mildewcide and ultraviolet (UV) stabilizers to provide added protection. Semi-transparent stains (opposite top, center two) provide a degree of protection against sun damage that clear finishes, even those containing UV stabilizers, cannot match.

Film-forming finishes. Paint and solid-color stains are finishes that seal wood with a protective film on the surface. In general, latex exterior paints and stains work fine on trim and siding, and they can be good choices for railings, but no latex paint is hard enough for a surface that people will walk on. Alkyd- or polyurethane-based

Clear   Redwood   Cedar   Solid color

"porch and deck" paint is much more durable, but is banned in many areas because of environmental concerns.

Solid-color deck stain (above, right) makes the decking look painted from a distance, but up close you can see the wood grain. Be sure to use a product made specifically for deck surfaces; solid stains made for fences will not hold up. Some products combine oil- and acrylic-based ingredients.

For a premium price, you can purchase a two-coat finish that looks like penetrating stain, but also forms a film to produce a slightly shiny "wet" look. Apply the second coat a day or so after the first coat. These sorts of products last longer than single-application stains.

When to Apply the Finish

It is sometimes said that you should let a deck weather in the sun awhile before applying the first coat of finish. However, unless the lumber has a factory-applied water repellent, this is bad advice. Pressure-treated wood may need to dry for a week or two, but untreated wood usually should be finished right away. Test the wood for dryness by sprinkling it with some water. If the water soaks in quickly, the wood is ready to be finished. Once you have selected the finish to put on your deck, applying it is a matter of purchasing the right tools, waiting for the right weather, and then allowing yourself the time to do it correctly.

Applicator Options

Rollers, brushes, and pump sprayers all can be used to apply deck finishes. Brushes are the most effective, since they do a better job of working the finish into the wood. Whichever tool you choose, you will need a brush to apply the finish to railings and other smaller sections of the deck.

For best long-term results, use a brush to apply at least the first coat of finish to your new deck. Or, for a nice combination of speed and thoroughness, have a partner use a roller or sprayer to apply the finish while you work it into the wood with a brush. If you are brushing on an oil-based stain, use a natural-bristle brush. For water-borne finishes, synthetic-bristle brushes work best. If you securely tape a brush onto a pole, you can brush while standing up.

For New Wood Decks

The ideal weather for applying deck finish is slightly overcast, with no rain in the immediate forecast. Avoid applying finish while the sun is beating down. Apply a fairly thin layer, let it dry, then apply a second coat soon afterward. Work plenty of finish into exposed end grain and into any joints where water could later be trapped.

1 **SAND THE DECKING.** New lumber often has a slight glaze on the surface. The wood will better absorb the finish if you sand it lightly to remove the glaze before applying the first coat. A pole sander allows you to sand while standing up. Use 100-grit sandpaper, and change the paper when it loses its effectiveness.

PRO TIP

The underside of a deck is often subjected to moisture, temperature variations, and insects. If at all possible, apply finish to all underside surfaces. A pump sprayer is particularly suited to reaching remote sections.

2 **REMOVE ALL DUST.** Sweep the deck thoroughly with a broom. Use a shop vacuum or a putty knife to clean out sawdust and other debris between boards. If you pick up dust when you run your hand over the wood surface, sweep again.

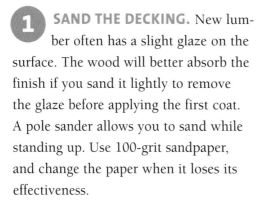

3 **APPLY THE FINISH.** If you are using a stain, try to minimize the lap marks that occur when you brush new finish over previously applied finish that has already begun to dry. For best results, apply the stain along the full length of a couple of boards at a time. Never let the stain puddle on the surface.

Refinishing Composite Decking

Many composite decks can be stained or painted with products made specifically for them. Pure vinyl decks generally cannot be refinished. Check with the manufacturer to see if you should use an oil-based or acrylic finish on your deck. Apply the stain much as you would to a wood deck: Clean the surface with a standard deck cleaner or a cleaner made for composite decking, wait a day or so for the surface to completely dry, and apply the stain with a brush or roller.

For Existing Wood Decks

If left alone, a wood deck will turn driftwood-gray as it weathers. Even if you like this look, it is better for the long-term survival of the deck if the wood is regularly cleaned and refinished.

A deck stripper will remove the finish entirely, allowing a deck-cleaning product to do a more thorough job. To remove paint, use a water-neutralized paint stripper as directed by the manufacturer. You may still need to scrape or sand paint away in some areas.

1 **GET RID OF THE GUNK.** Use a putty knife or a screwdriver to remove debris that has accumulated on joists between decking boards and in other nooks and crannies. It is tedious to do this sort of cleaning, but it is a vital step—these spots are prime candidates for rot.

2 **APPLY DECK CLEANER OR WOOD BLEACH.** Some deck cleaners should be diluted with water, others applied full strength. Follow the manufacturer's directions. Apply with a pump sprayer at a time when the deck boards are cool and in shade (cleaners evaporate too quickly under dry, sunny conditions).

3 **SCRUB.** Let the cleaner sit on the deck for about 15 minutes, then scrub thoroughly with a stiff-bristled brush. Use a large brush for the decking; you'll want a smaller one for the railings and stairs. Always brush the wood in the direction of the grain.

4 **RINSE OR PRESSURE-WASH.** A pressure washer is ideal for rinsing the deck, but only if you know how to avoid damaging the wood (cedar and redwood are easily dented). Use a fan-type nozzle and test on scrap pieces. A spray nozzle on a garden hose is a suitable and less risky alternative. Rinse away the cleaner, avoiding garden plants.

5 **APPLY THE FINISH.** Let the deck dry for a day or two (but not much longer). If the wood is still not really clean—if it hasn't turned pale, with no evidence of grime—scrub it again using deck cleaner or wood bleach. Apply the finish as described on the opposite page. If you use a roller or a pump sprayer to apply the finish to the deck surface, use a brush to work it between the boards and into other parts of the deck.

INSPECTING AND REPAIRING

EVEN THE BEST-BUILT DECKS REQUIRE PERIODIC MAINTE-NANCE. Wood shrinks and expands, making once-tight joints separate. Fasteners lose their grip and may start rusting. Rot can develop in out-of-sight parts of the deck. While you cannot stop the aging process, you can slow it down by performing a thorough inspection and fixing minor problems once a year. The following pages cover repairing or replacing decking, stair treads, joists, posts, and beams. For damaged or missing railing parts, see chapter 8 for installation methods. For significant foundation problems or other major structural concerns, consult a professional.

Inspection Checklist

Use this checklist to assess the more important and trouble-prone parts of the deck.

FOUNDATION
Are the concrete piers free of major cracks or deterioration?

Is there any sign that footings and piers have sunk or shifted (for example, has the deck developed a slope)?

LEDGERS AND BEAMS
Is the ledger free of rot and signs of splitting?

Are the bolts connecting the ledger to the house tight and secure?

Is there any sign that the ledger has separated from the house?

Is the flashing solid, with its edges sealed?

Is the beam sagging, cracked, or rotted?

POSTS
Are the posts, especially at the ends, free of rot and signs of splitting?

Are the fasteners tight and secure?

Are the posts fairly plumb?

JOISTS
Is the wood, especially at the ends and where the joists contact the beams and decking, free of rot and signs of splitting?

Are the joist hanger connections and fasteners tight and secure?

Is the header joist tight against the joist ends?

DECKING
Have the fastener heads worked their way above the deck surface?

Is the wood free of rot and signs of splitting?

Have the ends of deck boards begun warping?

Is the wood free of splinters and excessive cupping?

STAIRS
Do the stairs and stair rail meet current code?

Have mold and mildew made the treads slippery?

Is the wood, especially the stringers, free of rot and signs of splitting?

Are the treads fastened securely to the stringers?

Are the treads cracked and/or showing signs of rot?

RAILINGS
Does the railing wobble when you lean against it?

Does it meet current code?

Are the posts securely bolted to the deck frame?

Is the wood free of rot and signs of splitting?

Are the rail and baluster connections tight and solid?

A Deck Inspection

Walk around your deck with a wrench and tighten all the bolts and lag screws. If a fastener no longer seems to be holding tight, check for rot in the wood. Also check for rot by probing questionable spots with a pocket knife or a screwdriver. Soft, spongy areas should be repaired or replaced right away. Be aware that if you find rot on one piece (such as a stair tread or decking board), it is quite possible that an underlying piece (such as a stringer or joist) is also rotten.

Repairs to Decking

When deck boards get splinters, smooth them with a hand or power sander. Cups and small warped areas can be leveled with a power sander or a plane. If you find that nails keep pulling away from the decking, replace them with deck screws. If screws are not holding, try driving longer screws (if that doesn't help, it's a good sign that the underlying joist may be rotten). When a decking board is severely warped, rotted, or split, it should be replaced. Use the same type of decking material and finish as on the rest of the deck. New boards will be different in appearance at first, but they should blend in within a year or so.

Begin by removing all nails or screws holding the board in place. You may need a cat's paw to grasp nail heads. If you are unable to pull nails out, use a nail punch to drive them farther into the joist. Then remove the board. A flat pry bar works well for getting boards out. Let the replacement decking board overhang the side of the deck while it is being attached. Then you can accurately cut it to length.

When one or both boards are coming up at a butt joint, try drilling pilot holes and driving new screws at an angle into the joist. If this doesn't work, install 2 × 2 cleats as shown at right.

Removing Nails and Screws

A cat's paw nail remover will efficiently extract a nail, but it will also gouge the decking. To remove a nail without damaging the wood, pry up on the board using a flat pry bar and a scrap of wood to protect the decking; tap the board back down, and the nail head may pop up so you can remove it with a hammer or pry bar. If that doesn't do it, you can simply leave the nail in place and drive another one next to it.

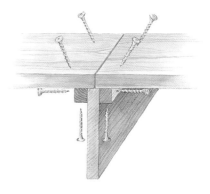

In cases where a screw's head is stripped so that the Phillips bit cannot bite into it, try drilling a small hole in the middle of the head. If the screw spins but doesn't back out, pry up on the board as you try to unscrew it. Worst case, you may have to leave a screw in place and drive another one next to it.

Replacing Stair Treads

Damaged stair treads should be replaced as soon as they are discovered. Pry loose a nailed-in tread or back the screws out of a screwed-in tread. With the tread removed, take the opportunity to check the condition of the stringers. If a stringer is too rotten to hold a screw, it should be replaced. If the stringer is fine, cut a replacement tread to length, using the same material as the old tread, and attach it to the stringer.

Repairing Joists

A joist may be rotted at its top, where the decking rests on it, or at its end, where it ties into the ledger or the header joist. If you detect rot on a joist early enough, the repair is easy to make. Remove the rotted material with a hammer and chisel, then coat the newly exposed wood with a water-repellent preservative. Using the same size lumber, cut a "sister" joist to the same length as the damaged joist, or cut one that extends at least 4 feet in either direction from the damaged area. Position the sister joist into place against the old joist and attach with a pair of 2½-inch deck screws every foot or so. Attach the decking to the sister joist. If the sister runs into the ledger, attach it to the ledger using an angle bracket. If rot is extensive, the joist should be replaced—a major job. Check nearby joists; you may discover that you need to replace the entire deck.

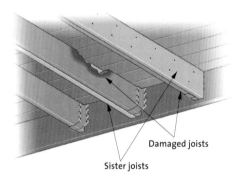

Damaged joists

Sister joists

Removing a Deck

Sometimes the only solution for a worn-out deck is to tear it down and start anew. Removing a deck will produce a huge amount of trash to be disposed of, but the actual demolition can usually be performed by two people in less than a day. Wear protective clothing, and take care to avoid stepping on nails. Cut off power to any electrical fixtures on the deck, disconnect the wiring, and remove the fixtures. Also remove any plumbing, overheads, benches, planters, or other features. Cut the railings into removable sections. Snap chalk lines on the decking to identify joist locations, then cut through and remove the decking on each side of each joist. Cut and remove the joists, one at a time. Remove treads and risers from stairs and cut stringers loose from the deck. Cut up the beam and then the posts. Remove fasteners holding the ledger to the house and carefully pry the ledger off. Finally, remove old flashing.

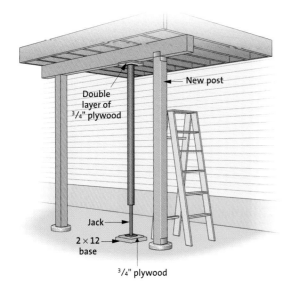

Double layer of ³/₄" plywood

New post

Jack

2 × 12 base

³/₄" plywood

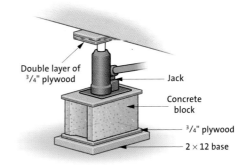

Double layer of ³/₄" plywood

Jack

Concrete block

³/₄" plywood

2 × 12 base

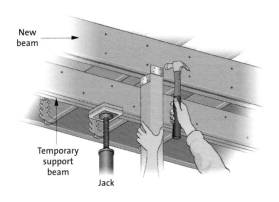

New beam

Temporary support beam

Jack

Replacing a Post

If you have discovered a failing deck post, replace it as soon as you can. Begin by jacking up the beam. On a low deck, use a hydraulic bottle jack and concrete block along with pieces of wood, as shown above. For a higher deck, use a telescoping jack (above, left). Apply just enough pressure with the jack to lift the beam very slightly off the post. Remove the post and install a new post base if the old one is damaged. Cut the new post to length and set it in place, with a new post cap on top (left). When it is plumb, lower the beam so that it rests on the post, but keep the jack in place. Attach the post to the beam, then remove the jack.

For an old post that was buried in concrete, dig out as much of the buried wood as possible, fill up the cavity with fresh concrete, and add a new anchor bolt and a new post base. Then attach the new post to the post base.

Replacing a Beam

A rotted or severely cracked beam should be replaced. If you inherited an old deck with a sagging beam, it is possible that the beam was undersize when the deck was built, in which case it should be replaced with a stronger beam.

Build a temporary replacement beam by nailing together three 2 × 8s that are at least as long as the old beam. Have the new beam ready to install before you start removing the old one (see pages 112–117 for a full discussion of beams).

Set the temporary beam on top of jacks close to the old beam. Raise the jacks just enough to release the pressure of the old beam on the posts. Remove fasteners and hardware securing the beam to the posts and joists, then remove the beam. Set the new beam and the new post caps in place. Make sure that all the posts are plumb before fastening the beam to the joists and the posts. Then remove the temporary beam and the jacks.

Railing Repairs

Individual balusters, rails, and cap pieces can be replaced with little trouble. Use a hammer, with medium pressure, and a flat pry bar to loosen and separate the parts. You may be able to remove screws using a drill with a screwdriver attachment, but often old screws are rusty or stripped and won't unscrew. Install new pieces using screws rather than nails so you won't shake the structure as you work.

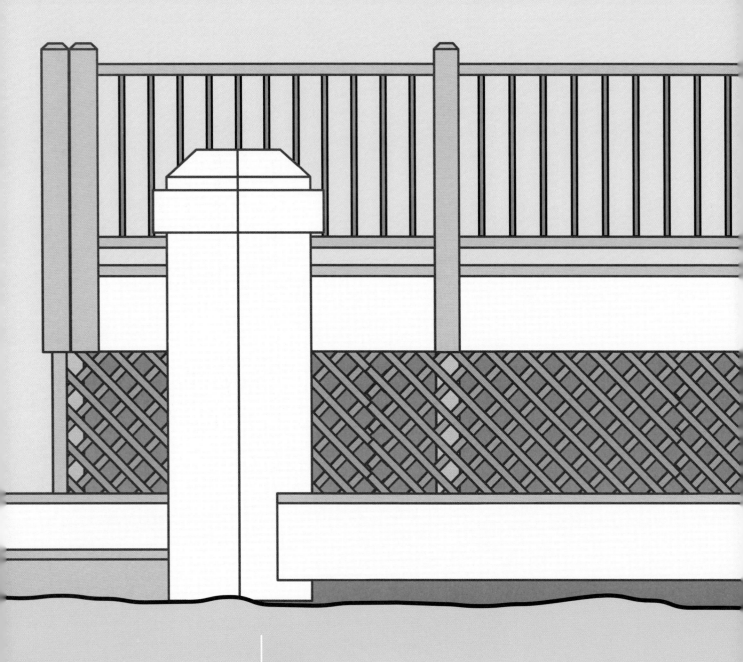

deck plans

THE REAL-LIFE DESIGNS IN THIS CHAPTER, WHICH
INCLUDES DRAWINGS, PHOTOGRAPHS, AND DETAILED
MATERIALS LISTS, CAN HELP YOU PLAN YOU OWN DECK.
YOU MAY FIND A DECK THAT CLOSELY MATCHES WHAT
YOU WANT TO ACHIEVE, OR USE THE IDEAS HERE TO
ENHANCE YOUR DESIGN.

SIMPLE AND MODERN

THIS DECK IS AS BASIC AS IT CAN BE, BUT IT IS SOLID, FUNCTIONAL, AND FAMILY FRIENDLY. Attached to the master bedroom, the deck has high railings and gates to keep children and pets safe.

Materials List

LUMBER	
Posts	4 × 6
Beams	4 × 6, or doubled 2 × 6s
Joists and ledgers	2 × 6
Fascia and borders	2 × 2, 2 × 6
Decking	2 × 6
Stairs	2 × 12 stringers; 2 × 6 treads
Railings	4 × 4 posts; 2 × 4 rails; 2 × 2 balusters; 2 × 6 cap rails
Gates	2 × 4 frames; 2 × 2 balusters, nailers, and braces
MASONRY	
Concrete	Piers, footings
HARDWARE	
Nails	16d (framing); as appropriate for connectors
Bolts and screws	2$\frac{1}{2}$" stainless-steel screws (decking); $\frac{1}{2}$" lag screws (ledger)
Connectors	Post connectors; joist hangers
Other	Gate hardware

To Adapt this Plan

The deck can be built low to the ground or, with cross-braced posts, can be made higher. Stairs can be left off or attached at any point on the perimeter. The gates probably will not be needed if children and pets are not a concern.

Building Notes

The framing and foundation in this deck are textbook simple and should pass code in most areas. As with any deck-building project, however, be sure the location, size, and spacing of your foundation, posts, beams, and joists are appropriate to the materials you use and meet local code.

DESIGNER: TIBOR AMBRUS

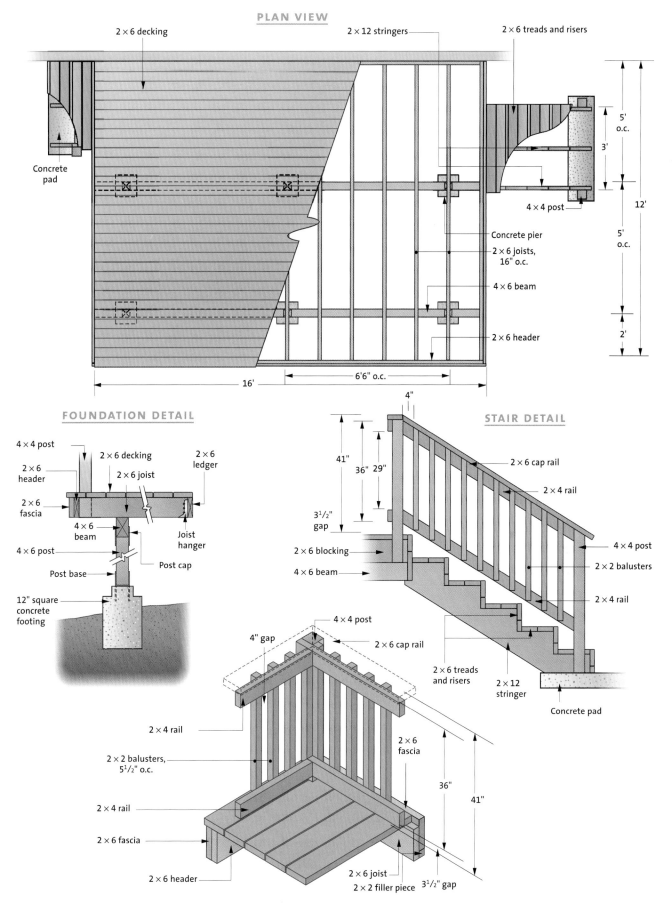

PLAN VIEW

2 × 6 decking

2 × 12 stringers

2 × 6 treads and risers

Concrete pad

5' o.c.

3'

4 × 4 post

Concrete pier

2 × 6 joists, 16" o.c.

4 × 6 beam

2 × 6 header

12'

5' o.c.

2'

16'

6'6" o.c.

FOUNDATION DETAIL

4 × 4 post

2 × 6 header

2 × 6 fascia

4 × 6 post

Post base

12" square concrete footing

2 × 6 decking

2 × 6 joist

4 × 6 beam

Post cap

2 × 6 ledger

Joist hanger

STAIR DETAIL

4"

41"

36" 29"

3½" gap

2 × 6 blocking

4 × 6 beam

2 × 6 cap rail

2 × 4 rail

4 × 4 post

2 × 2 balusters

2 × 4 rail

2 × 6 treads and risers

2 × 12 stringer

Concrete pad

4 × 4 post

4" gap

2 × 6 cap rail

2 × 4 rail

2 × 2 balusters, 5½" o.c.

2 × 4 rail

2 × 6 fascia

2 × 6 header

2 × 6 fascia

2 × 6 joist

2 × 2 filler piece

3½" gap

36"

41"

RAILING CONSTRUCTION

HARDWOOD ENTRY DECK

THIS ELEGANT ENTRY DECK along the front of a suburban home was built to replace a small concrete porch, which was left in place underneath the deck. The tropical hardwood surface of pau lope is practical, beautiful, and enduring. Crisply painted white railings add a tailored look appropriate for the public side of the house.

Materials List

LUMBER

Posts	4 × 4
Beams	4 × 6, or doubled 2 × 6s
Joists and ledgers	2 × 6
Decking and fascia	⁵⁄₄ × 6
Stairs and risers	2 × 12 stringers; ⁵⁄₄ × 6 treads
Railings	6 × 6 posts, with caps; 2 × 2 balusters; 2 × 4 rails; 2 × 6 cap rails
Other	Lattice skirting; 2 × 4 nailers

MASONRY

Concrete	Piers

HARDWARE

Nails	16d (framing); as appropriate for connectors
Bolts and screws	Metal-bracket screws (decking); ¹⁄₂" bolts and lag screws (framing/ledgers)
Connectors	Metal-bracket fasteners (decking); post connectors; joist hangers; seismic ties
Other	#4 rebar; #3 hoops

To Adapt this Plan

The deck is designed to fit a particular house front, and the outer edge is angled to provide useful space, create visual interest, and distinguish between areas. The shape of your house face is undoubtedly different, so you will need to adjust the deck plan accordingly.

Building Notes

Since the concrete porch was not removed, the system shown in the plans was used to cover it up. If you are building from scratch (or tearing out a porch), you will need to fill in that area with framing and foundations. The hardwood decking permits 24-inch joist spacing. Different decking materials may require a different joist spacing.

DESIGNER: PETER KOENIG DESIGNS, WITH BRYAN GORDON, B. GORDON BUILDERS

PLAN VIEW

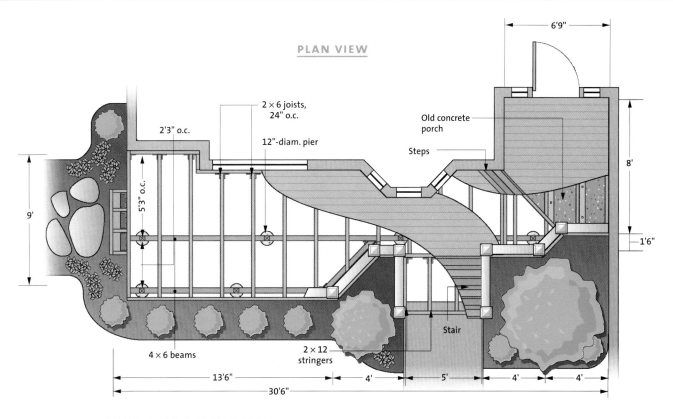

6'9"

2 × 6 joists, 24" o.c.

Old concrete porch

Steps

2'3" o.c.

12"-diam. pier

5'3" o.c.

8'

9'

1'6"

Stair

4 × 6 beams

2 × 12 stringers

13'6"

4'

5'

4'

4'

30'6"

BUILT-OVER PORCH DETAIL

Decorative cap

2 × 6 cap rail

2 × 4 rail

2 × 4 nailer screwed to concrete

House

2 × 2 baluster

2 × 6 joist, shaped to follow slope of porch

6 × 6 post

2 × 4 rail

Lag screw

⁵/₄ × 6 decking used as fascia

Brick veneer

Old concrete porch

FRAME AND RAILING CONSTRUCTION

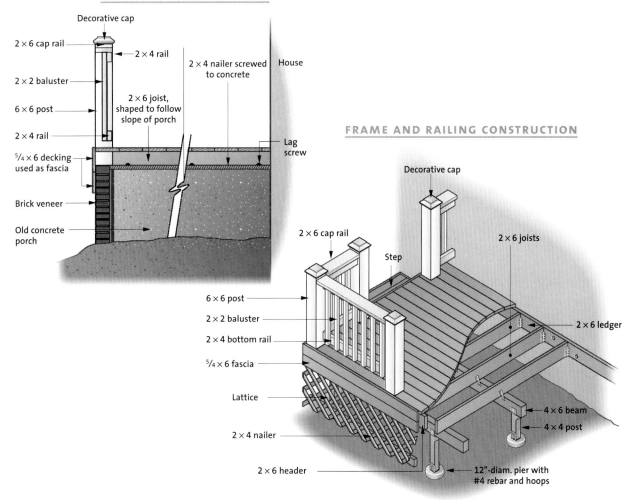

Decorative cap

2 × 6 cap rail

Step

2 × 6 joists

6 × 6 post

2 × 2 baluster

2 × 4 bottom rail

2 × 6 ledger

⁵/₄ × 6 fascia

Lattice

4 × 6 beam

4 × 4 post

2 × 4 nailer

2 × 6 header

12"-diam. pier with #4 rebar and hoops

SEATING DECK

SET ABOVE A LARGE DECK ON AN ANGLED PLATFORM, THIS HANDSOME SEATING UNIT is in effect a mini-deck itself. The design provides front-row seats for eight or more with cantilevered benches that are easy to sweep under. The sturdy overhead can support heavy, mature foliage for shade in summer.

Materials List

LUMBER	
Joists	2 × 10
Fascia	2 × 12
Decking	2 × 6
Stairs	2 × 6 treads and risers
Overhead	4 × 6 (posts, beams), 4 × 4 (braces, rafters),
Bench	4 × 4 (supports); 2 × 4 with ⅛" spacers (seating); 2 × 6 (trim)

HARDWARE	
Nails	16d (framing), 16d (fascia and risers) as appropriate for connectors
Bolts and screws	2½" stainless-steel screws (decking); ½" bolts (framing)
Connectors	Joist hangers; post caps; angle clips

EXTRAS	
Recessed, low-voltage stair lights	

To Adapt this Plan

This versatile design could be adapted in several ways. It was originally built as a platform on top of a large deck, but you can adapt it to stand alone by setting the joists on beams supported by posts, piers, and footings, with a stair added if necessary. You can also extend the deck, benches, and overhead in either direction; be sure to stick to the same spacing. The unit need not be angled and could instead be built straight. Finally, the bench and overhead alone could make a handsome addition to a new or an existing deck. Be sure to provide a strong connection between the overhead posts and the framing underneath them. In this deck, the posts are attached to plates atop a perimeter foundation that supports the main deck.

Building Notes

Be sure to buy good-quality, straight-grain seasoned lumber for this project. Since the assembly is exposed to view, any warping or other defects will show clearly. Accurate cutting and assembly are important, too. A power miter saw set up as shown on page 76 is ideal for reproducing the identical parts required in this design.

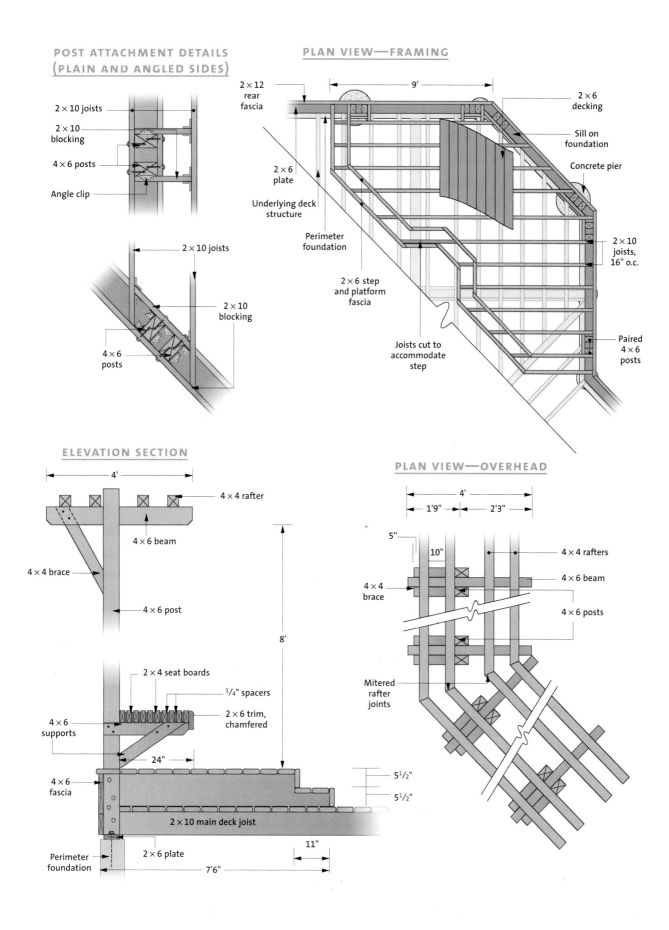

POST ATTACHMENT DETAILS
(PLAIN AND ANGLED SIDES)

2 × 10 joists
2 × 10 blocking
4 × 6 posts
Angle clip

2 × 10 joists
2 × 10 blocking
4 × 6 posts

PLAN VIEW—FRAMING

2 × 12 rear fascia
9'
2 × 6 decking
Sill on foundation
Concrete pier
2 × 6 plate
Underlying deck structure
Perimeter foundation
2 × 6 step and platform fascia
Joists cut to accommodate step
2 × 10 joists, 16" o.c.
Paired 4 × 6 posts

ELEVATION SECTION

4'
4 × 4 rafter
4 × 6 beam
4 × 4 brace
4 × 6 post
8'
2 × 4 seat boards
¼" spacers
2 × 6 trim, chamfered
4 × 6 supports
24"
4 × 6 fascia
2 × 10 main deck joist
Perimeter foundation
2 × 6 plate
11"
7'6"
5½"
5½"

PLAN VIEW—OVERHEAD

4'
1'9"
2'3"
5"
10"
4 × 4 rafters
4 × 4 brace
4 × 6 beam
4 × 6 posts
Mitered rafter joints

DECK FOR A SLOPING SITE

BUILT AT THE EDGE OF A HILL, this deck serves as an outdoor room that carries the home's floor level outward to light, fresh air, and a fine view. A balcony supported by angled "kicker" posts punctuates the far side of the deck. A pathway deck leads around the house on one side, while a simple step gives access to the backyard on the other side. A "saddlebag" storage unit on that same side supports a built-in barbecue. Simple details—such as the water-shedding bevels on the top rails and post tops—distinguish the design and add to its character.

To Adapt This Plan

A single, floating platform like this is adaptable to houses of nearly any size and shape. Enlarging it is a matter of extending the framing and foundations. The barbecue unit and pathway deck are optional and can be replaced with sections of railing.

Building Notes

This deck was built on a hillside in a zone where earthquakes may occur, so it required a substantial pier-and-tie-beam foundation that might be excessive in your location. (A tie beam is a reinforced concrete beam that ties together individual piers or footings so as to distribute forces among them.)

Your local building department can advise you on the most suitable approach for your situation. You will need a table saw to create the beveled rails.

Materials List

LUMBER	
Posts	6 × 6
Beams	6 × 8 or tripled 2 × 8s
Joists	2 × 8
Ledgers	2 × 8
Braces	2 × 6
Decking	2 × 6
Railings	6 × 6 posts; 4 × 4 top rails; 3 × 4 bottom rails; 2 × 2 balusters; $^5/_8$" × $^5/_8$" stops; 1" × 1$^1/_2$" spacers
Other	Clapboard siding

MASONRY	
Concrete	Tie beams, piers

HARDWARE	
Nails	16d (framing), 10d (decking); as appropriate for connectors
Bolts	$^1/_2$" bolts (framing)
Connectors	Post connectors; joist hangers
Other	#3, #4, #5 rebar

EXTRAS	
Built-in barbecue unit; gas lines	

On one side, the deck wraps around a corner of the house to provide access to a bedroom.

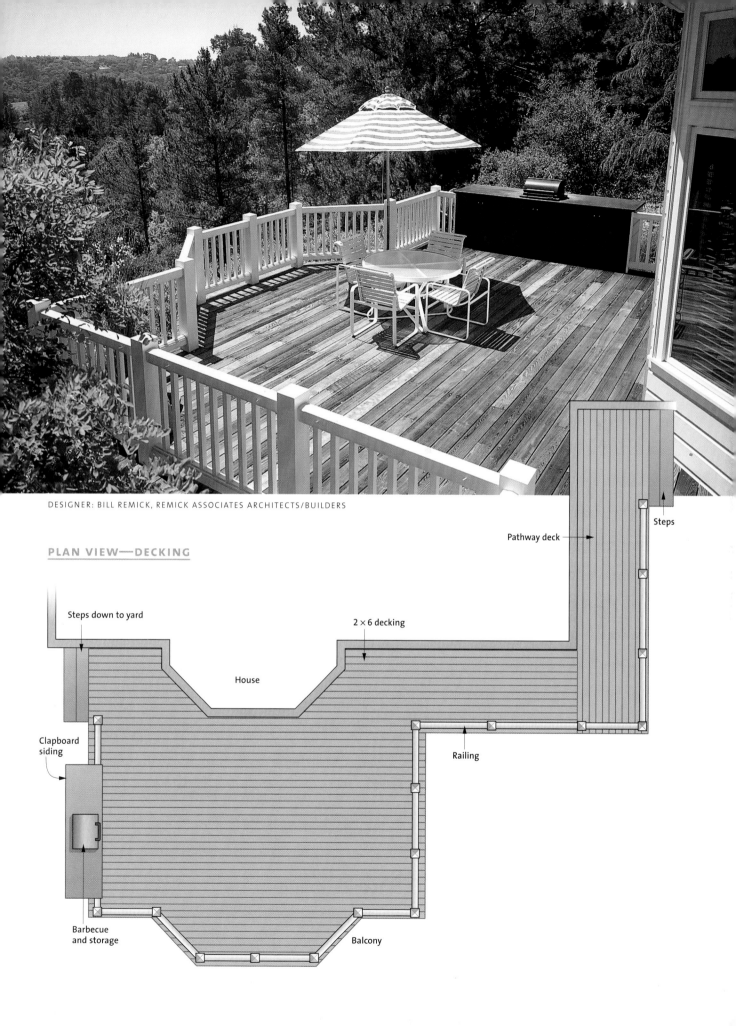

DESIGNER: BILL REMICK, REMICK ASSOCIATES ARCHITECTS/BUILDERS

PLAN VIEW—DECKING

Steps down to yard

House

2 × 6 decking

Pathway deck

Steps

Clapboard siding

Railing

Barbecue and storage

Balcony

DECK FOR A SLOPING SITE

The ledger-attached framing is supported by strategically placed beams. The outermost beam is supported by kicker posts.

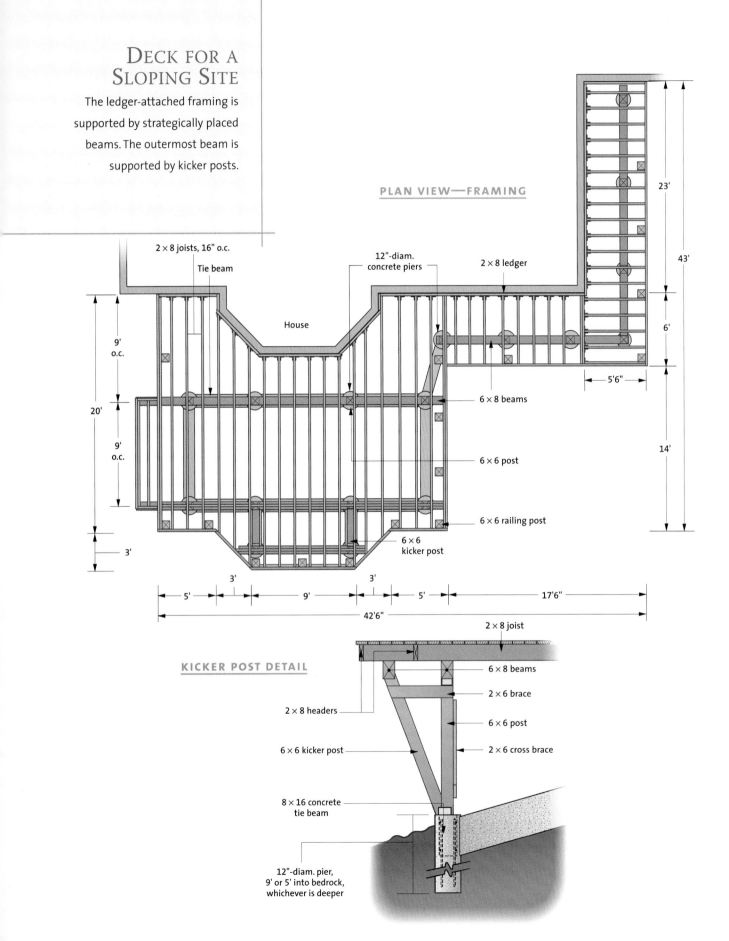

PLAN VIEW—FRAMING

2 × 8 joists, 16" o.c.

Tie beam

12"-diam. concrete piers

2 × 8 ledger

House

6 × 8 beams

6 × 6 post

6 × 6 railing post

6 × 6 kicker post

23'

43'

6'

5'6"

14'

9' o.c.

20'

9' o.c.

3'

3'

3'

5'

9'

5'

17'6"

42'6"

KICKER POST DETAIL

2 × 8 joist

6 × 8 beams

2 × 6 brace

6 × 6 post

2 × 6 cross brace

2 × 8 headers

6 × 6 kicker post

8 × 16 concrete tie beam

12"-diam. pier, 9' or 5' into bedrock, whichever is deeper

ELEVATION

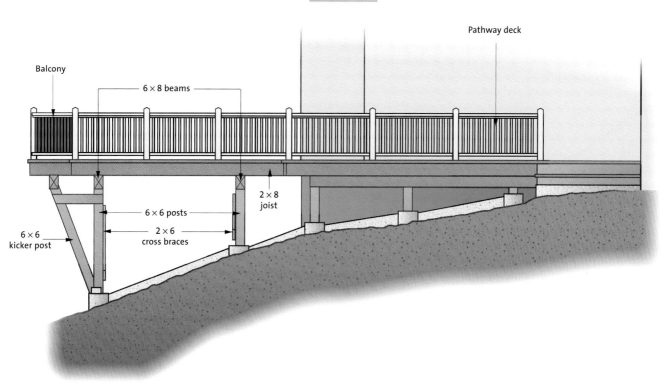

Balcony

6 × 8 beams

Pathway deck

2 × 8 joist

6 × 6 posts

2 × 6 cross braces

6 × 6 kicker post

RAILING CONSTRUCTION

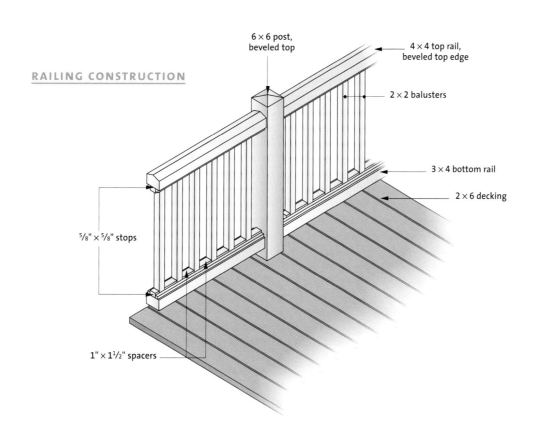

6 × 6 post, beveled top

4 × 4 top rail, beveled top edge

2 × 2 balusters

3 × 4 bottom rail

2 × 6 decking

$5/8" × 5/8"$ stops

$1" × 1^{1}/_{2}"$ spacers

SPLIT-LEVEL SPA DECK

THIS DECK COMBINES A BROAD, LEVEL EXPANSE that extends over a highly uneven backyard, with an upper level that houses a spa. Composite decking provides a low-maintenance, splinter-free surface that also handles chlorinated splashes from the spa without discoloring, as wood might do.

Materials List

LUMBER	
Posts	4 × 4
Beams	4 × 8, 4 × 10, or doubled 2× stock
Joists and ledgers	2 × 8
Decking and fascia	2 × 6, 2 × 8, or composite decking
Stairs	2 × 12 stringers; 2 × 6 treads; 1 × 6 risers
Railings	4 × 4 posts; 1 × 6 boards with 1 × 2 stops; 2 × 6 cap rails

MASONRY	
Concrete	Piers

HARDWARE	
Nails	16d (framing); as appropriate for connectors
Bolts and screws	2½" stainless-steel screws (decking); ½" bolts (framing)
Connectors	Post connectors; joist hangers
Other	#4 rebar; 2" steel pipe (stair handrail)

To Adapt this Plan

This deck is tailored to a very particular backyard full of challenging slopes, but you can adapt its outline and bilevel structure to suit any similar situation. You may even turn the deck around to work as a down-slope solution. Adjust deck levels and their relationship to each other by adding or subtracting stairs and changing post heights (as always, these changes will have ripple effects on other parts of the framing). You can also take out the spa and its reinforced framing. If you do that, you will need to fill in the space where the spa was with the framing found on either side and extend the stairs to full width.

Building Notes

This spa is supported by reinforced framing. You may choose to rest your spa on a concrete slab instead (page 115).

DESIGNER: GARY MARSH, ALL DECKED OUT

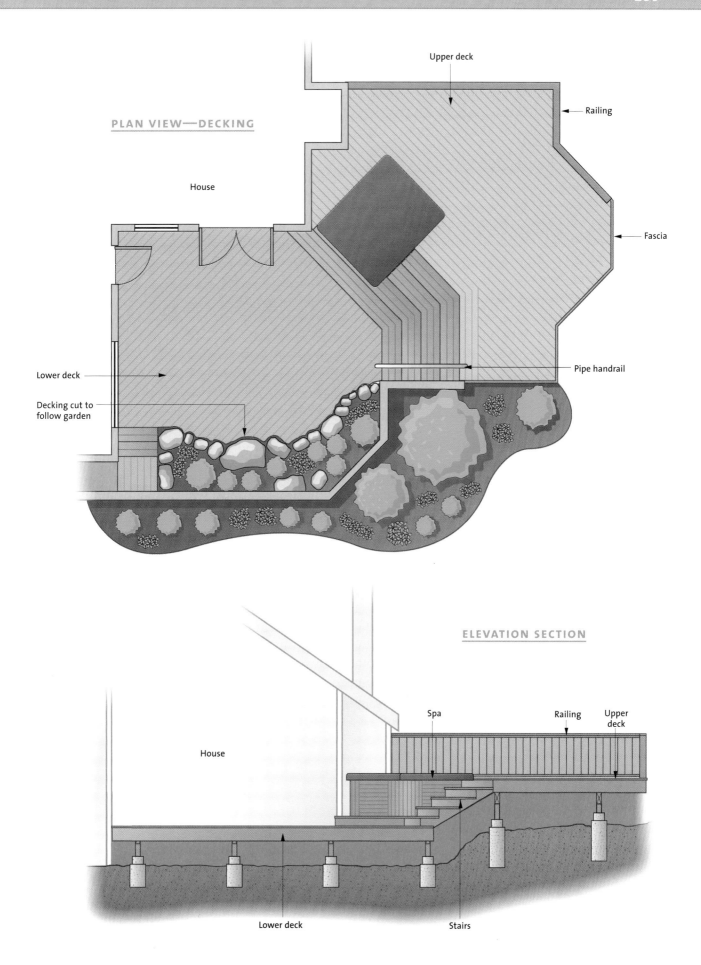

PLAN VIEW—DECKING

Upper deck

Railing

House

Fascia

Lower deck

Pipe handrail

Decking cut to
follow garden

ELEVATION SECTION

Spa

Railing

Upper
deck

House

Lower deck

Stairs

SPLIT-LEVEL SPA DECK

Where the deck is low to the ground, flush beams are used to save vertical space. Elsewhere, joists rest on top of the beams.

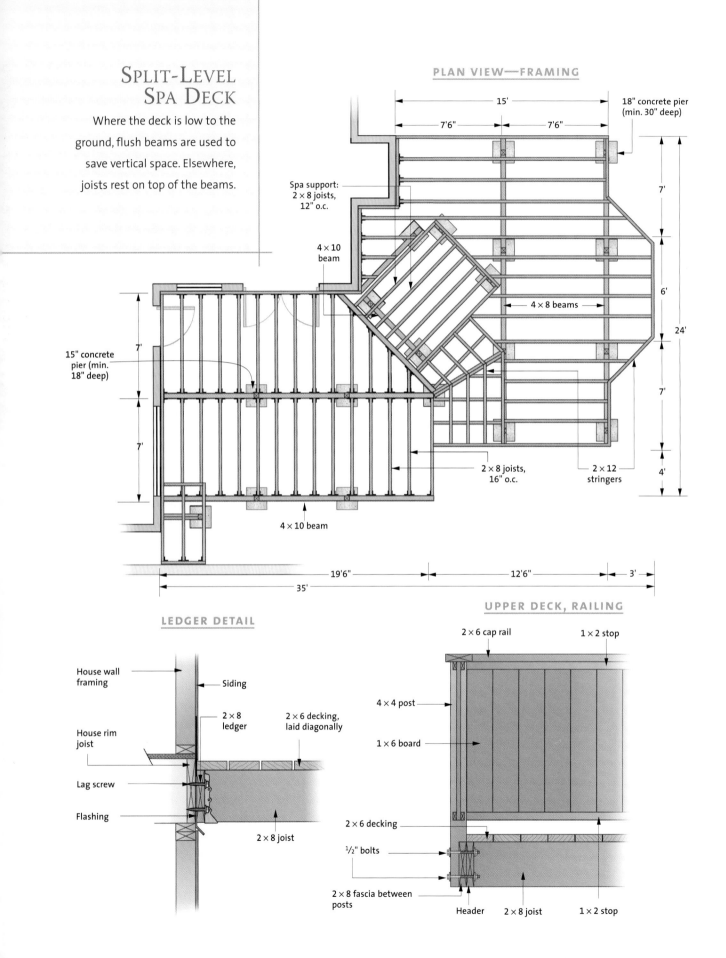

PLAN VIEW—FRAMING

15'

7'6"   7'6"

18" concrete pier (min. 30" deep)

Spa support: 2 × 8 joists, 12" o.c.

4 × 10 beam

4 × 8 beams

7'

6'

24'

7'

15" concrete pier (min. 18" deep)

7'

7'

2 × 8 joists, 16" o.c.

2 × 12 stringers

4'

4 × 10 beam

19'6"   12'6"   3'

35'

LEDGER DETAIL

House wall framing

Siding

House rim joist

2 × 8 ledger

2 × 6 decking, laid diagonally

Lag screw

Flashing

2 × 8 joist

UPPER DECK, RAILING

2 × 6 cap rail

1 × 2 stop

4 × 4 post

1 × 6 board

2 × 6 decking

½" bolts

2 × 8 fascia between posts

Header   2 × 8 joist   1 × 2 stop

UPPER DECK, SUPPORT DETAIL

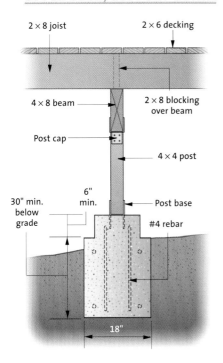

2 × 8 joist

2 × 6 decking

4 × 8 beam

2 × 8 blocking over beam

Post cap

4 × 4 post

30" min. below grade

6" min.

Post base

#4 rebar

18"

Because the top of the spa is virtually level with the upper decking, the spa's controls are easily accessible from the lower level.

LOWER DECK, FLUSH BEAM DETAIL

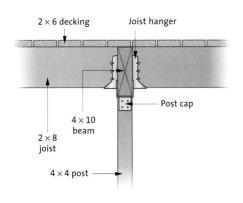

2 × 6 decking

Joist hanger

Post cap

4 × 10 beam

2 × 8 joist

4 × 4 post

STAIR CONSTRUCTION

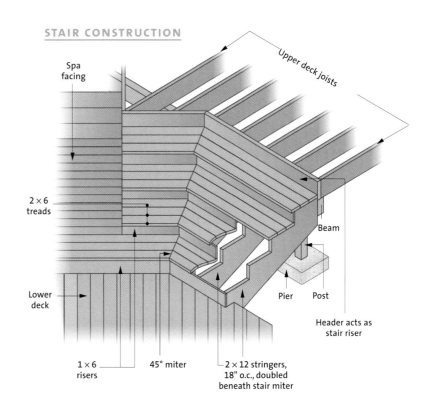

Spa facing

Upper deck joists

2 × 6 treads

Beam

Lower deck

Pier

Post

Header acts as stair riser

1 × 6 risers

45° miter

2 × 12 stringers, 18" o.c., doubled beneath stair miter

DECK WITH RAMPS

RAMPS CAN BE A GOOD SUBSTITUTE FOR STAIRS ON A DECK, PROVIDING FUNCTIONAL ACCESS FOR A WHEELCHAIR AND A GRACEFUL DESIGN TOUCH AS WELL. This deck uses three ramps to link separate areas for grilling, dining, and relaxing. The top level, shaded by the home's roof, is close to the kitchen and both indoor and outdoor eating areas. From it, an upper ramp descends to a dining platform with seating for 10. A second ramp then leads to a lower level, which is set low enough to do without railings. A third, shorter ramp connects the deck to the yard.

To Adapt this Plan

You can adjust the size, shape, and number of levels of this deck by proper adaptation of the framing—but make sure that any changes you make do not result in steeper ramps than those shown here. You may choose to reduce the ramp slopes for your deck as well. The stucco-clad pillars are visual elements meant to tie together the look of the deck and the house, and are not needed for structural support; you can keep or omit them as you wish.

Building Notes

The doubled posts and side-by-side piers and footings serve the same purpose as would larger foundations and single 6 × 6 posts. On this deck a planter functions as a barrier between the top deck and the first ramp; depending on your local codes, you may need to install an additional railing in this area. As built, this deck also includes a tree cutout in the lower deck.

Materials List

LUMBER	
Posts	4 × 4
Beams	2 × 8, 2 × 10
Joists and ledgers	2 × 6 (ramp joists); 2 × 8 (ledger, deck joists)
Decking	2 × 6
Stairs	2 × 12 stringers; 2 × 6 treads
Railings	4 × 4 posts; 2 × 4 rails; 1" pipe balusters; 2 × 6 cap rails
Fascia	Pressure-treated plywood
Columns	Plywood (sheathing); 2 × 4 (framing); 2 × 8 (tops)
Other	Lattice skirting
MASONRY	
Concrete	Piers, slabs
Stucco	Columns, fascia
HARDWARE	
Nails	16d (framing); as appropriate for connectors
Bolts and screws	$1/2$" bolts (framing); $5/8$" lag screws and epoxy anchors (framing-to-masonry)
Connectors	Post connectors; joist hangers
Other	Hidden fasteners (decking); #4 rebar; stucco mesh
EXTRAS	
Light fixtures and wiring	

DESIGNER: RUSS SINKOLA

PLAN VIEW—DECKING

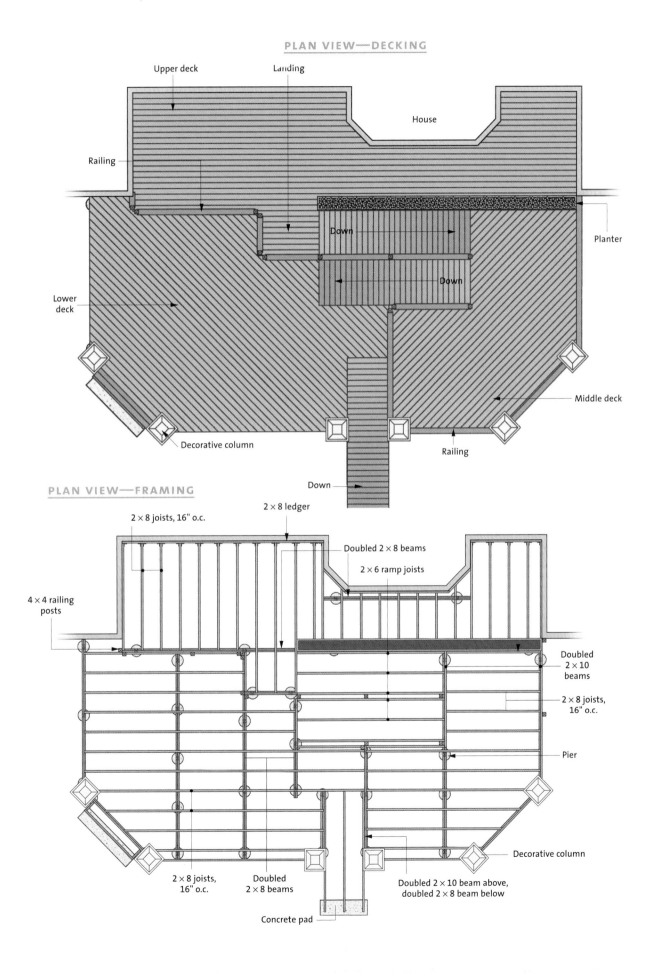

Upper deck

Landing

House

Railing

Planter

Down

Down

Lower deck

Middle deck

Decorative column

Railing

Down

PLAN VIEW—FRAMING

2 × 8 ledger

2 × 8 joists, 16" o.c.

Doubled 2 × 8 beams

2 × 6 ramp joists

4 × 4 railing posts

Doubled 2 × 10 beams

2 × 8 joists, 16" o.c.

Pier

Decorative column

2 × 8 joists, 16" o.c.

Doubled 2 × 8 beams

Doubled 2 × 10 beam above, doubled 2 × 8 beam below

Concrete pad

DECK WITH RAMPS

Ramps are simple to build—they are essentially decking sections set at angles. The only tricky part is cutting the ramp joists at each end.

ELEVATION

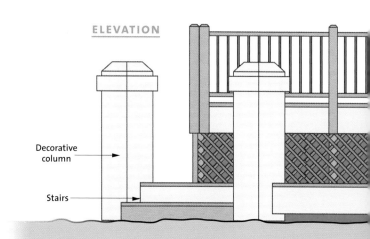

Decorative column

Stairs

LOWER DECK SUPPORT DETAIL

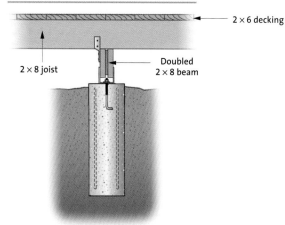

2 × 6 decking

2 × 8 joist

Doubled 2 × 8 beam

MIDDLE DECK DETAIL

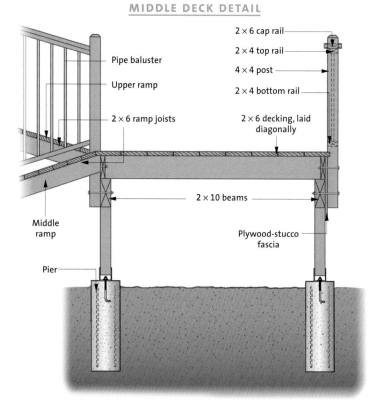

Pipe baluster

Upper ramp

2 × 6 ramp joists

2 × 6 cap rail

2 × 4 top rail

4 × 4 post

2 × 4 bottom rail

2 × 6 decking, laid diagonally

2 × 10 beams

Plywood-stucco fascia

Middle ramp

Pier

UPPER DECK SUPPORT DETAIL

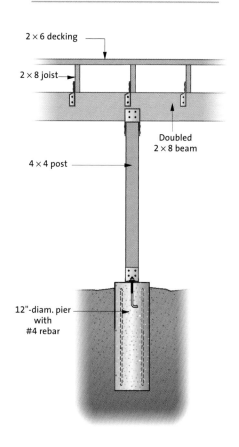

2 × 6 decking

2 × 8 joist

Doubled 2 × 8 beam

4 × 4 post

12"-diam. pier with #4 rebar

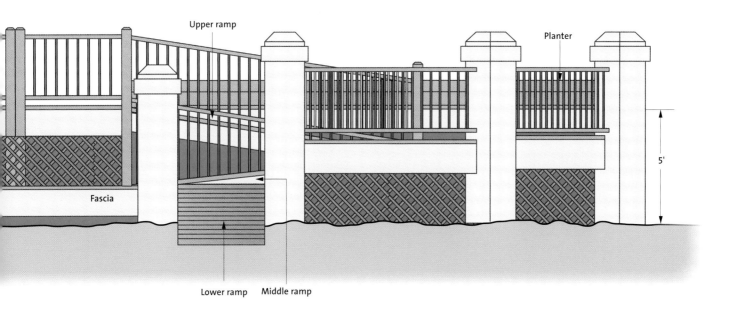

Upper ramp

Planter

5'

Fascia

Lower ramp   Middle ramp

RAMP FRAMING DETAIL

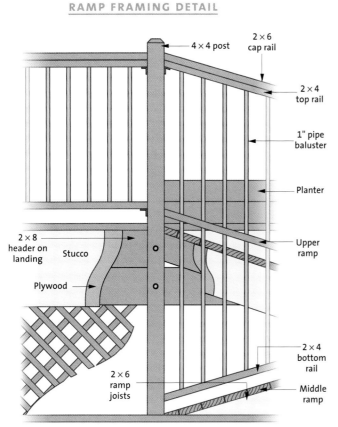

4 × 4 post

2 × 6 cap rail

2 × 4 top rail

1" pipe baluster

Planter

Upper ramp

2 × 8 header on landing

Stucco

Plywood

2 × 4 bottom rail

2 × 6 ramp joists

Middle ramp

DECORATIVE COLUMN DETAIL

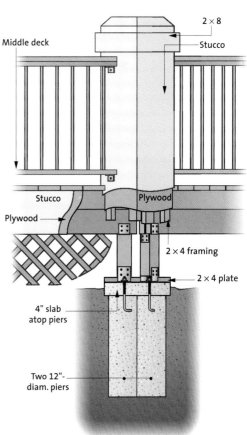

Middle deck

2 × 8

Stucco

Stucco

Plywood

Plywood

2 × 4 framing

2 × 4 plate

4" slab atop piers

Two 12"-diam. piers

TRANSITIONAL DECK

THIS PARTLY SHELTERED DECK serves as an indoor-outdoor space connecting a family room with a patio. Classically simple, it is a great transitional element for nearly any style of house.

Materials List

LUMBER

Beams	4 × 6, or doubled 2 × 6s
Joists and ledgers	2 × 6
Decking	2 × 6, with 2 × 8 trim boards
Steps	2 × 12 treads; 2 × 6 risers; 1 × 4 and 1 × 6 fascias

MASONRY

Concrete	Perimeter foundation

HARDWARE

Nails	16d (framing), 10d finish (blind-nailed decking); as appropriate for connectors
Connectors	Joist hangers
Other	#4 rebar

To Adapt this Plan

You can wrap this deck plan around almost any house on fairly flat ground. The key lies in establishing the shape of the deck. As shown here, wide places invite socializing, while traffic areas are narrower. If the floors in your home are higher than in this design, you can set the beams on posts with appropriate piers and footings, and then add steps as needed. For a higher deck, check whether a railing may be necessary. This plan includes a perimeter foundation to support the beams, an arrangement that provides maximum support and ease in leveling the structure, but you could use individual piers and footings instead.

Building Notes

Where a perimeter trim board runs perpendicular to the rest of the decking, an extra joist must be provided beneath the joint.

DESIGNER: TODD FRY, ASLA

PLAN VIEW

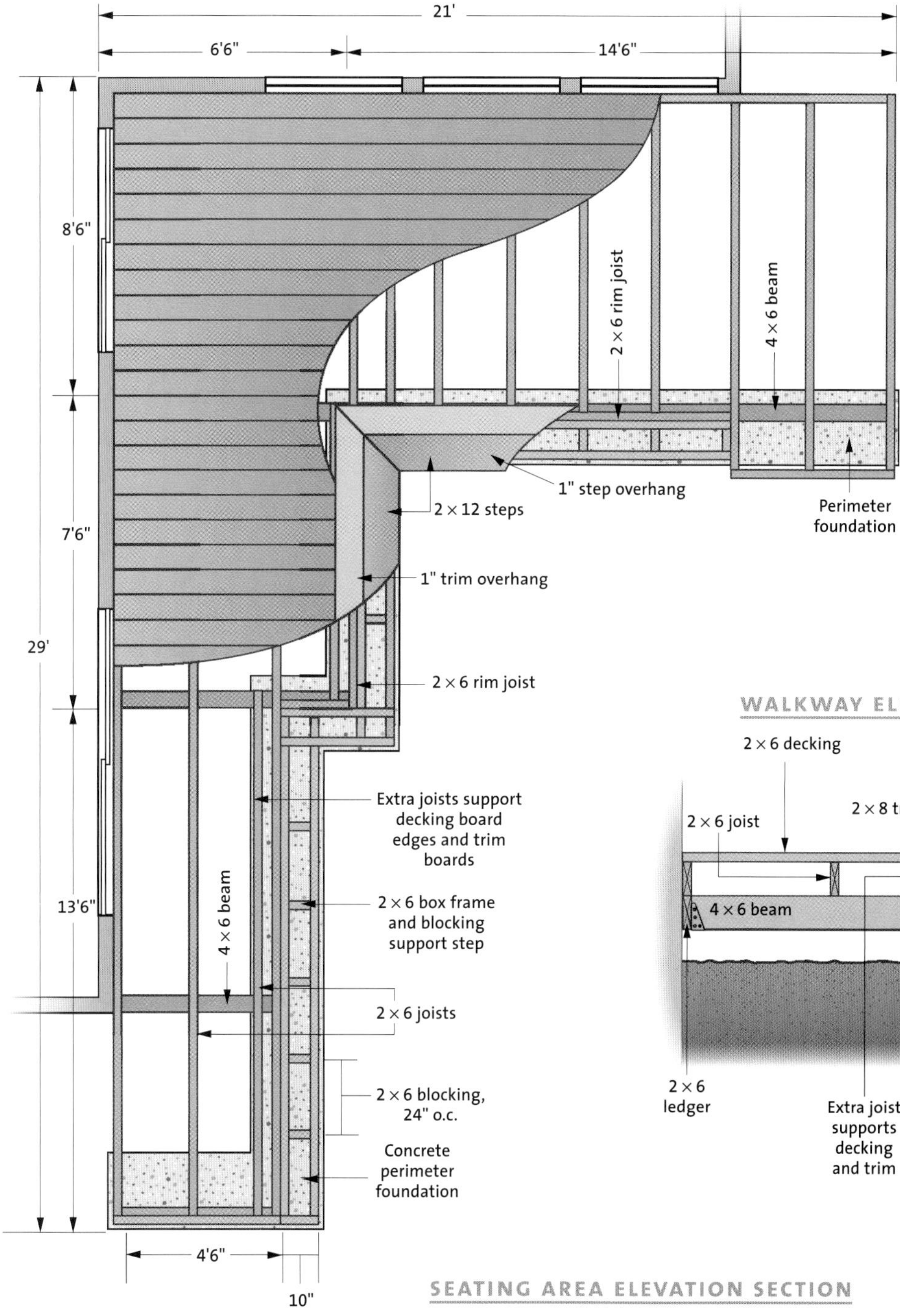

21'

6'6"   14'6"

8'6"

2 × 6 rim joist

4 × 6 beam

8.6"

14"

1" step overhang

2 × 12 steps

Perimeter
foundation

7'6"

1" trim overhang

29'

2 × 6 rim joist

Extra joists support
decking board
edges and trim
boards

4 × 6 beam

2 × 6 box frame
and blocking
support step

13'6"

2 × 6 joists

2 × 6 blocking,
24" o.c.

Concrete
perimeter
foundation

4'6"

10"

WALKWAY ELEVATION SECTION

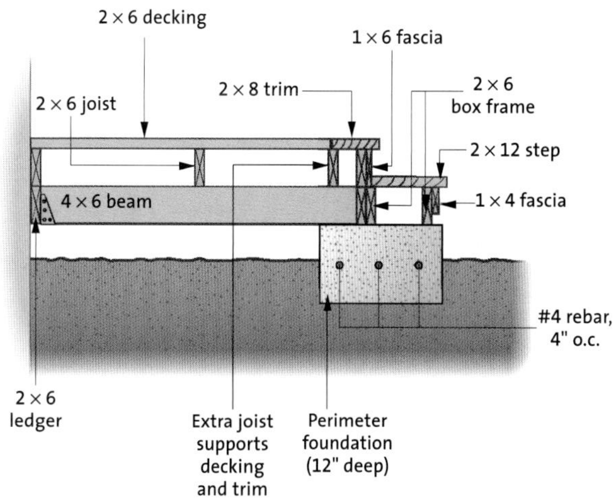

2 × 6 decking

1 × 6 fascia

2 × 6 joist

2 × 8 trim

2 × 6
box frame

2 × 12 step

4 × 6 beam

1 × 4 fascia

#4 rebar,
4" o.c.

2 × 6
ledger

Extra joist
supports
decking
and trim

Perimeter
foundation
(12" deep)

SEATING AREA ELEVATION SECTION

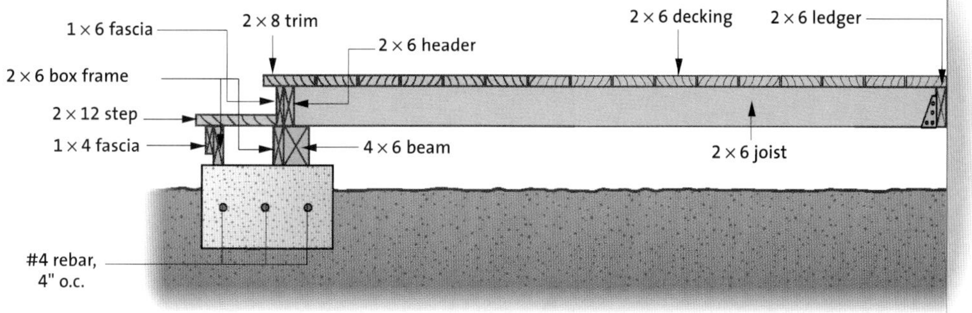

1 × 6 fascia

2 × 8 trim

2 × 6 header

2 × 6 decking

2 × 6 ledger

2 × 6 box frame

2 × 12 step

1 × 4 fascia

4 × 6 beam

2 × 6 joist

#4 rebar,
4" o.c.

RESOURCE GUIDE

WOOD DECKING AND LUMBER

Infinite Decking
800/338-3355
parksite.com

Scenic Mahogany Decking
800/338-3355
parksite.com

Southern Pine Council
504/443-4464
southernpine.com

Stein Wood Products
423/648-0375
siberianlarchproducts.com

Wonder Deck
866/605-3325
wonderdeck.com

DECK FINISHES AND CLEANERS

Gemini TWP
800/262-5710
www.gemini-coatings.com

Sikkens
866/745-5367
sikkens.com

Superdeck
800/825-5380
superdeck.com

Thompson's WaterSeal
800/367-6297
thompsonswaterseal.com

ALTERNATIVE DECKING AND RAILING MATERIALS

Brock Deck Systems
800/488-5245
www.royalcrownltd.com

CertainTeed Corp.
800/233-8990
certainteed.com

Correct Deck
877/332-5877
correctdeck.com

DeckStone
800/572-9029
dekstone.com

Fiberon
704/463-7120
fibercomposites.com

Nexwood
866/866-3369
nexwoodnw.com

Oasis
800/962-6973
alcoa.com

Procell Decking Systems
251/943-2916
procelldeck.com

TimberTech
800/307-7780
timbertech.com

Trex Co.
800/289-8739
trex.com

LP WeatherBest Decking
888/820-0325
lpcorp.com

Weyerhaeuser ChoiceDek
800/951-5117
choicedek.com

Xtendex
877/728-3498
xtendex.com

Yardcrafters Railing Systems
800/461-5706
gswinc.com

FASTENERS AND CONNECTORS

Dec-Klip
425/776-5340
dec-klip.com

DeckLok Bracket Systems
866/617-3325
deck-lok.com

Deckmaster
800/869-1375
deckmaster.com

Deck One
888/335-3217
deckone.com

EB-TY
888/438-3289
ebty.com

EZ Stairs
866/693-9570
ez-stairs.com

McFeely's Square Drive Screws
800/443-7937
mcfeelys.com

Siggi Screw
802/388-7515
diggsigg.com

Tebo Decker
800/873-2239
spotnails.com

The Ipe Clip® Company
716/822-7841
ipeclip.com

TigerClaw
800/928-4437
deckfastener.com

DECORATIVE RAILING PRODUCTS

AGS Stainless Inc.
888/842-9492
agsstainless.com

Deckorators
888/332-5724
deckorators.com

Island Post Cap
800/555-3694
islandpostcap.com

Railing in a Box
800/338-3355
parksite.com

Woodway Products
800/459-8718
woodwayproducts.com

LIGHTING

Aurora Deck Lighting
800/603-3520
auroradecklighting.com

Hadco Outdoor Lighting
800/331-4185
hadco.com

Highpoint Deck Lighting
888/582-5850
hpdlighting.com

SPECIALIZED TOOLS

BoWrench
800/466-9626
cepcotool.com

PamDrive Screw Gun
704/394-3141
pamfast.com

ACKNOWLEDGMENTS

We would like to extend special thanks to the pros who showed us how it's done and appeared in many of this book's photos. Jay Oliver, Josh Oliver, and Keith Camacho of Long Island Decking (Oceanside, New York; longislanddecking.com) built the cedar deck with inground posts introduced on page 48. Adam Fechner, Brian McMahon, and Chris Bordonaro of The Deck and Door Company (Apple Valley, Minnesota; deckanddoor.com) built the composite deck with aboveground posts introduced on page 50. And Jacob Porter, Aaron Stites, and Dennis Schaefer of Creative Wood Products (Fenton, Michigan; creativewood products.com) built the low patterned composite deck with built-in benches featured on pages 166–169.

ILLUSTRATIONS

Tracy La Rue Hohn: 34–35, 43 bottom (3), 83 top right, 84 bottom left, 86 center, 101 center left, 114 bottom, 126 top left, 133 top right, 174 right (2), 187 top right, 188 top left, 203 bottom right (3), 207 bottom right, 243; **Jim Kopp, Kopp Illustration, Inc.:** 32 bottom right, 43 top, 44 bottom, 46 center, 47 top and bottom, 58 bottom right, 59 all, 70 center, 71 top right (2), 74 bottom, 82 top left, 83 center (3) and bottom, 84 bottom right, 85 all, 94 top left, 99 all, 100 bottom (2), 101 right and bottom (3), 113 bottom (2), 114 all except bottom, 115 right and bottom right, 116 all, 117 top, 130–131 all, 134 bottom (2), 139–149 all, 172–173 all, 174 top and bottom left (3), 180–181 all, 189 bottom left, 193 top, 200 center (2), 203 top right (6), 207 second from bottom right, 208–209 all, 212–213 all, 216–217 all, 244–245 all, 246–267 all; **Bill Oetinger:** 226 bottom right, 227 top left and bottom right; **Ian Worpole:** 222–223 all, 224 all

PHOTOGRAPHY CREDITS

Unless otherwise credited, all photographs are by **Steve Cory**.
courtesy AGS Stainless Inc.: 170 bottom left, 175 middle left, 194 top, 199 top left; **Jim Alinder**: 14 top; **courtesy Aurora Deck Lighting**: 197 bottom left; **Laurie Black**: cover, 146–147; **Ernest Braun/California Redwood Association**: 194 bottom right, 226 top left; **Marion Brenner**: 11 top, 24 top, 28 bottom, 52-53; **Brian Vanden Brink**: 195 top; **courtesy Certainteed**: 165 bottom; **Tom Chiatalas**: 166 top left; **courtesy CorrectDeck**: 15, 175 top and bottom right; **Crandall & Crandall**: 214 bottom right; **Ben Davidson**: 246 bottom left, 247 bottom right, 248 bottom, 250 bottom, 252 bottom, 254 bottom, 255 top, 258 bottom, 261 top right; **R. Todd Davis Photography**: 25 top, 28 top, 216 top left; **courtesy Deck and Door**: 49 top, 87 center left bottom, 230 bottom right; **courtesy DeckLok Bracket Systems**: 107 bottom, 193 bottom left and right; **courtesy Deckorators**: 65 center, 190 bottom right, 196 bottom right, 197 right and bottom right, 202 top left, 206 top left; **courtesy Decks by Kiefer**: 234 bottom left, 236–237; **courtesy Deckstone**: 161 top right; **Andrew Drake**: 7 bottom, 29 bottom, 139 top right, 170 bottom right, 178 bottom right, 214 bottom left, 220 top left; **courtesy EB-TY**: 164–165; **Catriona Tudor Erler**: 21 top and bottom, 30 bottom, 175 right middle; **Cheryl Fenton**: 52 bottom right, 55 top right, 63 (4), 66 bottom left, 67 (3), 196 (post caps), 231 top right, 233 top middle, 239 top right; **courtesy Fiber Composites**: 149 top right, 162 top left, 195 left, 198 top left and bottom, 199 bottom right; **Bob Firth**: 145 top left and left center; **Scott Fitzgerrell**: 55 upper center right, 56 bottom right, 57 second from top left and lower center right, 62 (7), 63 (8), 64 top right, 65 top and bottom, 66 (5), 67 (9), 68 top right, 70 top right, 74 top left and center right, 196 left and second from left, 239 bottom; **Roger Foley**: 4 bottom right, 18 top; **Frank Gaglione**: 68 (4), 88 all, 89 center left, 178 all except bottom, 179 all; **John Granen**: 5 bottom right, 6 top, 29 top, 32 bottom center, 40 top right; **courtesy Hadco Lighting**: 231 second from top right and center right; **Philip Harvey**: 62 (3), 68 bottom right, 69 top right; **courtesy hpdlighting. com**: 215 bottom right, 230 center inset, 231 top left and center left, 233 bottom; **courtesy Infinite Decking**: 234 center left; **Andrea Jones**: 14 bottom right, 20 top; **Rob Karosis Photography**: 4–5, 22 top, 192 top left, 201 top left; **Douglas Kiester/Corner House Stock Photo, Inc.**: 201 bottom right; **Andrew Eban Lieberman**: 39 inset; **courtesy Long Island Decking**: 33 bottom right, 40 bottom, 41 bottom, 46 top, 50 top, 201 center left, 212 top left, 221 top left; **Janet Loughrey Photography**: 19 top, 142 top left, 185 top right, 217 bottom right; **Allan Mandell**: 8 top, 19 bottom; **Nicole & Patrick Mioulane/M.A.P.**: 30 top; **Clive Nichols/M.A.P.**: 12 bottom; **courtesy Oasis**: 52 bottom left, 61 center right and bottom; **Jerry O'Brien**: 220 left and bottom right; **courtesy PAM Fastening Technology, Inc.**: 69 center; **Jerry Pavia**: 20 bottom, 44 top, 115 top, 140 bottom left; **Robert Perron**: 16 inset; **Norman A. Plate**: 225 all; **courtesy Portland Cement Association**: 95 center right; **courtesy Procell Decking Systems**: 60 bottom left, 158 top left, 192 bottom left; **courtesy Railing in a Box**: 197 top, 199 top inset; **Jon Reis/PHOTOLINK**: 200 bottom right; **Kenneth Rice**: 32–33, 231 bottom right; **Lisa Romerein**: 9 inset, 22 bottom; **Eric Roth**: 6 bottom, 13 top, 26 all, 40 center, 80–81, 144 bottom, 190–191, 200 top left; **Bill Rothschild**: 4 bottom center, 17 top, 27 top, 106 bottom left, 148 top left; **Mark Rutherford**: 32 bottom left, 42 bottom, 69 top left, 73 bottom left, 75 center right, 76 center right, 78 bottom right, 79 top left, 91 top, 92 top left, 93 bottom right, 94 bottom left, 95 top left, 97 bottom right, 110 bottom right, 127 bottom right, 133 right inset, 134 top left, 140 top right, 141 bottom (3), 143 top left, 146 bottom center, 151 right second from top and bottom (2), 152 all except bottom left, 153 right, 153 bottom center and right, 155 top right (2), 160 all, 163 bottom right (2), 170 bottom center, 171 bottom right, 185 bottom right (2), 204 all, 205 top (3), 208 top left, 213 top right (3), 229 top right and center right, 232 left top, 236 bottom (3), 237 bottom right, 240–241 all, 243 all, 244 top right; **Mark Samu Studios**: 41 top, 170–171, 188 right middle, 228 top left; **Loren Santow**: 176–177 all, 221 al except top; **courtesy Scenic Mahogany Decking**: 57 upper center right; **David Schiff**: 66 (2), 67 (2); **Alan Shortall/Corner House Stock Photo, Inc.**: 13 bottom, 27 bottom; **courtesy Southern Pine Council**: 38 bottom, 76 bottom, 125 bottom, 150 bottom left; **courtesy Stein Wood Products**: 57 bottom right; **©1996 Forest Stewardship Council A.C.**: 56 bottom left; **Thomas J. Story**: 68 (1); **Tim Street-Porter**: 9, 214–215; **Dan Stultz**: bottom left (2); **courtesy Superdeck Brand Products**: 56 top left; **courtesy The Ipe Clip® Company**: 165 bottom inset; **Michael S. Thompson**: 230 center right; **courtesy Thompson's WaterSeal**: 4 bottom left, 8 bottom, 10, bottom, 18, bottom, 24 bottom, 31 inset, 58 top left, 110–111, 133 bottom, 202 bottom right, 238 bottom left (2); **courtesy Tiger Claw, Inc.**: 63 top left, 162 bottom left (3), 164 top left; **courtesy TimberTech**: 36 left; **Dave Toht**: 81 bottom right, 109 all, 235 top right (2), **courtesy Trex Company, Inc.**: 11 bottom, 12 top, 25 bottom, 39 top right, 61 top (2), 199 second from bottom right (2); **Mark Turner**: 195 right; **Jessie Walker**: 10 top, 23 top, 31, 90 top, 173 top, 195 bottom left, 201 center right, 217 top left; **Deidra Walpole Photography**: 16 bottom, 17 bottom, 23 bottom, 42 top, 238 top right; **courtesy Weyerhaeuser**: 198 left; **Judy White/ GardenPhotos.com**: 7 top, 14 bottom left, 39 bottom; **David Winger**: 246 bottom right, 262 bottom; **courtesy WonderDeck**: 161 bottom right (3); **courtesy Woodway Products**: 190 bottom left, 196 bottom left, 197 top left; **Tom Wyatt**: 246 bottom center, 266 bottom; **courtesy Xtendex**: 190 bottom center, 199 top right

DESIGN CREDITS

cover Northwest Exteriors by John Breiling **4 bottom right** Clyde Timmons/Design Works **6 top** Architect: Winton Scott **7 top** Sarah Eberle **8 top** Jan Hopkins **11 top** Barbara Jackel Design **12 bottom** Charlotte Sanderson **14 top** Turnbull Griffin Haesloop Architects, tgharchs.com **16 bottom** Gordon Kurtis Landscape Design **17 bottom** Jonny Appleseed Design **18 top** Clyde Timmons/Design Works **19 top** Thomas Vetter **19 bottom** Clark Matschek **24 top** Barbara Jackel Design **28 bottom** Thayer Design **39 inset** Andrew Eban Lieberman **42 top** Mark David Levine Design Group **50 top** Long Island Decking **52–53** Barbara Jackel Design **142 top left** Philip Thornburg **146–147** Northwest Exteriors by John Breiling **166 top left** Creative Wood Products **185 top right** Philip Thornburg **217 bottom right** Philip Thornburg **246–247** Russ Sinkola **246 bottom left** Ward-Young Architecture & Planning **246 bottom center** Todd Fry, ASLA **246 bottom right** Russ Sinkola **247 bottom right** Bill Remick, Remick Associates Architects/Builders **248–249** Tibor Ambrus **250–251** Peter Koenig Designs, with Bryan Gordon, B. Gordon Builders **252–253** Ward-Young Architecture & Planning **254–257** Bill Remick, Remick Associates Architects/Builders **258–261** Gary Marsh, All Decked Out **262–265** Russ Sinkola **266–267** Todd Fry, ASLA

INDEX

A

Accessibility, 262–265
Anchors. *See* Beams,
    Connection to; Foun-
    dations; Masonry;
    Posts, Connection to
Arbor, 225
Arch. *See* Crown
Auger, 50
    hiring professional
        with, 93
    power, 48, 90, 93

B

Balusters
    about, 34–35, 49,
        200–203
    examples, 195–197
    installation, 51, 208–213
Bar, for excavation, 68
Batterboards, 84, 88–89
Beams
    about, 34–35, 36, 38,
        113, 116–117
    built-up, 117
    connection to, 34
    on curved decks,
        140–141
    double and triple, 116,
        121
    how to trim, 117
    installing, 128
    for overhead, 222–223
    replacement, 245
    shared, 114
    side-by-side, 38, 113,
        117
    spans, 45
    splicing, 117
Bench, 6, 28, 31, 151,
    216–219, 252–253
Bevel, 66
Bits, 79, 108
Blocking, 139, 141, 203.
    See also Bracing
Bolts, 50, 63, 74, 96–97,
    99, 106
Bow, 59

Bracing, 99, 120, 131, 139
Brackets, 34–35, 75, 107,
    163, 187, 193
Breadboard edging, 157
Brick landing pad,
    178–179
Building codes, 34–35,
    44–45, 192–193

C

Cambara, 57
Cantilever design
    about, 38, 47
Cap rail, 35, 54, 200–201
Carriage bolts. *See* Bolts
Carriages. *See* Stringers
Cat's paw, 67
Caulking gun, 67
Cedar, 6, 7, 8, 39, 48–49,
    54, 57, 58, 152
    spans, 45
Chalk line, 49, 66, 156,
    157
Checking, 59
Checking for square, 71
Chisel, 67, 137
Clamps, 67
Cleat supports, 113
Composite decking, 50–51
    about, 35, 39, 60–61
    examples of, 11, 15, 25
    installation, 158–161,
        166–169
    railings, 210–211
    refinishing, 240
Concrete. *See also*
    Footings; Piers
    about, 65, 94–99,
        122–123
    curing, 123, 177
    delivered, 95
    estimation of needs, 94,
        96, 177
    footing preparation,
        34–37, 96–97
    landing pad, 35, 176–177
    mixing, 94–95
    setting posts in, 36–37,
        50
    tools, 94–99
    tube forms, 90, 96–97
Corners, 85, 130–131, 140

Crook, 59
Crown, 117
Cup, 59
Curved decks
    examples, 20–21, 28
    how to build, 140–141

D

Deck(s)
    curved (*See* Curved
        decks)
    destination, 20–21
    elevated (*See* Elevated
        decks)
    freestanding, 8, 83, 86–87
    low (ground-level), 6,
        14, 142–143, 145, 192
    multilevel (*See* Multilevel
        decks)
    parts of a, 34–37
    removal, 244
    size, 8–9
    stacked, 114
    weight (*See* Load)
    wraparound, 85
Decking
    about, 34–35, 39
    the last row, 155
    laying out, 152–157
    materials, 39, 47 (*See*
        Composite decking;
        Lumber; Vinyl)
    modular, 161
    pregrooved, 165
    repair, 242–245
    spans, 44–45
    tongue-and-groove, 160
    webbed hollow-core, 160
Decking caps
Decking pattern
    choosing, 39, 148
    examples of, 11
    framing V-shape,
        166–169
    types, 148–149
Deck plans
    deck with ramps,
        262–265
    entry deck, 250–251
    plan view, 47
    seating deck, 252–253
    simple deck, 248–249

for sloping sites, 254–257
    split-level spa deck,
        258–261
    transitional deck,
        266–267
Digging holes, 90–91
Dining, 7
Drainage, 93, 101
Drills, 69, 74, 152, 154
Duckboards. *See* Decking,
    Modular

E

Edges, sealing, 107
Elevated decks, 84
Elevated walkways. *See*
    Pathways, decks as
Elevation drawing, 46
Extension cords, 79

F

Fascia board, 34–35, 40,
    49, 51, 58, 157
Fasteners, 156
    galvanized, 55, 62, 151
    hidden, 15, 63, 158,
        162–165
    power, 69
    stainless steel, 55, 62
    types, 62, 120, 151
Finishes. *See also* Paint
    about, 58
    application, 240–241
    choosing, 55, 65,
        238–239
Fir, 54–55
    spans, 45
Flashing, 34–35, 48, 64,
    104–105, 107
Footings. *See also* Piers
    about, 35–37, 82–83
    absence of, 143
    holes, 90–93
    inground, 98
Foundations, 82–83.
    See also Footings;
    Piers
Framing
    about, 34–35, 112–145
    corners and angles,
        130–131

for a counter, 234–235
curves, 140–141
hardwood, 63
for a hot tub or spa, 115,
258–261
level changes, 120
around obstacles, 138
openings, 138–139
for an overhead,
222–223
for a stair landing,
188–189
Framing box, 89,
118–119, 122

G

Gazebo, 10, 25, 197
Girders. See Beams
Gloves, 69
Goggles, 69
Gravel, 64, 176
Grill, 31, 234

H

Hammer, 66–67
Handrails, 213
Hangerboard, 174, 183,
184
Hot tubs, 106, 115,
258–261
Hurricane ties, 34, 130,
137

I

Inspections, 44–45
Ipé, 57, 165
Ironwood, 16

J

J-bolt. See Bolts
Jig for joist installation,
134
Joints
butt, 158, 243
Joist hangers, 34–35, 38,
63, 75, 129, 134, 138
Joists
about, 130
around openings, 139

attaching to beam, 129,
136–137
with curved deck,
140–141
double, 130
hanging, 130–131
header, 51, 136–137
jig for installation, 134
laying out, 71, 132
in level changes, 120
repair, 24
"sister," 293
spacing, 130
spans, 44–45
trimming, 113, 132–133

K

Knee pads, 69
Knot, 59

L

Landing, 189
Landing pads, 176–179
Lattice, 196–197
fence, 201
skirting, 40
Laying out, 84–89
a curve, 140–141
decking, 152
joists, 71, 105, 132
methods, 86–89
for mitered corners, 85
railing post, 202–203
stringers, 172–175
Ledger
about, 34–37, 48
held-off, 37
how to attach, 37–38,
100–109
for overhead, 223
Level, finding, 66, 70, 127
Level changes, 120
Levels, 66, 68, 70, 127
Lighting, 49, 172, 175,
197, 230–233
Load, 82
Lumber
alternatives to, 158–161.
(See Composite
decking; Vinyl)
choosing, 58–59, 130

crown side up, 117, 121,
130
environmental impact of,
56
kiln dried, 58
span and wood type, 45
treated, 54–56, 63
untreated softwoods,
56–57

M

Magnesium float, 177
Mahogany, 39, 57
Masonry, 108
Mason's line, 66
Membrane, 64
Mending plate, 123,
128
Meranti, 57
Mixer, 68, 94–95
Moisture barriers, 64
Mortar tub and hoe, 68,
94–95
Multilevel decks, 114,
156
about, 24–25, 105
deck plans, 258–265
examples, 10, 11, 13, 23,
24–25, 28, 175
Mushrooms, 61

N

Nail gun, 39, 62, 69, 75,
78, 151
Nailing plate. See Mending
plate
Nails, 62, 134, 243
Nailset, 67, 152
Notching, 155, 182–183

O

Octagonal decks,
166–167, 169,
175
Outdoor counters,
234–235
Outdoor rooms, 22–23
Overhang. See Cantilever
design

Overheads
about, 222–227
examples, 7, 16–17, 19,
22–23
repairing, 245

P

Paint, 238–239
Paintbrushes, 239
Pathways, decks as, 14,
15, 20–21
Patios, 87
Pau Lopé, 57
Pavers. See Decking,
modular
Pergola, 226–227
Pickets. See Balusters
Piers. See also Footings
about, 34–35, 36
precast, 83, 144
Pilot holes, 74–75, 108,
116
Pine, 54–55
spans, 45
Planning
choosing a location, 43
drawing deck plans,
42–43, 46–47,
making a site plan, 42
trial run, 43
using your computer, 46
when to hire a profes-
sional, 46
Plans. See Deck plans
Planters
examples, 28–29, 41
how to build, 220–221
Plumb, establishing, 66
Plumb bob, 70
Pools, ponds and spas,
18–19, 115
plans, 258–261
Post anchors, 34, 50, 98,
203
Post base, 98, 126
Post cap, 65, 116, 123,
196–197
Post sleeve, 49, 197
Post-hole digger, 68, 91
Posts
about, 34–37, 113
aboveground, 126–127

absence of, 143
connection to, 34–35, 99
cutting, 123, 126
dressing up, 125
on footings, 36–37,
    82–83, 112
in freestanding decks,
    82–83, 86–87
inground, 36, 123–125
lumber for, 36
notched, 113, 123,
    204–205
for overhead, 224
on piers, 34–35, 82–83
for railing, 193, 204–205
    (See Railing posts)
replacement, 245
setting, 99
shared, 114, 212
on stairs, 212
Pressure-treated lumber,
    36, 54–58, 116,
    238–239
Pressure washer, 241
Pry bar, 67, 109
Pump sprayer, 239, 240

R
Racking, 157
Rail cap, 207
Railing posts
    installation, 151, 174,
        202–207
    notched, 204–205
    for stairs, 174, 192–193
Railings. See also
    Balusters; Cap rail;
    Railing posts
    about, 34–35, 40, 49
    cable or wire, 40, 175,
        194, 199
    clear panels, 40, 195,
        197, 198
    composite, 40, 51,
        198–199
    corners, 203
    curved, 194
    hybrid, 212–213
    metal, 195, 196, 197, 199
    products, 196–197
    safety and codes,
        192–193

for stairs, 175
styles, 194–195
Rebar, 97, 99
Redwood, 152
    about, 56, 58
    examples of, 9, 18–19,
        39
    spans, 45
Refinishing, 241
Removing a deck, 244
Repairs, 242–245
Rise of a stairway,
    172–173
Risers, 34–35, 186–187
Rooftop decks, 13, 26–27
Router, 79
Run of a stairway,
    172–173. See also
    Treads

S
Safety issues
    handrails, 213
    lighting, 175
    power tools, 69, 72
    railings, 192–193
    stairs, 172
    working with concrete,
        69
    working with treated
        wood, 54–55
Sanders, 67
    power, 78
Saws
    blades, 72, 109
    circular, 72, 96, 109
    hand, 67, 96
    jigsaw, 73, 155
    power miter, 76
    reciprocating, 77, 96,
        109
    table, 77
    using, 72–73
Screed, 177
Screw gun, 39, 69, 74
Screws
    deck, 62–63
    lag, 63, 106, 108, 120
    removing, 243
    for synthetic decking,
        61, 151, 158–159
Seismic ties, 130, 137

Sheathing, 104, 109
Siberian larch, 57
Siding, 103–105
Site, 144–145
Skirting, 34, 40, 228–229
Slopes, 254–257
Snugging, 101
Sod removal, 143
Spa. See Pools, ponds
    and spas
Spacers, 51, 101, 153
Spacing, 44–45
Spades, 68, 91
Spans, 44–45
Spindles. See Balusters
Split, 59
Sprinkler lines, 91
Square, checking for, 71
Squares, 66
Stain. See Finishes
Stairs
    about, 34–35, 172–173
    building codes, 172
    components, 172–173
    examples, 175
    finding the dimensions,
        180–181
    landing pad, 41, 173,
        174, 176–177, 189
    railings for, 172
    styles, 49, 175
    variations, 188–189
Storage space, 229
Straps, metal, 63
Striking, 97
Stringers
    about, 34–35, 173
    attaching, 174, 185
    cut, 182–183
    notched, 41, 173,
        182–187
Stucco, 109
Sun or shade considera-
    tions, 16–17, 224
Synthetic decking,
    railings and fascia,
    60–61, 158–159,
    210–211

T
Tamper, 98
Tape measure, 66, 104

Tape measure method,
    86–87
Teak, 57
Temporary supports, 36,
    48–49, 112
Tin snips, 67
Toenailing, 75, 135, 163
Tools
    cutting and joining, 67
    excavation and concrete,
        68, 94–99
    layout, 67
    masonry, 108–109
    rental, 95, 106
    for straightening boards,
        153
Top cap. See Cap rail
Trammel, 141
Treads, 172–173, 186,
    187, 244
Trees growing through
    deck, 30
Triangulation method, 48,
    50, 86–87
Tropical hardwoods, 39,
    57
Tube forms. See Concrete
Twist, 59

U
Utility lines, 91

V
V-shape pattern, 166–169
Vinyl, 39, 60–61, 102,
    158–159, 166–169
    railing, 210–211

W
Walks. See Pathways,
    decks as
Wane, 59
Webbed. See Decking
Weeds, 64, 93
Weight of the deck. See
    Load
Wheelbarrel, 95
Wraparound, 85, 175,
    189
Wrenches, 67